The Economics of
Macro Issues

The Pearson Series in Economics

Abel/Bernanke/Croushore
*Macroeconomics**

Acemoglu/Laibson/List
*Economics**

Bade/Parkin
*Foundations of Economics**

Berck/Helfand
The Economics of the Environment

Bierman/Fernandez
Game Theory with Economic Applications

Blanchard
*Macroeconomics**

Boyer
Principles of Transportation Economics

Branson
Macroeconomic Theory and Policy

Bruce
Public Finance and the American Economy

Carlton/Perloff
Modern Industrial Organization

Case/Fair/Oster
*Principles of Economics**

Chapman
Environmental Economics: Theory, Application, and Policy

Daniels/VanHoose
International Monetary & Financial Economics

Downs
An Economic Theory of Democracy

Farnham
Economics for Managers

Froyen
Macroeconomics: Theories and Policies

Fusfeld
The Age of the Economist

Gerber
*International Economics**

Gordon
*Macroeconomics**

Greene
Econometric Analysis

Gregory/Stuart
Russian and Soviet Economic Performance and Structure

Hartwick/Olewiler
The Economics of Natural Resource Use

Heilbroner/Milberg
The Making of the Economic Society

Heyne/Boettke/Prychitko
The Economic Way of Thinking

Hubbard/O'Brien
*Economics**

InEcon

*Money, Banking, and the Financial System**

Hubbard/O'Brien/Rafferty
*Macroeconomics**

Hughes/Cain
American Economic History

Husted/Melvin
International Economics

Jehle/Reny
Advanced Microeconomic Theory

Keat/Young/Erfle
Managerial Economics

Klein
Mathematical Methods for Economics

Krugman/Obstfeld/Melitz
International Economics: Theory & Policy*

Laidler
The Demand for Money

Lynn
Economic Development: Theory and Practice for a Divided World

Miller
Economics Today*

Miller/Benjamin
The Economics of Macro Issues

Miller/Benjamin/North
The Economics of Public Issues

Mishkin
The Economics of Money, Banking, and Financial Markets*

The Economics of Money, Banking, and Financial Markets, Business School Edition*

Macroeconomics: Policy and Practice*

Murray
Econometrics: A Modern Introduction

O'Sullivan/Sheffrin/Perez
Economics: Principles, Applications and Tools*

Parkin
Economics*

Perloff
Microeconomics*

Microeconomics: Theory and Applications with Calculus*

Perloff/Brander
Managerial Economics and Strategy*

Pindyck/Rubinfeld
Microeconomics*

Riddell/Shackelford/Stamos/ Schneider
Economics: A Tool for Critically Understanding Society

Roberts
The Choice: A Fable of Free Trade and Protection

Scherer
Industry Structure, Strategy, and Public Policy

Schiller
The Economics of Poverty and Discrimination

Sherman
Market Regulation

Stock/Watson
Introduction to Econometrics

Studenmund
Using Econometrics: A Practical Guide

Todaro/Smith
Economic Development

Walters/Walters/Appel/Callahan/ Centanni/Maex/O'Neill
Econversations: Today's Students Discuss Today's Issues

Williamson
Macroeconomics

*denotes **MyLab Economics** titles
Visit **www.pearson.com/mylab/economics** to learn more.

The Economics of
Macro Issues

EIGHTH EDITION

Roger LeRoy Miller
Research Professor of Economics
University of Texas—Arlington

Daniel K. Benjamin
Clemson University, South Carolina
and PERC, Bozeman, Montana

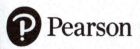 Pearson

New York, NY

Vice President, Business Publishing:
Donna Battista
Director of Portfolio Management:
Adrienne D'Ambrosio
Specialist Portfolio Manager: David Alexander
Editorial Assistant: Nicole Nedwidek
Vice President, Product Marketing:
Roxanne McCarley
Senior Product Marketer: Tricia Murphy
Executive Field Marketing Manager:
Carlie Marvel
Product Marketing Assistant: Marianela
Silvestri
Manager of Field Marketing, Business
Publishing: Adam Goldstein
Vice President, Production and Digital Studio,
Arts and Business: Etain O'Dea
Director of Production, Business: Jeff Holcomb
Managing Producer, Business: Alison Kalil
Content Producer: Christine Donovan
Operations Specialist: Carol Melville

Creative Director: Kathryn Foot
Manager, Learning Tools: Brian Surette
Content Developer, Learning Tools:
Sarah Peterson
Managing Producer, Digital Studio, Arts and
Business: Diane Lombardo
Digital Studio Producer: Melissa Honig
Digital Studio Producer: Alana Coles
Digital Content Team Lead: Noel Lotz
Digital Content Project Lead: Courtney Kamauf
Project Manager: Kathy Smith, Cenveo®
Publisher Services
Interior Design: Cenveo® Publisher Services
Cover Design: Cenveo® Publisher Services
Cover Art: Rick Elkins/Getty Images; GrAl/
Shutterstock; Ariel Skelley/Getty Images;
Hisham Ibrahim/Getty Images; TheaDesign/
Shutterstock
Printer/Binder: LSC Communications, Inc./
North Chelmsford
Cover Printer: LSC Communications, Inc.

Library of Congress Cataloging-in-Publication Data
Names: Miller, Roger LeRoy, author. | Benjamin, Daniel K., author.
Title: The economics of macro issues / Roger LeRoy Miller, Research Professor of Economics, University of Texas, Arlington, Daniel K. Benjamin, Clemson University, South Carolina, and PERC, Bozeman, Montana.
Description: Eighth Edition. | New York : Pearson, [2017] | Revised edition of The economics of macro issues, [2016] | Includes bibliographical references and index.
Identifiers: LCCN 2017021871 | ISBN 9780134531991 | ISBN 013453199X
Subjects: LCSH: Macroeconomics.
Classification: LCC HB172.5.M53 2017 | DDC 339--dc23
LC record available at https://lccn.loc.gov/2017021871

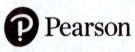 **Pearson**

ISBN 10: 0-13-453199-X
ISBN 13: 978-0-13-453199-1

To

Jay Hagenbuch,

Topics for long discussions over a glass of Domaine Leroy

(and more to follow in the many years ahead of us).

R.L.M.

To

Ferd Johns,

Who has heard almost all of it,

And believes almost none of it.

D.K.B.

CONTENTS

Preface   xii

PART ONE

The Miracle of Economic Growth   1

1. Rich Nation, Poor Nation   3
   (the importance of institutions in promoting economic growth)

2. Innovation and Growth   9
   (the path from invention to prosperity is paved with innovation)

3. Outsourcing and Economic Growth   16
   (the impact of competition and voluntary exchange on wealth)

4. Poverty, Capitalism, and Growth   23
   (does a rising tide lift all boats?)

5. The Threat to Growth   30
   (why higher taxes can mean less prosperity)

6. Hello Boomers, Goodbye Prosperity   37
   (the world is aging—and the world's economy is suffering)

PART TWO

The Business Cycle, Unemployment, and Inflation   43

7. What Should GDP Include?   45
   (Lady Gaga and the shadow economy)

8. What's in a Word? Plenty, When It's the "R" Word   51
   (how is a recession defined and why we care)

9. The Disappearing Middle Class   56
   (why the middle class no longer rules)

10. Capital, Wealth, and Inequality   64
    (will taxing capital help labor?)

11. The Great Stagnation   71
    (the role of economic policy in economic recovery)

12. The Case of the Missing Workers   79
    (misleading measures of unemployment)

13. The Gig Economy   85
    (how jobs are changing, and what it means for the future)

14. Mobility in America   91
    (can workers still make it to the top in the modern economy?)

15. Inflation and the Debt Bomb   98
    (why soaring government debt means that inflation must *go up)*

16. Is It Real, or Is It Nominal?   105
    (why record-high prices aren't always what they seem)

Part Three
Fiscal Policy   **111**

17. Can We Afford the Affordable Care Act?   113
    *(what the Affordable Care Act does—and doesn't—mean for
    health care)*

18. Who *Really* Pays Taxes?   120
    *(contrary to politicians' claims, it's the rich who foot the bill
    for Uncle Sam)*

19. Are You Stimulated Yet?   126
    (why stimulus packages do—or don't—work)

20. Higher Taxes Are in Your Future   133
    (why you can expect to pay higher and higher taxes in the future)

21. The Myths of Social Security   139
    (it's not what government says it is, nor will it ever be)

Part Four
Monetary Policy and Financial Institutions   **145**

22. The Fed and Financial Panics   147
    (why the Fed was founded, and what it learned from its failures)

23. The Fed Feeding Frenzy   152
    (why monetary policy no longer looks like it used to)

24. Deposit Insurance and Financial Markets   157
(economic implications of subsidized deposit insurance)

25. Revolutionizing the Way We Pay   164
(no credit cards, no currency—no problem)

26. Cryptocurrencies   168
(are Bitcoin, Zcash, and Litecoin here to stay?)

PART FIVE

Globalization and International Finance   **175**

27. The Value of the Dollar   177
(why exchange rates move and what it means for America)

28. The Eurozone after Brexit   184
(what Britain's exit from the EU means for the Eurozone)

29. The Global Power of the Big Mac   192
*(how a simple burger illuminates the mysteries of foreign
exchange markets)*

30. The Opposition to Globalization   198
(why people object to globalization)

31. The $750,000 Job   205
(economic consequences of attempts to restrict free trade)

Glossary   210

Selected References and Web Links   224

Index   235

SUGGESTIONS FOR USE

At the request of our readers, we include the following table to help you incorporate the chapters of this book into your syllabus. Depending on the breadth of your course, you may also want to consult the companion paperback, *The Economics of Public Issues*, 20th edition, which features microeconomics topics and a similar table in its preface.

Economics Topics	Recommended Chapters in The Economics of Macro Issues, 8th Edition
Taxes and Public Spending	5, 6, 11, 17, 18, 19
Unemployment, Inflation, and Deflation	13, 15, 16, 27
Measuring the Economy's Performance	2, 7, 9 16, 26
Economic Growth and Development	1, 2, 3, 4, 6, 9, 10, 13, 14
Classical and Keynesian Macro Analyses	8, 11, 18, 19, 20
Fiscal Policy	10, 11, 14, 15, 16, 17, 18
Deficits and the Public Debt	5, 6, 11, 15, 17, 19
Money and Banking	8, 21, 22, 25, 26
Money Creation and Deposit Insurance	24, 25, 26
Monetary Policy: Domestic and International	21, 22, 23, 26, 27, 28
Stabilization and the Global Economy	11, 14, 19, 22, 23, 27, 29
International Trade	1, 3, 4, 10, 30, 31
International Finance	22, 27, 28, 29
Recession	8, 11, 12, 13, 19, 25

PREFACE

By the time you read this slim volume about macroeconomic issues, there probably will have been significant changes in many subjects discussed herein. Congress and the president may have already changed our federal income tax structure. Interest rates might be higher than they were several years ago. The value of the dollar relative to other countries' currencies could have changed. The rate of economic growth might be different than it was in recent years.

While economy-wide facts, like the ones mentioned above, may change, the analysis does not. Individuals (and businesses) react predictably to changes in incentives. If interest rates rise relative to what they were a few years ago, people will change their saving and buying plans. If overall prices rise faster (there is more inflation), businesses will rethink previous management decisions. If the dollar is stronger relative to other currencies, more American families will choose to travel abroad, while fewer families in other nations will visit the United States.

In this new edition, you will learn how to analyze current issues in the macro economy. Those issues are ones that we have chosen for their currency and importance. Consequently, not only does this edition have important new chapters, but all previous chapters have been fully updated. Five of them have undergone major revisions.

New to This Edition

- Chapter 6: Hello Boomers, Goodbye Prosperity *(the world is aging—and the world's economy is suffering)*
- Chapter 9: The Disappearing Middle Class *(why the middle class no longer rules)*
- Chapter 13: The Gig Economy *(how jobs are changing, and what it means for the future)*
- Chapter 26: Cryptocurrencies *(are Bitcoin, Zcash, and Litecoin here to stay?)*
- Five additional chapters have been completely revised.
- All chapters have been updated to reflect the latest developments and data available.

Chapters That Have Undergone Major Revisions

The following chapters have been completely revised for this eighth edition.

- Chapter 10: Capital, Wealth, and Inequality
- Chapter 12: The Case of the Missing Workers

- Chapter 17: Can We Afford the Affordable Care Act?
- Chapter 28: The Eurozone after Brexit
- Chapter 30: The Opposition to Globalization

Of course, every chapter has been revised to incorporate the latest data and developments. We have also continued to update references and Web links and improve our glossary. Quite simply, our objective is to provide a book that reflects in every dimension the major events that have taken place in the American economy over the past few years. The result, we believe, will stimulate our readers in unprecedented ways.

INSTRUCTOR'S MANUAL

An Instructor's Manual accompanies this 8th edition. It is available online to all adopters of the book from the Instructor's Resource Center (**www.pearsonhighered.com**). For each chapter, the manual provides the following:

- A synopsis that cuts to the core of the economics issues presented in the chapter.
- A concise exposition of the "behind the scenes" economic foundations of the text.
- Answers to all of the end-of-chapter discussion questions. Most suggest new avenues of discussion.

THE REVIEW TEAM

Every revision of this book requires lots of help from many economists. We received helpful comments and detailed analyses from reviewers of the last edition, including:

Tina Esparza, Hartnell College
Ninos Malek, San Jose State University
Cyril Morong, San Antonio College

We have also received numerous comments from professors who have successfully used this book in their classrooms. We thank you for taking the time to provide us with such comments.

THE PRODUCTION TEAM

Our thanks also go to the individuals involved in the hands-on production process. As usual, Sue Jasin of K&M Consulting contributed expert typing and editing. And Robbie Benjamin was unstinting in her demand for clarity of thought and exposition. We thank Kathy Smith, our production editor, for her professionalism. Finally, our editors at Pearson, David Alexander and Christine Donovan, provided continuous guidance and help on this revision. Thank you again, as always.

R.L.M.
D.K.B.

PART ONE

The Miracle of Economic Growth

CHAPTER 1

Rich Nation, Poor Nation

Why do the citizens of some nations grow rich while the inhabitants of others remain poor? Your initial answer might be "because of differences in the **natural-resource endowments** of the nations." It is true that ample endowments of energy, timber, and fertile land all help increase **wealth.** But natural resources can be only a very small part of the answer, as witnessed by many counterexamples. Switzerland and Luxembourg, for example, are nearly devoid of key natural resources, and yet, decade after decade, the real income of citizens of those lands has grown rapidly, propelling them to great prosperity. Similarly, Hong Kong, which consists of but a few square miles of rock and hillside, is one of the economic miracles of modern times, while in Russia, a land amply endowed with vast quantities of virtually every important resource, most people remain mired in economic misery.

UNRAVELING THE MYSTERY OF GROWTH

Recent studies have begun to unravel the mystery of **economic growth.** Repeatedly, they have found that it is the fundamental political and legal **institutions** of society that are conducive to growth. Of these, political stability, secure private property rights, and legal systems based on the **rule of law** are among the most important. Such institutions encourage people to make long-term investments in improvements to land and in all forms of **physical** and **human capital.** These investments raise the **capital stock,** which in turn provides for more growth long into the future. In addition, the cumulative effects of this growth over time eventually yield much higher **standards of living.**

Table 1–1   Differing Legal Systems

Common Law Nations	Civil Law Nations
Australia	Brazil
Canada	Egypt
India	France
Israel	Greece
New Zealand	Italy
United Kingdom	Mexico
United States	Sweden

Professor Paul Mahoney of the University of Virginia, for example, has studied the contrasting effects of different legal systems on economic growth. Many legal systems around the world today are based on one of two models: the English **common law system** and the French **civil law system.** Common law systems reflect a conscious decision in favor of a limited role for government and emphasize the importance of the judiciary in constraining the power of the executive and legislative branches of government. In contrast, civil law systems favor the creation of a strong centralized government in which the legislature and the executive branch have the power to grant preferential treatment to special interests. Table 1–1 shows a sample of common law and civil law nations.

The Importance of Secure Property Rights

Mahoney finds that the security of property rights is much stronger in nations with common law systems, such as the United Kingdom and its former colonies, including the United States. In nations such as France and its former colonies, the civil law systems are much more likely to yield unpredictable changes in the rules of the game—the structure of **property and contract rights.** This, in turn, reduces the willingness of people to make long-term fixed investments in nations with civil law systems, a fact that ultimately slows their growth and lowers the standard of living of their citizens.

The reasoning is simple. If the police will not help you protect your rights to a home or car, you are less likely to acquire those **assets.** Similarly, if you cannot easily enforce business or employment contracts, you are much less likely to enter into those contracts—and thus less likely to produce as many goods or services. Furthermore, if you cannot plan for the future because you do not know what the rules of the game will be ten years or perhaps even one year from now, you are far less likely to make productive long-term investments that require years to pay off. And if you cannot be assured of the rewards from developing successful new goods and services, innovation will be stifled (see Chapter 2). Common law systems seem to do a better job at enforcing contracts and securing property rights and thus would be expected to promote economic activity now and economic growth over time.

When Mahoney examined the economic performance of nations around the world, he found that economic growth has been one-third higher in the common law nations than it has been in civil law nations. Over the three decades covered by his study, the increase in the standard of living—measured by **real per capita income**—was more than 20 percent greater in common law nations than in civil law nations. If such a pattern persisted over the span of a century, it would produce a staggering 80 percent difference in real per capita income in favor of nations with secure property rights.

THE IMPORTANCE OF OTHER INSTITUTIONS

The economists William Easterly and Ross Levine have taken a much broader view, both across time and across institutions, assessing the economic growth of a variety of nations since their days as colonies. These authors examine how institutions such as political stability, protection of persons and property against violence or theft, security of contracts, and freedom from regulatory burdens contribute to sustained economic growth. They find that it is key institutions such as these, rather than natural-resource endowments, that explain long-term differences in growth and thus present-day differences in levels of real income. To illustrate the powerful effect of institutions, consider the contrast between Mexico, with a real per capita income of about $18,000 today, and the United States, with a real per capita income of about $56,000. Easterly and Levine conclude that if Mexico had developed the same political and legal institutions that the United States has enjoyed, per capita income in Mexico today would be equal to that in the United States.

THE HISTORICAL ROOTS OF TODAY'S INSTITUTIONS

In light of the tremendous importance of institutions in determining long-term growth, Easterly and Levine go on to ask another important question: How have countries gotten the political and legal institutions they have today? The answer has to do with disease, of all things.

The seventy-two countries Easterly and Levine examined are all former European colonies in which a variety of colonial strategies were pursued. In Australia, New Zealand, and North America, the colonists found geography and climate that were conducive to good health. Permanent settlement in such locations was attractive, so the settlers created institutions to protect private property and curb the power of the state. But when Europeans arrived in Africa and South America, they encountered tropical diseases—such as malaria and yellow fever—that produced high mortality among the settlers. This discouraged permanent settlement and encouraged a mentality focused on extracting metals, cash crops, and other resources. This, in turn, provided little incentive to promote democratic institutions or stable long-term property rights systems. The differing initial institutions helped shape economic growth over the years, and their persistence continues to shape the political and legal character and the standard of living in these nations today.

WHY NATIONS FAIL

Scholars Daron Acemoglu and James Robinson have summarized the varieties of institutions found around the world into two broad categories: "inclusive" and "extractive." Nations with inclusive institutions tend to be democracies based on common law. Most importantly they have legal structures that create incentives for everyone to invest in the future. Nations with extractive institutions are often based on civil law and have centralized government powers, but the key is that their institutions protect the political and economic power of a small elite that takes resources from everyone else.

Acemoglu and Robinson found that whether we look at the sweep of history or the span of nations today, the results are the same. Prosperity is much greater and lasts longer in nations with inclusive institutions compared to those with extractive institutions. Remarkably, the authors conclude that experts cannot engineer prosperity by offering the right advice to rulers on policies or institutions, because rulers actually "get it wrong" on purpose, not by mistake.

Change, and thus prosperity, can happen only when a broad coalition of citizens insists on inclusive institutions. This reasoning leads the authors to a striking conclusion regarding China, where economic growth has been so robust over the last thirty-five years. Because the Chinese government has maintained tight, centralized political control even while allowing economic freedom in some areas of the country, Acemoglu and Robinson conclude that the economic gains of that nation are unlikely to continue. Indeed, they boldly assert that over the coming decades "the spectacular growth rates in China will slowly evaporate."

No Property Rights, No Property

Whatever the future of China turns out to be, there is little doubt that extractive political and legal institutions can dramatically alter outcomes in the wrong direction. When Zimbabwe won its independence from Great Britain in 1980, it was one of the most prosperous nations in Africa. Soon after taking power as Zimbabwe's first (and thus far only) president, Robert Mugabe began disassembling that nation's rule of law, tearing apart the institutions that had helped it grow rich. He reduced the security of property rights in land and eventually confiscated those rights altogether. Mugabe also gradually took control of the prices of most goods and services in his nation. The Mugabe government has even confiscated large **stocks** of food and most other things of value that might be exported out of or imported into Zimbabwe. In short, anything that is produced or saved became subject to confiscation, so the incentives to do either are—to put it mildly—reduced.

As a result, between 1980 and 1996, real per capita income in Zimbabwe fell by one-third, and since 1996 it has fallen by an additional third, and now is only $500. Eighty percent of the workforce is unemployed, investment is nonexistent, and the annual inflation rate reached 231 *million* percent in 2008—just before the monetary system collapsed completely. Decades of labor and capital investment have been destroyed because the very institutions that made progress possible have been eliminated. It is a lesson we ignore at our peril.

For Critical Analysis

1. Consider two countries, A and B, and suppose that both have identical *physical* endowments of, say, iron ore. In country A, however, any profits made from mining the ore are subject to confiscation by the government, while in country B, there is no such risk. How does the risk of expropriation affect the *economic* endowments of the two nations? In which nation are people likely to be richer?

2. In light of your answer to question 1, how do you explain the fact that in some countries there is widespread political support for government policies that expropriate resources from some groups for the purpose of handing them out to other groups?

3. Going to college in the United States raises average lifetime earnings by about two-thirds, given our current political and economic institutions. Now suppose that ownership of the added income generated by your college education suddenly became uncertain. Specifically, suppose a law was passed in your state that enabled the governor to

select 10 percent of the graduating class from all of the state's colleges and universities each year and impose a tax of up to 50 percent on the difference between the earnings of these people in their first job and the average earnings of people in the state who have only a high school education. What would happen to immigration into or out of the state? What would happen to attendance at colleges and universities within the state? If the governor were allowed to arbitrarily decide who got hit with the new tax, what would happen to campaign contributions to the governor? What would happen to the number of people "volunteering" to work in the governor's next campaign? Would your decision to invest in a college education change? Explain your responses.

4. Go to a source such as the CIA *World Factbook* or the World Bank and collect per capita income and population data for each of the nations listed in Table 1–1. Compare the average per capita income of the common law nations with the average per capita income of the civil law countries. Based on the discussion in this chapter, identify at least two other factors that you think are important to take into account when assessing whether the differences you observe are likely due to the systems of the countries.

5. Most international attempts to aid people living in low-income nations have come in one of two forms: (i) gifts of consumer goods (such as food), and (ii) assistance in constructing or obtaining capital goods (such as tractors or dams or roads). Based on what you have learned in this chapter, how likely are such efforts to *permanently* raise the standard of living in such countries? Explain.

6. Louisiana and Quebec both have systems of local law (state and provincial, respectively) that are heavily influenced by their common French heritage, which includes civil law. What do you predict is true about per capita income in Louisiana compared to the other U.S. states, and per capita income in Quebec, compared to the other Canadian provinces? Is this prediction confirmed by the facts (which can be readily ascertained with a few quick Web searches)? Identify at least two other factors that you think are important to take into account when assessing whether the differences you observe are likely due to the influence of civil law institutions.

CHAPTER 2

Innovation and Growth

Would you be better off without your smartphone and other digital devices? Would you be better off without access to the world's greatest library—the Internet? Would you be better off without social media?

Most of you will answer these questions with a resounding "no." The Internet and rapid telecommunications have changed most people's lives, in the United States and around the world, for the better. Note, though, that none of what is technologically available today came out of the blue. Rather, someone in the past created an **invention.** As the saying goes, however, inventions are literally "a dime a dozen." They have little value in their raw, idea form. Rather, **innovation** is necessary—that is, the transformation of something new, such as an invention, into something that benefits us. The technical novelty of the invention must be developed into the practical application that creates value for human beings. Innovations can either reduce the cost of producing what we already have—think telephone calls—or provide new goods and services—think the Internet.

INVENTION TO WIDESPREAD USE—NOT ALWAYS FAST

Just because someone has invented something that seems useful does not guarantee a quick transition from invention to widespread use. The incandescent light bulb was originally invented by Humphrey Davy in 1802. But it took more than seventy-five years, plus the considerable technical and commercial talents of Thomas Edison, to implement a practical application for the bulb. Even then, the widespread diffusion of the light bulb took additional decades—and it has not yet occurred in many locations around the world.

Consider also the transistor, which is the fundamental building block of modern electronic devices. When it was invented in 1947, its creators thought that it might help make a better hearing aid. The *New York Times* thought the invention merited no more than a tiny article buried deep in the newspaper's back pages. Now the transistor is the basis for the billions of computers instrumental to the operation of devices ranging from the cell phone to the airplane.

When the laser was invented, nobody knew what to do with it. Indeed, people told the inventor that it was "a solution in search of a problem." One early application was in chemical research. Then people realized it could be used for measurement and navigation. Today, lasers are employed in optical data transmission, surgery, printing, reproduction of music, retail sales, telecommunications, and much more.

The evolution of the light bulb, transistor, and the laser is repeated for virtually all inventions that have been transformed by innovation. The initial perceived and actual applicability of the invention is narrow, ludicrously so in hindsight. Only after significant technical refinements and the development of ingenious and previously unforeseen applications—the process of innovation—does the invention add substantively to human welfare.

RESEARCH AND DEVELOPMENT AND YOUR STANDARD OF LIVING

Innovation does not arise spontaneously. To paraphrase Edison, it emerges only after substantial inspiration and even more perspiration. As a practical matter, both inventions and innovations are closely tied to how much we spend on research and development (R&D).

Large companies and the federal government are well known for spending billions on the R&D process. A typical large company may see many hundreds of inventions come out of its R&D laboratories each year. Only a few of these inventions are developed into formal proposals for new processes or products. In the end, a carefully chosen dozen or so are further developed and become either more efficient production processes or novel new products. Of those, perhaps one or two may succeed commercially.

Of course, not all R&D is done by large firms and the government. Much is undertaken by single individuals or small start-up companies whose sole initial assets may be no more than the glimmer of an idea in the inventor's mind. Most of these ideas go nowhere. Even so, a large and steady stream of innovation comes to market through the efforts of small companies. Indeed, in some fields, such as pharmaceuticals and computers, the large firms of today were originally founded on a single idea that over years of research and development, eventually became transformed by innovation into a highly successful product.

INNOVATION AND GROWTH

Whoever undertakes the R&D, there is no doubt that the amount of resources devoted to the process has an important impact on our future standard of living. **Economic growth** is the annual increase in the amount of goods and services produced per person each year. The rate of such growth is what determines our future standard of living. For example, if Country A grows by just 1 percentage point per year faster than neighboring country B, its prosperity will *double* relative to its neighbor's in the course of a single human lifespan.

Innovation is essential to economic growth for two reasons. First, innovation is the principal source of new products and of resource-conserving cost reductions for existing products. Second, the prospect of profits from innovation is a chief motivator of the new investment needed to produce more output in the future.

We need only look back to the years before the Industrial Revolution to see the importance of innovation. For most of history until about 1750, the pace of innovation was slow, relatively little new investment took place, and the standard of living hardly moved from one decade—or even century—to the next. Since then, the rate of innovation has been high and the standard of living has soared. Thus, innovation is not just a minor aspect of our economy. It is a fundamental basis of economic growth and prosperity.

INCENTIVES AND INNOVATION

By definition, the innovative process is unpredictable. To the outside observer, then, innovation seems to be totally random. In fact, it is driven by **incentives.** Innovation does not arise spontaneously. It is the result of purposive behavior, motivated by the prospect that the rewards will exceed the costs.

Three elements must be present for sustained, widespread innovation to emerge. First, there must be protection for the ideas that are the source of both inventions and innovation. Second, there must be the prospect of commercial success for the innovation. And finally, this commercial success must actually yield rewards to the innovator.

THE IMPORTANCE OF PATENTS

Many innovative ideas are protected by secrecy. For example, the Coca-Cola Company is the only firm that may produce its flagship product, because it is the only company that knows the formula for that product.

Much of the time, however, the innovative process begins when an inventor applies for a **patent** for her invention. A patent is the protection that the government gives an inventor for the exclusive right to make, use, or sell an item for a limited period of time. This period of time is currently twenty years in the United States. Once the patent is granted, the owner of the patent can sell or license the invention without fear of someone using it without payment.

The American patent system, which dates back to our nation's founding, is generally regarded as the most effective in the world. It is relatively cheap and simple to use, and it offers superior levels of legal protection for patent holders. Hence, the U.S. patent system is acknowledged as playing a crucial role in stimulating innovation in America over the last two centuries.

Although the average rate of innovation in the United States has been high, the emergence of new ideas, at least as measured by patents, has been highly uneven over our history. For example, from 1800 to 1900, new patents grew at a rate of about 6.5 percent per year. From 1900 to 1980, the growth slowed sharply to just over 1 percent per year. World Wars I and II, plus the Great Depression, no doubt played important roles in slowing patent growth, for these events all greatly reduced normal commercial activities, and thus the incentive to invent. Since 1980, the inventive process has again accelerated, with patent growth averaging about 4.5 percent per year.

IS THERE A MARKET?

Innovations are inherently unexpected and thus disruptive. They may pose a threat to existing ways of doing business, as Uber and Lyft have done in the personal transportation market, thereby threatening the profits of existing businesses. Or they may raise the prospect of possible threats to human health or safety, as many people feel that genetically modified organisms (GMOs) have done.

Politicians and bureaucrats often respond to disruption by attempting to suppress it—the simplest way being to prevent the innovative process by sharply limiting the commercial introduction of new goods and services. This type of political or regulatory suppression clearly reduces the potential rewards to innovation and thus cuts the incentives to undertake it. Many observers believe that European efforts to stifle disruptive innovation have played a key role in reducing both innovation and economic growth on that continent in recent decades.

WHO GETS THE PROFITS?

Even if an innovation is legally protected and makes it to the market, there remains a further hurdle. All governments must have tax revenues to operate, and taxes on profits and on the incomes of business owners are important sources of government revenue. Higher taxes mean less after-tax profits, and this in turn means reduced incentives to innovate.

Consider again Europe, where overall taxes are generally much higher than in America. One French economist has estimated that had Bill Gates—the founder of Microsoft Corporation—started that company in France, he would have ended up with only 20 percent of his accumulated wealth. Now, you may say, Gates made so many billions that a few billions less would not have mattered. Yet would Gates have worked twelve hours a day, seven days a week, for the first twenty years of his career had he thought the government was going to take away an extra 80 percent of what he earned? And how many other would-be innovators have simply not bothered to try at all in the face of high tax rates, knowing that 100 percent of the hard work would fall on them, but only 20 percent of the benefits—if any—would be theirs?

HAVE ALL THE EASY INVENTIONS BEEN DISCOVERED?

The six most basic "simple machines," including the wheel, the pulley, the lever, and the screw, were all invented thousands of years ago. Their profound positive impact on human welfare can never be repeated. More recently, the automobile, the telephone, and the electric light bulb were all invented more than one hundred years ago, yielding benefits not easily replicated by other innovations.

Examples such as these have led some observers to argue that "all the important stuff has already been invented." According to this view, from now on it is going to become harder and harder to invent anything that matters very much. There will not be anything like the discovery of electricity or antibiotics in the future. And given this, the benefits of future innovation will likely be far less than those in the past. If this pessimistic view of the world is correct, we might thus expect future rates of economic growth to be far lower than the ones we have enjoyed previously.

Not everyone agrees that the future is so bleak, however. Consider the automobile, invented late in the nineteenth century. Pessimists argue that cars today are really just refinements of that initial invention. The "big bang" of the car is gone, and something of comparable magnitude cannot realistically be expected again. But this ignores the fact that the first auto was no more than an existing engine bolted onto a wagon frame, using a method of transmitting engine power to wheels that had been adapted from other processes. Even the original steering system was borrowed from wagons. In short, the automobile was simply a new idea built on the platform of old ideas—with a twist. If we fast-forward 130 years, "automobiles" are still with us, but their transformation—one innovation at a time—is nothing short of staggering.

Indeed, the automobile episode characterizes a fundamental feature of every innovation: commercial, artistic, intellectual, or otherwise. *All* of them have built on the ideas of the past. But this means that with the creation of each new idea (invention or innovation), the stock of ideas on which still more new ideas can be built is increased. For this reason, the optimists argue, we can actually expect *more* innovation in the future than in the past, because the foundation for it grows with each new idea.

WHAT DOES THE FUTURE HOLD?

Because innovations are, by their very nature, unexpected, neither we nor anyone else can know the future of innovation. By using the principles of economics, however, we *are* able to make some predictions about how government policies will influence that future.

As we noted above, just as innovation is the engine of economic growth, so too are incentives the engine of innovation. If property rights to new ideas are protected, if fear does not cause us to suppress novelty, and if innovators are allowed to keep the fruits of their labor, then the future of innovation is bright. But if these conditions are not met, innovation will languish, along with the possibility of a more prosperous future. Thus, even if few of us may individually be responsible for important innovations of the future, it is within the power of all of us to encourage government policies that will make such innovation possible.

FOR CRITICAL ANALYSIS

1. If you had the choice of living today or 100 years ago, which would you prefer and why? What about the choice between now and 100 years in the future?

2. Why is it true that inventions are "a dime a dozen"?

3. Are those resources that are spent on R&D but do not yield profitable innovations wasted? Why or why not?

4. Why does it matter to you if the long-run economic growth rate falls from its historical 2.1 percent to, say, only 0.9 percent? How does your answer differ depending on whether you are looking ahead to the end of this year or are looking ahead to the entirety of your working career?

5. Suppose you are about to start an innovative, high-tech company in one of two countries. You expect before-tax profits to be about $100,000 per year. Both nations have similar living conditions, climate, and other amenities, but the tax rate in nation A is 17 percent, while the tax rate in nation B is 7 percent. By how much will your annual after-tax profits differ between the two countries? From a business perspective, which country is a preferred location? How will your choice affect economic growth in the two nations, even if by only the tiniest of margins?

6. What are the innovations from the last five years that you think are the most important in your life and why? Can you put a rough dollar value on the personal loss you would suffer if these innovations had *not* occurred, perhaps because they were suppressed or discouraged by government policies?

CHAPTER 3

Outsourcing and Economic Growth

One prominent business commentator keeps a "hit list" of corporations that send jobs overseas. Such actions are decidedly un-American, he opines, whenever he gets a chance to express his views against **outsourcing.** A Democratic presidential nominee over a decade ago had a name for heads of companies that outsourced telemarketing projects, customer services, and other white-collar jobs to foreign countries: "Benedict Arnold CEOs." More recently, President Trump has made it clear that "Made in America" is the only acceptable business model.

Congress even tried to pass a bill to prevent any type of outsourcing by the Department of State and the Department of Defense. One Republican representative at the time said, "You can't just continue to outsource overseas time after time after time, lose your strategic military base, and then expect this Congress to sit back and see the jobs lost and do nothing." When an adviser to the president publicly stated that the foreign outsourcing of service jobs was not such a bad idea, numerous politicians lambasted him for even the suggestion that outsourcing could be viewed in a positive light.

What Is This "Outsourcing"?

The concept of outsourcing is simple: Instead of hiring American workers at home, American corporations hire foreign workers to do the same jobs. For example, some of these foreign workers are in India and do call center work, answering technical questions for computer purchasers. Another job such workers do well (and cheaply) is software development and debugging. Because of low-cost communication, especially over the

Internet, software programmers can be just about anywhere in the world and still work for U.S. corporations.

Besides the fear that outsourcing "robs Americans of jobs," it is also claimed that outsourcing reduces **economic growth** in the United States. Because outsourcing is part and parcel of international trade in goods and services, the real question becomes: Can the United States have higher growth rates if it restricts American corporations from "sending jobs abroad"?

As we set out to answer this question, we must keep one simple fact in mind: Outsourcing is nothing more or less than the purchase of labor services from the residents of a foreign nation. When the Detroit Red Wings host the Vancouver Canucks, fans at the game are outsourcing. They are purchasing labor services from Canadians. In this sense, Canadian hockey players are no different from Indian software engineers. They are citizens of foreign nations who are competing with citizens of the United States in the supply of labor services. Just as important, outsourcing is no different from any other form of international trade.

The Link between Economic Growth and Outsourcing

International trade has been around for thousands of years. This means that the concept of outsourcing is certainly not new, even though the term seems to be. After all, the exchange of services between countries is a part of international trade. In any event, if we decide to restrict this type of international trade in services, we will be restricting international trade in general. Experts who study economic growth today have found that the openness of an economy is a key determinant of its rate of economic growth. Any restriction on outsourcing is a type of **trade barrier,** one that will reduce the benefits we obtain from international trade.

There is a clear historical link between economic growth and trade barriers. Figure 3–1 shows the relationship between the openness of an economy—fewer or more trade barriers—and the rate of economic growth. Along the horizontal axis of the graph is a trade barrier index, which for the United States is equal to 100. On the vertical axis, you see the average annual growth of **per capita income** in percentage terms.

It is evident from this graph that countries that have fewer international trade barriers have also had higher rates of economic growth. The lesson of history is quite clear: International trade increases economic growth, and growth boosts economic well-being. Government efforts to restrict outsourcing will restrict international trade, and this will make Americans poorer, not richer.

Figure 3–1 Relationship between Economic Growth and Barriers to International Trade

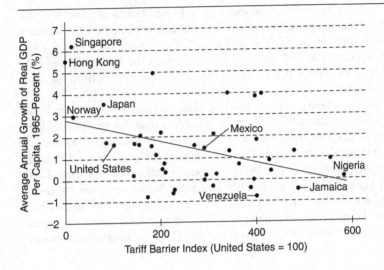

WILL THE UNITED STATES BECOME A THIRD WORLD COUNTRY?

In spite of the evidence just shown, one prominent economic commentator declared "the United States will be a third world economy in twenty years." His prediction was based on the idea that entire classes of high-wage service-sector employees will eventually find themselves in competition with highly skilled workers abroad who command lower salaries than their U.S. counterparts. He contended that U.S. software programmers and radiologists, for example, will not be able to compete in the global economy. Thus, he argued, the United States will lose millions of white-collar jobs due to outsourcing of service-sector employment to India and China.

Jeffrey E. Garten, former dean of the Yale School of Management, reiterated and expanded on this prediction. He believes that the transfer of jobs abroad will accelerate for generations to come. He argues that in countries from China to the Czech Republic, there is a "virtually unlimited supply of industrious and educated labor working at a fraction of U.S. wages." Similarly, according to Craig Barrett, former board chair at the chipmaker Intel, American workers today face the prospect of "300 million well-educated people in India, China, and Russia who can do effectively any job that can be done" in the United States.

Still other commentators have claimed that India alone will soak up as many as four million jobs from the U.S. labor market within the next few years. Some even believe that this number may exceed ten million. If true, one might expect American software developers and call center technicians to start moving to India!

SOME OVERLOOKED FACTS

Much of the outsourcing discussion has ignored two simple facts that turn out to be important if we really want to understand what the future will bring.

1. *Outsourcing is the result of trade liberalization in foreign nations.* After decades of isolation, the markets in China, India, and Eastern Europe have begun to open up to international trade. As often happens when governments finally allow their people to trade internationally, these governments have pushed hard to stimulate exports—of labor services as well as goods. Nonetheless, this cannot be a long-term equilibrium strategy because the workers producing those goods and supplying those services are doing it because they want to become consumers. Soon enough, and this is already happening, they want to spend their hard-earned income on goods and services, many of which are produced abroad. Thus, today's outsourcing of jobs to those nations is turning into exports of goods and services to those same nations. This in turns implies more export-industry jobs for their trading partners.

2. *Prices adjust to keep markets in balance.* The supply curve of labor is upward-sloping. Thus, as U.S. corporations hire foreign workers (either directly by outsourcing or indirectly by importing goods), market wages in foreign lands must rise. Between 2003 and 2010, for example, Indian labor-outsourcing companies saw wages rise more than 50 percent. Over a longer span, real wages in southern China (which has been open to trade far longer than India) are now *six times higher* than they were just twenty years ago. These higher wages obviously reduce the competitiveness of the firms that must pay them. As a result, over the last few years, an increasing number of jobs are now being outsourced from China to other nations. Most of these jobs are going to low-wage Vietnam, Cambodia, or Indonesia. But some are even being outsourced to the United States, because slower wage growth here has made American workers more competitive.

Of course, adjustments are never instantaneous. Moreover, they are occurring because some American firms are moving output and employment abroad. Hence, at least some U.S. workers are moving to lower-paying jobs, often with a spell of unemployment along the way. How big is the impact in the short run, before all of the price adjustments take place? According to the Bureau of Labor Statistics, in a typical recent year, the number of jobs lost to outsourcing is measured in the thousands—out of a workforce of 160 million. So if you are currently a U.S. software developer, you do not have to worry about packing your bags for Mumbai, at least not soon.

INSOURCING BY FOREIGN FIRMS

U.S. firms are not the only ones that engage in outsourcing. Many foreign firms do the same. When a foreign firm outsources to the United States, we can call it **insourcing.** For example, Mexican firms routinely send data to U.S. accounting businesses for calculation of payrolls and for maintenance of financial records. Many foreign hospitals pay American radiologists to read X-rays and MRI images. Foreign firms use American firms to provide a host of other services, many of which involve consulting. Also, when a foreign automobile manufacturer builds an assembly plant in the United States, it is in effect outsourcing automobile assembly to American workers. Thus, American workers in the South Carolina BMW plant, the Alabama Mercedes-Benz plant, or the Toyota or Honda plants in Tennessee and Ohio have benefitted because those foreign companies have insourced jobs to the United States.

Indeed, all across the country and around the world, hundreds of millions of workers are employed by "foreign" corporations—although it is becoming difficult to tell the nationality of any company, given the far-flung nature of today's global enterprises.

WHAT REALLY MATTERS: THE LONG RUN

If you own the only grocery store in your small town, you are clearly harmed if a competing store opens across the street. If you work in a small telephone equipment store and a large company starts taking away business via Internet sales, you will obviously be worse off. If you formerly were employed at a call center for customer service at Walmart and have just lost your job because Walmart outsourced to a cheaper Indian firm, you will have to look for a new job.

These kinds of "losses" of income or jobs have occurred since the beginning of commerce. They will always exist in any dynamic economy. Indeed, if we look over the American economy as a whole, in a typical year roughly *1 million workers lose their jobs every week*. But in a typical year slightly *more* than 1 million people find a new job every week. On balance then, employment in the United States keeps growing, even though the average person changes jobs every three years—some, no doubt, because of international competition. Job turnover like this is an essential component of a labor market that is continually adjusting to economic change. It is a sign of health, not sickness, in the economy. If you find this hard to believe, you can look west or east. In Japan, efforts to "protect" workers from international trade resulted in economic stagnation and have depressed real income growth over the past twenty years. In Europe, similar efforts to "preserve" the jobs of existing workers have resulted in *higher*, not lower, unemployment because firms are unwilling to hire people that they cannot later fire.

It is true that the pattern of job losses and gains in a given year is altered during an economic recession. In particular, during the early stages of a recession, additional people lose their jobs in a given week and fewer people find a job each week, with the result being higher unemployment in the short run. But international trade is not the cause of recessions in the United States (although an economic recession can be made worse by *restrictions* on international trade, as it was in the early 1930s). On the contrary, international trade is an important source of economic prosperity.

If you are still wondering, simply look back at Figure 3–1. The lessons of history and of economics are clear: Trade creates **wealth,** and that is true whether the trade is interpersonal, interstate, or international. The reality is that labor outsourcing is simply part of a worldwide trend toward increased international trade in both goods and services. As international trade expands—assuming that politicians and bureaucrats allow it to expand—the result will be higher rates of growth and higher levels of income in the United States and elsewhere. American workers will continue to enjoy the fruits of that growth, just as they always have.

For Critical Analysis

1. What, if any, differences exist between competition among service workers across the fifty states and competition among service workers across nations?

2. When BMW decides to build a plant in the United States, who gains and who loses?

3. International Business Machines Corporation (IBM) recently stated that it expected to save almost $170 million annually by shifting several thousand high-paying programming jobs overseas. Explain why IBM would undertake this move. Then explain the short-run and long-run effects of this outsourcing.

4. Some companies that outsourced call centers during the 1990s have returned these centers to North America over the past decade. Who has gained and who has lost as a result of the return of the call centers to this continent? Explain.

5. The automaker BMW, whose corporate headquarters is in Germany, makes its X-series sport utility vehicles in South Carolina and sells many of them in China. Who is outsourcing what to whom? Explain.

6. What is the difference between outsourcing and international trade?

CHAPTER 4

Poverty, Capitalism, and Growth

Fifty years ago, nearly half of the world's population lived in abject poverty; today, the proportion is under 10 percent. In fact, compared to fifty years ago, even though the world's population has doubled, there are actually far fewer people now living below the poverty line. Despite the human misery that is evident to varying degrees in virtually every nation of the world, there is little doubt that economic prosperity has made great strides.

THE SWEEP OF HISTORY

The past half-century is but a small part of a story that has evolved over the course of more than 250 years. In the middle of the eighteenth century, perhaps 90 percent of the world's population lived in a state of **abject poverty,** subsisting on the equivalent of less than $700 per person per year, measured in today's terms. In fact, for most of human history, abject poverty—including inadequate nutrition and rudimentary shelter—was the norm for almost everyone, everywhere. This began to change in the eighteenth century with the **Industrial Revolution** and its associated mechanization of tasks that had always been laboriously done by humans or animals. Stimulated in the early years by the invention and application of the steam engine, the Industrial Revolution initiated a massive cascade of innovations in transportation, chemistry, biology, manufacturing processes, communications, and electronic technology. This continuing process of invention and innovation has made little headway in many parts of the world, but where it has taken hold, there has been a sustained rise in average **real per capita income** and a corresponding decline in poverty. By 1820, the extent of abject poverty had fallen to 80 percent. By 1900, it had dipped below 70 percent and has continued to decline since. Before the Industrial Revolution, nine out of ten people lived in abject poverty. Today, it is *one* out of ten.

UNEVEN PROGRESS

This story of human progress has been uneven across countries. Europe, North America, and a few other locations have witnessed the greatest increases in real per capita income and the greatest decreases in poverty. By contrast, the **standard of living** and the extent of poverty in many African nations have changed little over the past 250 years. Even within given countries, progress has sometimes been erratic. Ninety years ago, for example, the standard of living in Argentina was the sixth highest in the world. Today, that nation ranks sixtieth in living standards. In contrast, thirty years ago, 750 million people in China lived in abject poverty; that number has since been cut to about 150 million.

In Chapter 1, you saw the key institutional factors that determine average levels of **per capita income.** Secure **property and contract rights** and the **rule of law** were the **institutions** under which the Industrial Revolution flourished best, and it is thus in nations that have embraced these institutions that people are most likely to be prosperous. These same institutions are those typically associated with **capitalism,** economic systems that depend primarily (though not necessarily totally) on markets to allocate scarce **resources.** Of course, no country in the world is completely capitalist. In the United States, for example, only about 60 percent of resources are allocated by the private sector, while the rest are allocated by federal, state, or local governments. At the other end of the spectrum, even in Communist countries, such as Cuba, Vietnam, and North Korea, markets play at least some role in allocating resources.

Despite a few ambiguities, then, it is possible to measure the degree of capitalism (or, as some would term it, economic freedom) in each country around the world. Doing so yields measures that seem to correspond reasonably well with what many people would think is true about the economies of those countries. For example, using the measures constructed by Canada's Fraser Institute, Hong Kong's economy is rated the most capitalist. Singapore, Switzerland, New Zealand, Canada, and Australia are other nations whose economies are judged among the ten most capitalist in the world. If you know much about economic prosperity around the world, you will be aware that these countries are also among the world leaders in real per capita income. Indeed, the association of capitalism with prosperity is everywhere quite strong.

You may be surprised that the United States was not mentioned among the top ten capitalist nations. In fact, it used to be there, year after year. Beginning about 2001, however, the combination of rapidly growing government regulations and sharply higher federal spending began taking their toll on economic freedom. As a result the United States has dropped from third most capitalist to sixteenth on the list. Overall, we are now about as capitalist as several of the formerly communist countries of Eastern Europe, such as Lithuania, Estonia, and Romania.

Capitalism and Prosperity

When thinking about the impact of capitalism, it is convenient to divide all the nations in the world into four groups, ranging from "most capitalist" to "least capitalist." Data limitations prevent doing this with every single nation. Nevertheless, it is possible to do it for almost 160 of them, putting forty nations into each of the four groups. Thus, among the top forty "most capitalist" nations, in addition to the countries we mentioned earlier, many (but not all!) of the original members of the **European Union (EU)** would be included, along with Chile, Taiwan, and Panama. At the other end of the spectrum, the economies of Argentina, Iran, Venezuela, and Zimbabwe would all fall into the group of the forty "least capitalist" nations.

As we suggested earlier, people who live in the most capitalist nations in the world also tend to have the highest average income. For example, average per capita income for people living in the group including the forty most capitalist nations averages over $42,000 per year. For people living in the next most capitalist group of nations, per capita income averages about $21,000 per year. Once we get down to the forty least capitalist nations, average income has dropped to $5,900 per year. In addition, because rates of economic growth are *also* higher in more capitalist nations, the differences in income between the most and least capitalist nations are growing over time.[1]

Of course, this is a chapter about poverty, and the *average* income in a nation may bear little relation to the income earned by its poorest residents. Many people believe, for example, that capitalist nations promote excessively competitive behavior so that people who are not good at competing end up much poorer in capitalist than in noncapitalist nations. If the rich get richer in capitalist countries while the poor get poorer, then

---

1 All income comparisons are made using a method called **purchasing power parity (PPP)**, generally acknowledged to be the most accurate means of making comparisons across nations with very different income levels and consumption bundles.

even if the average person in capitalist nations is doing well, the same might not be true for people at the bottom of the income distribution. As it turns out, however, the poor do *not* do worse in capitalist countries. In fact, they do *better.*

Capitalism and Poverty

Consider the forty most capitalist nations in the world. On average, the poorest 10 percent of the population receives about 2.5 percent of total income in these countries. Indeed, if we look across *all* countries, we find that although there is some variation from nation to nation, the poorest 10 percent of the population typically gets between 2.0 and 2.5 percent of total income. One way to put this is that on average, capitalism does *not* lower the share of total income going to the people at the bottom of the income distribution. Capitalist or Communist, in Africa or in the Americas, the per capita income of the poorest 10 percent of the population in a nation ends up being about one-quarter of per capita income in the middle of the income distribution for that country.

Now if you followed the numbers earlier about average income and capitalism, you may already have figured out the next point: Because capitalism raises total income in a nation without reducing the *share* of income going to the poor, capitalism ends up raising income at *all* points in the income distribution. Thus, for the poorest 10 percent of the population in highly capitalist countries, average per capita income is about $12,000 per year (or $48,000 per year for a family of four). For the poorest 10 percent of the population in the least capitalist countries, average income is under $1,200 per year (about $4,800 for a family of four). Expressed somewhat differently, poor people in the most capitalist nations can expect average income levels *ten times higher* than poor people in the least capitalist nations.

Now and the Future

The radically better standard of living experienced by the poor in capitalist nations is reflected in many other statistics indicative of quality of life. For example, life expectancy in the forty most capitalist nations is a bit over 80 years. In the least capitalist, it is 64. Similarly, infant mortality rates are *eight times higher* in the least capitalist countries than in the most capitalist countries. Moreover, because people at the top of the income distribution have access to health care in both rich and poor nations, these differences in life expectancy and infant mortality are chiefly due to differences among people at the bottom of the income distribution. In capitalist nations, compared to noncapitalist countries, it is the poor whose newborns are surviving infancy and whose adults are surviving to old age.

There is another compelling difference between capitalist and noncapitalist countries that sheds light on what the future may bring. In the forty most capitalist countries of the world, fewer than 1 percent of children under the age of fifteen are working rather than in school. In the forty least capitalist nations, one child of every six under the age of fifteen is working rather than being in school—a rate nearly twenty times higher. Thus, in capitalist nations, children are much more likely to be getting the education needed to acquire the skills of the future. This in turn means that **economic growth** is likely to be higher in capitalist nations than in noncapitalist nations, and this is exactly what we observe. Growth in per capita income in the forty most capitalist countries averages about 3.6 percent per year, enough to double income at all levels over the next twenty-one years. In contrast, average per capita incomes have been growing barely 1.5 percent per year in the least capitalist nations. Incomes are rising around the world, but the gap—some might say the gulf—between the capitalist nations and noncapitalist nations is growing steadily.

MORE THAN NUMBERS

It is easy to get too wrapped up in numbers, so it may be useful to make a few simple head-to-head comparisons. Consider North Korea and South Korea. Both emerged from World War II with shattered economies, only to fight each other in the Korean War. When the war was over, South Korea embraced capitalism, building an economy based on the rule of law, secure property rights, and a reliance on the market as the primary means of allocating scarce resources. North Korea rejected all of these, choosing instead a Communist system that relied on centralized command and control to allocate resources—a system ruled not by law but by one man at the top. South Korea became a world economic powerhouse, with per capita income of $37,000 per year. North Korea stagnated and, with a per capita income of only $1,800 per year, must now rely on foreign aid to feed many of its people.

If we were to look at East Germany and West Germany between World War II and the fall of the Berlin Wall in 1989, we would see the same story repeated. West Germany embraced the central principles of a market-based capitalist economy and prospered. East Germany rejected those principles, and its people were impoverished. A similar tale of two countries can be told in comparing the economies of Taiwan and China between 1950 and 1980. Capitalist Taiwan prospered while Communist China stagnated—and people at the bottom of the income distribution suffered the most.

Indeed, China itself presents us with a tale of two countries: the Communist version before 1980 and the increasingly capitalist one of the years since. After decades of post–World War II stagnation under communism, the gradual move toward market-based resource allocation in China since 1980 is transforming life for people at all levels of income. Overall, real per capita income has roughly doubled every decade since 1980. Moreover, at least in those areas of the country where the Communists have let the capitalists try their hand, this economic progress has been widespread and sustained. Thus, even though political freedom in China is not present, the growing economic freedom in that nation is having the same impact it has had around the world and over time: When people are able to enjoy secure property rights, the rule of law, and a reliance on markets as allocators of scarce resources, people at *all* points in the distribution benefit.

For Critical Analysis

1. The income measures discussed in this chapter do not include non-cash benefits that are often available to low-income individuals, such as food stamps and Medicaid. Do you think such noncash benefits are more likely to be made available to poor people in a rich nation or in a poor nation? Explain your answer. (*Hint:* Do people get more or less charitable as their incomes rise?) Then ask yourself: How will the difference in noncash benefits in rich nations versus poor nations affect your conclusions regarding relative incomes of poor individuals in capitalist nations compared to noncapitalist nations? Explain this answer as well.

2. How would a political system in which there is the rule of law (i.e., in which the same rules apply to everyone) serve to protect people at the bottom of the income distribution most effectively?

3. In light of the analysis in Chapter 1 and the information presented in this chapter, what are some ways that people in developed nations might help people in developing nations achieve higher income levels? Give specific examples.

4. If capitalism is so good at creating economic prosperity, why don't more nations try it?

5. Over the past few years, the United States has slipped downward in the rankings of capitalist countries. As you read the rest of this book, use the knowledge you gain to compile a list of the specific reasons you think the U.S. ranking has dropped.

6. According to the CIA *World Factbook*, the Democratic Republic of the Congo ranks among the poorest nations in the world year after year. How do you suppose this country ranks in its degree of capitalism? Test your prediction by going to the Fraser Institute's Web site (www.fraserinstitute.org) and seeing where the Congo rates on the Institute's Index of Economic Freedom.

CHAPTER 5

The Threat to Growth

During Barack Obama's presidency, government spending hit levels virtually unprecedented in American history. At its peak, the federal government, for example, was spending fully *one-quarter* of gross domestic product (GDP), and state and local government spending accounted for an additional 15 percent of GDP. At no time in American history have state and local governments spent as much as they have recently. Only briefly, during the height of World War II, has federal spending as a share of GDP ever rivaled its recent heights. Remarkably, the big spending of 2009–2017 was just a continuation of an upsurge that began early in George Bush's two terms in office. Bailouts, subsidies, entitlements, bloated pensions, subsidized health care, and two ground wars in Asia (Iraq and Afghanistan) created a "perfect storm" of massive government spending at all levels.

THE BIG PICTURE

"So what," you might say. If the government was not spending it, someone else would be. Indeed, when government spends more, whatever the spending is on, there is ultimately only one place the government can obtain the resources. That place is you and everyone else who earns income each year in the United States. In the short run, just as you can borrow, so too can governments—an activity that is called running a **budget deficit.** Nevertheless, the ability to borrow does not change the fundamental **budget constraint** facing our society. What is spent today must be paid for now or in the future. And when it is government doing the spending, that means the higher spending today *must* eventually be matched with higher taxes. Hence, today's big spending means higher taxes (and lower private spending) for you and everyone else who earns income in the United States.

Now, if those higher taxes just meant that Peter would have less spending power so that Paul could have more, this chapter probably would not be worth writing. But Peter's income does not simply appear like a surprise birthday gift. Instead, his income is the result of hard work, investing, and innovation. When taxes rise, the **incentives** of taxpayers to work, invest, and innovate is reduced—and that in turn means lower economic growth and lower wealth now and in the future.

INCENTIVES ARE IMPORTANT

We have seen in the previous chapters that secure property rights and the rule of law are crucial in fostering economic growth. These institutions help ensure that individuals are confident that they will get to keep the fruits of their labor. Hence, people are willing to work hard, invest for the future, and engage in innovation. In addition, because all of these activities contribute to higher incomes and greater economic growth, they ensure more long-run prosperity. But note the key point: People work, invest, and innovate because they believe they will be rewarded with the fruits of their efforts. If these fruits are denied them—because, for example, taxes take much of what they produce—the incentives to work, invest, and innovate are sharply reduced and so too is economic growth and, ultimately, wealth.

Data from Europe illustrate how taxes shape incentives to work. Researchers have found that a tax increase of just over 12 percentage points induces the average adult in Europe to reduce work effort by over 120 hours per year—the equivalent of almost four weeks' work. Such a tax change also causes a sharp reduction in the number of people who work at all, and causes many others to join the **underground economy** or to devote their time to **tax evasion.** Overall, then, higher tax rates cause lower output and lower employment. Wealth is reduced now and in the future.

Taxes also affect the incentives to invest. A good case in point is Ireland, whose economy in the 1980s was a disaster and whose citizens were among the poorest of **European Union (EU)** citizens. In the 1990s, the Irish slashed the corporate **profits** tax to 12.5 percent, the lowest in Europe and only about one-third as high as the U.S. rate of 35 percent. Beginning in 2004, the Irish government also began offering a 20 percent tax credit for company spending on research and development, offering high-tech firms an opportunity to cut their taxes by starting up and expanding operations in Ireland. Almost immediately, Ireland became a magnet for new investment and for successful companies that did not want to hand over one-third or more of their profits to the tax collector.

The combination of lower corporate tax rates and tax breaks on research and development induced hundreds of multinational corporations to begin operations in Ireland. They brought with them hundreds of thousands of new jobs (and this to a nation of only four million residents), and Ireland quickly became number one among the EU's fifteen original members in being home to companies that conduct research and development. As for the people of Ireland, their per capita incomes went from the bottom ranks of the EU to the top.

INNOVATION IS ESSENTIAL

On one point, all economists agree: Innovation is a fundamental, indeed necessary, element of economic growth. Note that we say "innovation" rather than "invention." As we noted in Chapter 2, invention is the creation of a new idea—but plenty of new ideas go nowhere. Innovation is the transformation of a new idea into successful commercial, scientific, or artistic application. Although innovation may incorporate invention, it need not do so. A simple example may suffice.

Many people credit Thomas Edison with the invention in 1880 of the incandescent light bulb. In fact, Sir Humphry Davy created the first recognizable incandescent bulb in 1802, and Edison's bulb was much like one patented in 1875 by two Canadians. Shortly after Edison patented his version of the incandescent bulb, he bought the Canadians' patent rights from them for $5,000 (over $1 million in today's dollars)—and then proceeded to implement indoor electric lighting across America and around the world. The invention was the incandescent light bulb, old news before Edison was even born. The innovation was Edison's successful commercial application of that invention, an activity that included power generation and transmission, as well as the widespread commercial distribution of the bulbs themselves. Sitting in an English, Canadian, or New Jersey laboratory, the bulb was a bright idea. Once it lit up millions of homes and workplaces, however, it raised the world's wealth and contributed to sustained economic growth that continues to enrich us today.

INNOVATION AND WEALTH

Steve Jobs (Apple) did not invent the semiconductor, Bill Gates (Microsoft) did not invent the computer operating system, Oprah Winfrey (*The Oprah Show*) did not invent the talk show, and Mark Zuckerberg (Facebook) did not invent social networking. Yet each of these people became billionaires as innovators in their respective fields of work. To be sure, each has come up with plenty of new ideas, but what distinguishes them from all of the inventors you have never heard of is that the people on the list above have developed and applied their ideas and others' in ways that created enormous commercial success. In doing so, each got rich. More importantly for our purposes, they have contributed significantly to the wealth of millions of *other* people around the world by creating products that satisfied human wants.

Indeed, if we look more carefully at the world, we find that innovation is the source of most of our wealth. It could be the Mexican farmers who six thousand years ago began genetically engineering the precursors to corn. Or it might be Bill Hewlett and David Packard, who transformed semiconductors into calculators, business machines, and laser printers. But in each instance, it is innovation that has created the products that enable us to live like no other species on earth. In addition, although it is unlikely that many of the long-dead creators of corn got rich, many of the wealthiest people in the world are rich because of their innovations.

Even among the merely prosperous people of the world, innovation often plays a key role in creating their prosperity. Although **wealth** is obviously passed down from one generation to another, when we look at the **standard of living** of individuals, very little of that standard of living is determined by the financial inheritance they received from their ancestors. Instead, current living standards of people are primarily determined by the incomes they have earned for themselves. These incomes are chiefly the result of what they have produced in the workplace.[1] And most often, very high levels of workplace productivity are the result of innovative activity by those productive individuals.

TAXATION AND INNOVATION

Surely many things motivate all individuals, including innovators, great and small. One of these motivating factors may reasonably be assumed to be financial success. (We say this because there is a vast body of evidence that financial success is one of the motivators of human beings in virtually all walks of life.) This notion brings us back to taxes, where our story began. Innovators, like everyone else, only receive **after-tax income,** that is, income *after* the various government entities have collected the taxes they impose. These taxes may come in a variety of forms: income taxes, sales taxes, property taxes, and so forth. Whatever

---

1 We do inherit plenty of *nonfinancial* wealth from our parents, of course, including intelligence and work habits, which play a role in determining how much we produce and hence our standard of living.

their form or level of government at which they are levied, however, higher taxes mean lower after-tax incomes, and this reduces the incentive to innovate. Higher taxes also reduce the incentive to invest (because taxes cut into the after-tax income from investment) and even to work—because higher taxes mean lower after-tax income from work. Across the board, then, higher taxes discourage the very activities that create prosperity.

An easy way to think about the effect of taxes on behavior is to imagine that we decided to raise taxes on professional athletes. Recall from above that the most productive people are those who tend to earn the highest incomes. Almost surely, then, the biggest burden of higher taxes would be on those with the highest incomes—which also means those who are the most productive. The best runners and rebounders and hitters and passers would get the biggest increase in tax bills. What are the likely consequences? Overall performance would suffer. Athletes would spend less time working out in the off-season. They would spend less time practicing year round. They would devote less effort to studying their opponents—the list goes on and on. And the result would be a decline in the quality of the competition and less enjoyment for fans. Output, no matter how we measure it, would fall. To be sure, many players would still be motivated by pride and inherent competitive drive, but the extra edge offered by financial rewards would be gone—and so would the performance edge.

The same destruction of incentives occurs when taxes are raised on anyone who works, or invests, or innovates. As long as incomes are determined chiefly by performance (and the evidence is that they are), higher taxes reduce the incentive of people to engage in those activities that contribute to economic growth and thus increase our wealth. As in sports, the outcome is reduced performance and lower output, however measured.

THE RELEVANCE FOR TODAY

We started this chapter by discussing the historically high levels of government spending that we have been experiencing. Because this spending must eventually be paid for out of taxes, we can now see the threat to economic growth and prosperity that is posed by high levels of government spending. The result of this spending *must* be higher taxes, and higher taxes will reduce the incentives to work, invest, and innovate. This in turn means less economic growth and lower income and wealth.

Of course, the damage caused by higher taxes could be offset if the government spending represented productive investments in the future, as would occur, for example, if America's failing transportation infrastructure were being rebuilt. In fact, the upsurge in government spending since 2001 has most emphatically *not* been of this variety. Thus, once we account for the adverse effects of the higher taxes, we can conclude that our standard of living in the future will be lowered because of our government's spending today. President Trump has promised to direct more government spending to infrastructure improvements, but presidents Bush and Obama made the same promise—and failed to deliver.

Nearly a half century ago, President John F. Kennedy said, "An economy hampered by restrictive taxes will never produce enough revenue to balance our budget, just as it will never produce enough jobs or enough profits." It appears that this is a message that today's political leaders either do not understand or do not care to heed.

For Critical Analysis

1. Barack Obama campaigned for the presidency on the theme that he would bring "change" to the United States. One of the major changes occurring in President Obama's time in office was in the size of the federal debt. Largely because of higher federal spending over those years, federal debt almost *doubled* between January 20, 2009 and January 20, 2017 (an increase of about $30,000 for each person living in the United States). What does this higher debt imply must happen to the taxes you will pay over your lifetime?

2. Many European countries have imposed a **wealth tax.** It is typically based on everything a person owns, minus everything the person owes (the difference between what is owned and what is owed is called **net worth**). Put yourself in the shoes of an individual in a country that has just decided to impose a wealth tax. How does a wealth tax affect your incentive to accumulate wealth? How does it affect your incentive to work hard?

3. Explain why the incentives of individuals and businesses are chiefly affected by changes in **marginal tax rates**—that is, the share that must go to taxes out of the *next* income that is earned.

4. Fifty years ago in the United States, high-income people paid as much as 91 cents in federal personal income taxes on each additional dollar of income they earned. If you found yourself paying such a 91 percent marginal tax rate, how great would be your incentive to find legal **loopholes** to reduce your federal tax **liabilities?** If you found yourself in the lowest federal personal

income tax bracket of, say, 15 percent (paying 15 cents in taxes out of each additional dollar earned), would your incentive to find loopholes to reduce your tax bill be the same? Explain.

5. Let's suppose that income tax rates rise significantly over the next ten years. How can people at all levels of income react over time, not just immediately after taxes are raised? How will the size of the response differ, say, a year after the rise in tax rates compared to a week after the increase? Is it possible that some people will actually change their behavior *before* the higher tax rates go into effect? Explain.

6. How does the structure of a country's tax system affect who decides to immigrate into the nation or emigrate out of the nation? Contrast, for example, nations A and B. Assume that nation A applies a 20 percent tax rate on every dollar of income earned by an individual (i.e., 20 cents in taxes must be paid on each dollar of income). Nation B applies a 10 percent tax rate (10 cents per dollar) on the *first* $40,000 per year of income and a 40 percent tax rate (40 cents per dollar) on all income *above* $40,000 per year earned by an individual. Start by computing the tax bill in each country that must be paid by a person earning $40,000 per year and the tax bill that must be paid by a person earning $100,000 per year. Then consider the more general issue: If the language, culture, and climate of the two nations are similar and if a person can choose to live on one side or the other of a river separating the two nations, who is more likely to choose to live in A, and who is more likely to choose to live in B? To what extent does your reasoning apply if an ocean, rather than a river, separates the two countries? Does it apply if the language, culture, or climate in the two nations differ? Explain.

CHAPTER 6

Hello Boomers, Goodbye Prosperity

The baby boom generation comprises those people born from 1948 to 1964. It is a generation that brought the world free love, antiwar protests, environmental activism, women's rights, and one of the greatest periods of economic growth in recorded history. But as its members now retire, moving from the workforce into full-time rest and recreation, it is a generation that is helping to cause declining workforce productivity and sluggish—even negative—economic growth. And until recently, almost no one realized just how much the departing boomers had meant to the immediate past performance of the economy, or its likely performance over the next decade.

THE LIFE CYCLE OF LABOR

If we look at a generation of individuals such as the baby boomers, we can observe a predictable pattern of working behavior among them. Around the age of sixteen, people begin moving from school into the workforce. That is, the **labor force participation rate** of the generation (the fraction of the population that is either working or looking for work) begins rising sharply. Typically, the **labor productivity** of these early entrants is low because their education levels are low, as is their experience in the labor force.

Over the next thirty to forty years, two important developments take place in the working characteristics of the generation. First, as more people finish their education and then start families, the labor force participation rate moves up steadily, hitting a peak (of 80 percent or more) at around age forty-five. Second, the observed productivity of working individuals grows, partly because more educated people are starting work, and partly because people are gaining productive experience on the job.[1] The combined effect of these two forces means that the overall productivity of the generation hits a peak at around age fifty, somewhere in between the peak labor force participation year (forty-five) and the peak individual earnings year (fifty-five).

THE BOOMER CYCLE

Roughly speaking, the average birth year of the baby boomers was 1955—midway between the start (1946) and end (1964) of the surge in post–World War II birthrates. Once we recognize that the peak productivity of this generation occurred around age fifty, we can see that the peak productive contribution of the boomers must have occurred around 2005, which is fifty years beyond 1955.

From the 1960s until about 2005, the baby boomers played a key role in fueling **economic growth** around the world. In the United States, for example, their rising productivity kept **real per capita GDP** growing above its long-term rate of about 2 percent per year. Since 2005, fewer and fewer of the highly productive boomers have remained in the workforce, and those who stay are becoming less productive as they age past their peak of abilities. The combined effect has been to reduce economic growth *below* its long-term average. Moreover, because the last of the boomers won't depart the labor force until about 2030, we can expect this decreased growth to persist for the next decade or so.

Now, as we note in Chapter 11, the boomers are not the only source of reduced economic performance since 2005. Both the recession of 2007–2009 and the sharp increase in heavy-handed economic regulation under presidents Bush and Obama contributed significantly, too. Moreover, economic growth between now and 2030 will be influenced by the economic policies of President Trump and his successors. Still, the impact of the boomers is significant, and it is showing up in some unexpected ways.

THE IMPACT ON PRODUCTIVITY

The adverse productivity effects we have been discussing so far generally become apparent around age sixty, on average, so let's focus on that number. Thus, we'll divide the population into those people who are

---

1 Because people tend to get paid based on what they produce, this implies that wages and salaries are also rising as the generation ages, hitting a peak for the individual at around age fifty-five. See Chapter 14 for more on the life-cycle pattern of wages.

younger than sixty, versus those sixty and above, and call the latter group the "seniors." The proportion of the population comprised of people over sixty has been rising steadily for more than a century, primarily because of medical improvements that have led to increasing life expectancy. But the fraction consisting of seniors really began to accelerate around 2000, as the first members of the boomer wave approached sixty. And sure enough, this showed up in the productivity numbers.

It now appears that every 10 percent increase in the proportion of the population that is over sixty reduces per capita growth by about 5.5 percent. Because the proportion of seniors in the population jumped almost 25 percent between 2000 and 2015, this caused economic growth to drop by about 13 percent over this period. Interestingly, only about one-third of this reduced growth occurred because the retirements of the seniors reduced labor force participation rates. The rest of the drop in productivity occurred because the workers who *remained* became less productive when the seniors departed, because of on-the-job complementarity between older and younger workers. Let's see how this works.

EXPERIENCE AND PRODUCTIVITY

We noted earlier that workplace experience leads to higher productivity among workers. Despite all that can be learned in school, some things can be learned only on the job, and this learning continues over most, if not all, of a worker's career. Some of this learning occurs as a result of the mistakes that one makes along the way. But some also occurs because older, more experienced co-workers who have "been there and done that" pass along their knowledge to the workers coming up behind them. For example, at the start of their careers, rookie police officers are typically paired up with older veterans to help them learn how policing is done in real-world settings. Similarly, young physicians are mentored by experienced doctors, who can help them avoid common, sometimes deadly, errors.

In blue-collar and white-collar jobs alike, the knowledge passed along from older workers to younger workers raises productivity. When the older workers retire, they take their knowledge with them. In many cases, this means that younger workers must learn the hard way—by making mistakes. Such errors reduce output and raise costs, and the result is lower productivity and a lower standard of living. In the overall productivity figure for the economy, the loss in mentorship by older workers appears to account for about two-thirds of the productivity loss associated with the aging of the work force.

POLICY CONFUSION

The workforces in Europe and Japan are aging, as they are in the United States. The productivity in both of these geographical areas has sagged badly since 2005, and not just because of the recession of 2007–2009. Normally, recessions are followed by rapid growth in productivity and incomes, as full employment returns. But the recovery from this latest recession has been dismal in Europe, Japan, and the United States, importantly because worker productivity growth has been so sluggish. Productivity growth has been halved in America, cut by two-thirds in Europe, and actually become *negative* in Japan—workers produce less today than they did in 2005.

As we note in Chapter 11, the sluggish recovery of the American economy has been due in part to extensive new regulations here, and regulations have surely played a role in reducing productivity in Japan and Europe. Because workers are paid for what they produce, as productivity has slowed or fallen, wages and earnings have followed the same path, leading, of course, to widespread dissatisfaction among workers.

Policy makers around the world have failed to recognize the important role that the aging workforce has played in reducing productivity and thus earnings. In both the United States and Europe, for example, stagnant incomes have been blamed on both immigration and **globalization.** Yet in fact, immigration tends to raise incomes at all levels except the very bottom, while globalization raises incomes at all levels, especially at the bottom (see Chapter 29). Few politicians have fully appreciated the role of government regulations in reducing living standards (see Chapter 11), and none have realized that the aging of the workforce has compounded the adverse effects of regulation.

YOUNG VERSUS OLD?

There has always been a certain amount of tension between older workers and younger workers. Older workers, proud of their knowledge and experience, feel their higher pay is fully justified. Younger workers, steeped in the latest technology, view the older workers as being overpaid for their outdated skills. And each group sees the other as its fundamental workplace rival. The older workers worry that they will be displaced by the upcoming generation, while the younger workers view their elders as occupying the jobs they should have.

The latest research implies, however, that older and younger workers strongly complement one another in a mutually beneficial manner. By passing along their wisdom and experience, older workers can help younger workers avoid productivity-killing (and perhaps career-ending) mistakes. This is clearly to the benefit of the up-and-coming generation. Yet the older workers gain too, because their ability to help younger workers improve makes the seniors more valuable to employers, which translates into higher paychecks for the mentoring generation. And so, just as the seeming rivalry between buyers and sellers benefits both parties trading in markets, the seeming rivalry between older and younger workers benefits both age groups in the workplace, and in so doing, raises their standards of living. It may look like that old guy in the next cubicle is holding up your promotion, but it turns out he's getting you ready to be the boss.

FOR CRITICAL ANALYSIS

1. Go to Chapter 4 of the U.S. Department of Commerce report *65+ in the United States: 2010* (https://www.census.gov/content/dam/ Census/library/publications/2014/demo/p23-212.pdf) There you will observe data on the proportion of the population in each state that is over the age of sixty-five. Among the states with the most seniors are Florida, West Virginia, Maine, and Pennsylvania. Among the states with the lowest proportions of seniors are California, Colorado, Georgia, and Texas. What do the arguments of this chapter imply about the expected growth in productivity in the first group of states compared to the second group? Because people generally are paid for what they produce, income gains in these states should be roughly in line with productivity gains in recent years (say, between 2000 and 2010). Find information on per capita income in these states over this period and test your prediction.

2. Why would older people be willing to take valuable work time to help young people learn how to do their jobs better? One possible motive is that the seniors are altruistic. But there may be another motive: personal gain. How could older people benefit materially from behaving this way? (*Hint:* Do employers want this transfer of knowledge to happen? What incentives will they provide to make sure it does?)

3. In some occupations (such as elementary through high school teaching) and in many unionized industries, pay scales for employees depend in part on performance and formal training or education, but they also depend in part strictly on the number of years on the job (called "seniority"). Can you explain why seniority would be separately rewarded?

4. You saw in this chapter that productivity and pay both rise over people's working lives, peaking usually when individuals are in their fifties. Go to (https://en.wikipedia.org/wiki/List_of_countries_ by_median_age) and select ten nations that have widely differing median ages. What do you will predict will be true about average income levels in these countries, compared to one another? Go to (https://en.wikipedia.org/wiki/List_of_countries_by_GDP_(PPP)_ per_capita) and test your predictions.

5. After people retire, many of them soon take full- or part-time jobs, in part to stay active and in part to supplement their retirement income. Based on the principles in this chapter, explain why the hourly wages people earn in post-retirement jobs are normally much lower than what they earned in their pre-retirement jobs.

6. Most immigrants come to a country for economic reasons: Pay in their old home country is low and they expect to be able to work hard and improve their income in their new home country. If there is a surge of immigration into a nation, predict the impact of this on measured productivity (i) in the short run, say the first few years, and (ii) in the long run, say ten or twenty years down the road.

PART TWO

The Business Cycle, Unemployment, and Inflation

CHAPTER 7

What Should GDP Include?

Economists disagree about a lot. One important point of disagreement has to do with how to measure things. For example, suppose you were interested in how the economy was doing, either over time or in comparison to other nations. Or perhaps you want to know how well different people across the country feel they are doing. The most common way of addressing such issues would be with a measure linked to **gross domestic product (GDP).** For example, almost all macroeconomic policy is driven by policymakers' perceptions of what is happening to a few key variables, and GDP is on just about everyone's list of key variables. Moreover, as you saw in Chapters 1 and 4, the human condition varies dramatically around the globe, variation that can be understood only if we start with a clear awareness of what is being measured. That measurement starts with GDP.

WHAT DOES GDP MEASURE?

GDP is defined as the market value of new, domestically produced, final goods and services. There are four key elements of this definition:

1. *Market value*—GDP is calculated by multiplying the prices of goods and services by their quantities. Thus, it can rise or fall just because of changes in the prices of goods and services. Most of our discussion will focus on **real gross domestic product (real GDP),** which adjusts GDP for changes in the **price level.** This way, we know that we are talking about the actual amounts of goods and services that are being produced.

2. *New*—The only goods and services that get into GDP are those that are newly produced during the current accounting period, which

normally is the current calendar year. Even though used cars, old houses, and even antiques are a source of satisfaction for many people, GDP focuses on those goods and services that are currently produced.

3. *Domestically produced*—If you were to look carefully at the components of a new car, you would find that much of that car was actually made in other nations, even if it is an "American" car. Similarly, much of the typical "Japanese" car sold in America is actually made in America. The GDP of a nation includes only those parts of cars (and other goods and services) that are made in that nation.

4. *Final goods and services*—Many intermediate steps go into producing goods and services, and often these steps show up as separate transactions across the country. Nonetheless, because the value of each intermediate step is embedded in the value of the final product, we include only that final value in our measure of GDP. Otherwise, we would be double-counting the final good and all of the components that go into it.

WHAT'S MISSING?

Real GDP, that is, GDP corrected for changes in the price level, is the official measure of new, domestically produced, final goods and services in an economy. Although this number is widely used, you should be aware that it excludes some important economic activity. For example, do-it-yourself activities are not included in the official GDP measure, even though they clearly yield valuable output. The biggest category of such services consists of those performed in the house by homemakers. It is widely estimated, for example, that the *weekly* value of a home-maker's services is several hundred dollars, none of which is included in the official statistics.

Then there is the matter of the huge volume of transactions—hundreds of billions of dollars per year—in markets for illegal goods and services, including prostitution, illegal gambling, and drugs. In the United States we have made no effort to accurately incorporate this activity in our measure of GDP. But some nations, including Italy, Britain, the Netherlands, and Germany, have started including illegal activity in their official GDP numbers. Soon, many other members of the European Union will probably do likewise.

We are not talking about small sums. When Britain revised its numbers, accounting for prostitution, illegal drugs, and gambling added 0.7 percent to GDP. In Italy, the bump was a full 1 percent.

But when Germany added illegal activities to its GDP, the increase was only 0.1 percent. Why? Because in that nation, prostitution has been legal for a number of years and was already being measured in their GDP.

THERE IS MORE TO THE UNDERGROUND ECONOMY THAN ILLEGAL ACTIVITIES

Illegal activities of the sort just mentioned are typically considered part of the shadow or underground economy. But there are plenty of *legal* goods and services transacted in the underground economy on a scale that dwarfs the trade in drugs or sexual services. Indeed, recent estimates indicate that between 10 and 13 percent of all legally produced goods and services in the United States is not included in the official GDP statistics. This activity entails chiefly cash or barter deals on items including landscaping, child care, construction, housekeeping, food and beverages, indeed, almost anything you can think of. The goods and services themselves are lawful, but the transactions go unrecorded and thus unmeasured, usually because the market participants want to conceal them from the government.

Over the last twenty years, the share of total activity that is going unrecorded is believed to have risen substantially. There are a variety of reasons. For example, during the recession of 2008–2009, the duration of government unemployment benefits was hiked from 26 weeks to 99 weeks. Many people lost jobs and some who could not find a similar one signed up for unemployment benefits and also picked up a job "off the books"—getting paid in cash and invisible to government accountants.

In a similar vein, it has become much easier in recent years for people to collect tax-free disability payments from the federal government, a matter discussed more fully in Chapter 12. Some of the people collecting these benefits are able-bodied and, in fact, are working, perhaps for cash or in trade for goods and services. Either way, their production is unrecorded in the GDP figures.

The underground economy has also grown because government-licensing requirements have increased. About 30 percent of all occupations require a license. Many of these licenses require that the licensees undertake costly training courses that are partly or largely "make work," designed chiefly to reduce competition in the fields involved. Some people would rather forgo the time and cost of obtaining such licenses. So they work off the books, unlicensed and unrecorded in the statistics.

Finally, state and federal **marginal tax rates** have increased. Those increases have raised the incentives for individuals to get paid in cash—cash that is not reported and thus not taxed. But unrecorded cash deals also don't show up in the GDP numbers.

RESEARCH, DEVELOPMENT, AND LADY GAGA

Research and development (R&D) is an essential part of the innovative process, as we noted in Chapter 2. Historically, R&D expenditures have been treated as **intermediate goods,** consumed in the production process and thus not counted separately as part of GDP. Recently, however, the U.S. government has decided to reclassify R&D expenditures as **investment,** which, like **consumption,** is counted as part of GDP. The result has been an upward bump in the official GDP numbers.

Something similar has been done for the intellectual investment that occurs during the artistic process. Lady Gaga, J. K. Rowling, and other artists, writers, and performers devote great effort to their creative endeavors. Historically, the value of such activity has been picked up only in the final sales of their recordings, books, or paintings. Now, however, U.S. government accountants have added an additional measure of creative effort to GDP. Lacking information on how long Lady Gaga spends on her songwriting, the accountants have taken the tack of *estimating* how her sales might do in the *future.* Many economists are concerned about the speculative nature of such estimates. Nevertheless, the combined effect of taking into account R&D and creative activity has been to raise the official estimates of GDP by 3.6 percent. This is the equivalent of almost two years' worth of economic growth, all done with the bureaucratic stroke of a computer key.

BRINGING IN HAPPINESS

Even as economists have been focused on the GDP, a variety of other researchers—such as sociologists, psychologists, and political scientists—have been asking people how happy or satisfied they are with their lives. Now, answers to questions such as these must be taken with a big dose of caution, because "talk is cheap." That is, when you go to the store to buy something, you must make a real sacrifice to obtain the item. But when a person conducting a poll asks you about your happiness, it costs no more to check the box next to "happy" than it does to check the box next to "unhappy."

Keeping this caution in mind, economists Betsey Stevenson and Judson Wolfers thought it might be useful to see if there was any link between measures of income (such as **real per capita income [real GDP per capita]**) and measures of happiness. Stevenson and Wolfers found that there is indeed a strong and consistent positive relationship between real GDP per capita and reported levels of happiness. Using data spanning many decades and covering well over one hundred countries, the authors show that when per capita real GDP is higher, reported measures of satisfaction or happiness are higher also. Notably, there is no "satiation" point—that is, it appears that even the richest and happiest people have the opportunity to become even happier as their incomes rise further.

As you might imagine, there are numerous ways to do the measuring, and the authors tried a wide variety of them to cross-check their results. One simple measure is the proportion of people at each income level who report that they are "very satisfied" with their lives. It turns out that when income doubles, this measure of happiness increases by 25 percent, a finding that seems to be consistent across all income levels. Thus, when annual income per person doubles from $5,000 to $10,000, happiness rises by 25 percent. And when income doubles from $10,000 to $20,000 or from $20,000 to $40,000, happiness rises by 25 percent with each doubling—and it does so even when we look, say, at a move from $250,000 to $500,000 per year.

Obviously, real income is not the only factor that influences happiness. Gender, age, and many difficult-to-measure variables are important also. Moreover, it is entirely possible that some other factor is responsible for simultaneously creating high levels of income and happiness. It may be true that these same institutions that foster high per capita GDP (as discussed in Chapter 1) also happen to make people happier, perhaps because they enhance personal liberty. Nevertheless, even if "money can't buy happiness," the results of Stevenson and Wolfers make one point clear: Despite all of its imperfections, real GDP per capita is strongly linked to well-being, at least as perceived by the human beings being asked about such matters. Thus, although GDP may not be a perfect measure of anything, we keep on using it because it seems to beat all of the alternatives.

FOR CRITICAL ANALYSIS

1. How does one determine what is a final good or service and what is an intermediate good? In other words, where does one draw the line?

2. Why is it important to carefully distinguish between GDP and real GDP? Answer the same query for real GDP versus *per capita* real GDP.

3. Would you categorize each of the following expenditures as intermediate goods, investment goods, or consumption goods: (i) a spare tire, (ii) surgery to repair a badly broken arm, (iii) a Botox injection to remove forehead wrinkles, (iv) voice lessons, and (v) expenditures on your college education? Explain your reasoning in each instance. Would your answers to (iii) and (iv) change if you knew that the purchaser was a professional singer who made many public appearances? Why or why not?

4. Over the past forty years, growing numbers of women have entered the labor force, becoming employed outside the home. As a result, many women now hire people to do household tasks (such as child-care and house cleaning) that they used to do themselves. What impact does this "hiring out" of household tasks have on measures on GDP? Explain.

5. Over the past forty years, the levels of water and air pollution in the United States have declined substantially. Would these environmental improvements likely be reflected in reported measures of well-being or happiness? Would they likely be reflected in GDP?

6. Are nations with large underground economies likely to be happier or unhappier than one would expect, given their *measured* levels of real per capita GDP? Explain.

CHAPTER 8

What's in a Word? Plenty, When It's the "R" Word

Incumbent presidents (and members of their political party) hate the "R" word. We speak here of **recession,** a word used to describe a downturn or stagnation in overall, nationwide economic activity. Politicians' attitudes toward recessions are driven by the simple fact that people tend to "vote their pocketbooks." That is, when the economy is doing well, voters are likely to return incumbent politicians to office, but when the economy is doing poorly, voters are likely to "throw the bums out." Interestingly, although *recession* is the word most commonly used to describe a period of poor performance by the economy, most people do not really know what the word means.

THE NBER

Ever since its founding in 1920, a private organization called the National Bureau of Economic Research (NBER) has sought to accurately measure the state of overall economic conditions in the United States. (It also sponsors research on other economic issues.) Over time, the NBER developed a reputation for measuring the economy's performance in an evenhanded and useful way. As a result, most people now accept without argument what the NBER has to say about the state of the economy. Most notably, this means that it is the NBER that we rely on to tell us when we are in a recession.

If you are an avid reader of Internet news sites, you may have heard a recession defined as any period in which there are at least two quarters (three-month periods) of declining **real gross domestic**

product (real GDP). In fact, the NBER's recession-dating committee places little reliance on the performance of real (inflation-adjusted) GDP when deciding on the state of the economy. There are two reasons for this. First, the government measures GDP only on a quarterly basis, and the NBER prefers to focus on more timely data that are available at least monthly. Second, the official GDP numbers are subject to frequent and often substantial revisions, so what once looked like good economic performance might suddenly look bad, and vice versa.

Looking back at 2001 (a turbulent year), for example, the initial figures showed that real GDP declined in only one quarter during the year. But when the government finally finished all of its revisions to the data, it turned out that real GDP actually fell during *three* quarters of 2001. In 2007, the government issued a revision of its revised GDP figures for 2004–2006. Of the twelve quarters covered by this "revision of the revisions," the numbers for all twelve were changed: Two were revised upward and ten downward. The 2011 set of revisions altered virtually every GDP figure for the preceding decade. Then in 2013 the government made a major change to the entire *method* of estimating GDP (see Chapter 7). One can easily understand why an organization such as the NBER, which prides itself on reliability and accuracy, might be reluctant to place too much weight on measures of real GDP.

So what does the NBER use as its criteria in measuring a recession? Its official definition gives us some insight: "A recession is a significant decline in activity spread across the economy, lasting more than a few months, visible in industrial production, employment, real income, and wholesale–retail sales." Those are a lot of words to define just one term, but it is not too difficult to get a handle on it. The key point to note is that the NBER focuses chiefly on four separate pieces of information:

- Real income (inflation-adjusted personal income of consumers)
- Employment
- Industrial production
- Sales at the wholesale and retail levels

All of these figures are reliably available on a monthly basis, and thus every month the NBER uses the latest figures on each to take the pulse of the economy. When all four move upward, that is generally good news. When all move downward, that is definitely bad news. And when some move in one direction and some in another direction, that is when expert judgment comes into play.

THE THREE D'S

If the NBER recession-dating committee uses a strict formula to time the onset or end of a recession, the committee members do not reveal what it is. What they do reveal is that they look for three crucial elements, each starting with the letter D, when they officially announce the start or end of a recession:

1. *Depth.* If there is a downturn in one or more of the four key variables, the NBER focuses first on the magnitude of that downturn. For example, in an economy like ours with total employment of over 145 million, a drop of 50,000 in employment would not be crucial, but an employment drop of, say, 1 million surely would be considered significant.

2. *Duration.* Month-to-month fluctuations in economic activity are the norm in our economy. These fluctuations occur partly because our measures of economic activity are imperfect and partly because, in an economy as complex as ours, many things are happening all the time with the capacity to affect the overall performance of the economy. Thus, if real personal income moves up or down for a month or even two months in a row, the recession-dating committee is likely to decide that such a change is well within the bounds of normal variation. If a trend persists for, say, six months, the committee is likely to place a much heavier weight on that movement.

3. *Dispersion.* Because the NBER is trying to measure the overall state of the economy, it wants to make sure that it is not being misled by economic developments that may be important to many people but are not reliable indicators of the overall state of the economy. For example, America is becoming less dependent on industrial production and more reliant on service industries. In addition, it is well known that industrial production is sensitive to sharp fluctuations not shared by sectors elsewhere in the economy. Hence, the NBER tempers the importance of industrial production by simultaneously relying on measures such as wholesale and retail sales to make sure that it has a picture of what is happening throughout the economy.

A PRECISE ANSWER

Having blended its four measures of the economy in a way that reflects its focus on the three D's, the recession-dating committee makes its decision. A recession, in its view, begins "just after the economy reaches a peak of activity" and ends "as the economy reaches its trough" and starts expanding again. Between trough and peak, the economy is said to be in an **expansion.** Historically, the normal state of the economy is expansion. Most recessions are brief (usually ending within 12–18 months) and, in recent decades, they have been rare. Our most recent recession, coming after six years of economic expansion, began in December 2007 and ended in June 2009.

The four measures used by the NBER to date recessions generally move fairly closely together. Although individually they sometimes give conflicting signals for short periods of time, they soon enough start playing the same song. Nevertheless, some contention about the NBER's decisions remains. There are two sources of debate: One focuses on *potential* growth of economic activity and the other highlights the importance of population growth.

The NBER defines a recession as an absolute decline in economic activity. Yet some economists note that for the past couple of centuries, growth in economic activity from year to year has been the norm in most developed nations, including the United States. Hence, they argue, a recession should be declared whenever growth falls significantly below its long-term potential. The biggest problem with this proposed measure is that it is difficult to estimate with much confidence what the "potential" growth rate of any country might be.

The second point of contention starts with the observation that the population is growing in the United States, as it is in most countries. Hence, even if economic activity is growing, the well-being of the average citizen might not be. For example, suppose the population is growing 3 percent per year, but real personal income is growing only 2 percent per year. If the other measures of activity were performing like personal income, the NBER would say the economy was in an expansion phase, even though **real per capita income** was declining. Some economists would argue that this state of affairs should be declared a recession, given that the term is supposed to indicate a less-than-healthy economy. This point has some validity. Nevertheless, there have not been many prolonged periods when the NBER has said the economy was expanding while real per capita income was falling.

Ultimately, of course, even if the recession-dating committee somehow tinkered with its methods to better acknowledge the importance of potential growth and population changes, some other issue would undoubtedly be raised to dispute the NBER's conclusions. For now, most economists are content to rely on the NBER to make the call. Most politicians are, too—except, of course, when it suits them otherwise. As for ordinary voters, well, even if they do not know how a recession is defined, they surely know what one feels like—and are likely to vote accordingly.

For Critical Analysis

1. Why is it important, both for the political process and for our understanding of the economy, for the NBER to resist the temptation to change its definition of a recession to fit the latest political pressures or economic fads?

2. Do you think that voters care more about whether the NBER says the economy is in a state of recession or whether they and their friends and family members are employed in good jobs? Why do politicians make a big deal over whether the economy is "officially" in a recession or an expansion? (*Hint:* Is it hard for the average voter to tell what is going on in the economy outside his or her community, leaving the voter dependent on simple measures—or labels—of what is happening elsewhere in the economy?)

3. Examine the data from the last six recessions. (Good sources for data are www.nber.org/cycles/recessions.html and www.bea.gov for the United States, and http://data.worldbank.org/indicator for a global picture.) Rank them on the basis of both duration and severity. The first is easy; the second is more difficult: Is it possible that some people—either politicians or other citizens—might disagree about how to measure the severity of a particular recession? How would you measure it?

4. Return to the data you examined for question 3. Some people have called the recession of 2007–2009 the "Great Recession." Based on the data you think most relevant, is this latest recession worthy of being singled out as "Great"? Explain.

5. The stock market has been called a "leading indicator" of future economic activity, while the unemployment rate has been called a "lagging indicator" of past economic activity. Combine the data from questions 3 and 4, including data on the stock market and the unemployment rate to answer the following two questions:

   a. How well do movements in a stock price index (such as the DJIA or the S&P 500) predict ahead of time the beginning or end of each recession?

   b. How well do beginnings or endings of recessions predict future changes, up or down, in the unemployment rate?

6. Why do we bother to declare the beginning or end of something called a "recession"?

CHAPTER 9

The Disappearing Middle Class

The middle class is no longer the majority in America. For the first time ever, people in the middle of the income distribution are outnumbered by people in the tails of that distribution. According to the latest data there are 120.8 million adults in the middle and 121.3 million in lower- and upper-income classes combined. Since 1970, the middle class has shrunk from over 60 percent of America to just a bit less than 50 percent.

If you believe the Democrats, this has happened because declining job opportunities and stagnating wages forced people from the middle down into the lower-income classes. The Republicans, by contrast, would have you think that people have left the middle class for the prosperity of the upper-income classes. As it turns out, neither group of politicians is giving you the full picture.

WHAT IS THE MIDDLE CLASS?

Unlike **gross domestic product (GDP)** and the **unemployment rate,** there is no generally agreed upon definition of the "middle class." There is agreement, however, that it should include those people whose incomes are concentrated around the **median income**—that is, the income that exactly divides the population into the top and bottom halves. Some people then argue that the middle class comprises, say, the 60 percent of the population that is exactly centered on the median. Under this definition, the top 20 percent of the population would be in the upper class, and the bottom 20 percent of the population would reside in the lower class. The problem with this definition is that 60 percent of the population must *always* go into the middle class. Thus, the middle class can never shrink or grow relative to the other classes, no matter what is happening to incomes in the middle.

A more useful definition of the middle class is expressed in terms of incomes relative to the median income. For example, one widely used classification says that middle-income people are those whose incomes are at least two-thirds as great as the median income, but no more than double the median. For a family of three, for example, in 2016 median income was about $63,000. So a middle-class family of three had an annual income between $42,000 and $126,000.[1] For this same family, an income in the range from $126,000 to $188,000 put them in the upper-middle class range, while an income above $188,000 per year placed them in the upper class. On the downside, an income of $31,000 to $42,000 put the family in the lower-middle class group, while low-income families of this size had incomes below $31,000. We'll think in terms of these cut points in the discussion that follows, but a variety of other methods for classifying people by income levels yield quite similar conclusions.

CHANGES OVER TIME

By definition, there have been people in the middle of the income distribution as long as there has been income. But serious study of the middle class using modern, data-based definitions dates back only about half a century. Over those fifty years or so, a consistent pattern has emerged: The middle class is disappearing. In 1971, for example, 61 percent of all adults fell into the middle class. By 1981, when Ronald Reagan became president, the share had fallen to 59 percent. By 1991, the year before Bill Clinton was elected president, only 56 percent of adults were in the middle class. When George Bush took office in 2001, the number was down to 54 percent. At the end of Barack Obama's first term, only 51 percent of adults were in the middle class. By the time Donald Trump was elected, the middle class had become a minority, comprising just under 50 percent of all adults.

Clearly, the people in the middle didn't actually disappear. Instead they moved out of the middle class and into other income groups. Indeed, although one-third of the people who left the middle moved down into the lower-middle or lower class, two-thirds of the movers

---

1 Median income for a single person in 2016 was about $33,000 so middle-class single people had incomes in the range from $22,000 to $66,000.

headed *up*—into the upper-middle or upper class. The bottom two income-classes grew to 29 percent of the population from a starting point of 25 percent, while the top two classes increased to 21 percent, from an initial 14 percent. The very bottom income group (earning less than half the median income) rose from 16 percent of the population to 20 percent, while the very top group increased from 4 percent of the population to 9 percent. On balance then, there were more upward departures from the middle class than downward departures—almost twice as many people moved up, rather than down. And overall, the range of observed incomes increased relative to the median—the income distribution spread out.

Who Did Well and Who Didn't?

This migration of people out of the middle class over the last fifty years has occurred very differently across various groups within America. To help us see just how different these experiences have been, let's consider a hypothetical group that started in 1971 with 20 percent of its members in the bottom two classes, 60 percent in the middle, and 20 percent in the top two classes. Now imagine that by 2016, there were only 40 percent left in the middle, because 5 percent had dropped to the bottom classes, while 15 percent had gone up to the top classes. We would say that the *net* change for this group was +10 percentage points, which equals +15 points up, –5 points down. If some other group had 6 percent of its members move up, but 10 percent move down, we would say that its net change was –4 percentage points (= +6 – 10).

The biggest gainers—by far—over the last fifty years were senior citizens, those people 65 and older. They enjoyed a remarkable gain of almost 27 percentage points. The biggest losers were the people with the least education. Individuals with two years or less of college lost 16 percentage points, high school graduates lost 22 points, and those with less than a high school degree lost 18 points. Over this same period, blacks did better than whites, gaining more than 11 points, while whites gained less than 7 points. And women outperformed men, although the margin of difference was modest: +3.5 points versus +2.7 points.

What's Going On?

So far, we've seen that the middle class is shrinking, with more people moving up than down, and the spread of incomes from top to bottom seems to be growing. There is no generally agreed-upon explanation for all of these events, but we can outline some likely elements here (and you can find further discussion in Chapters 10 and 14).

The rapid pace of technological change involving computers has clearly played a key role, for it has enhanced the premium on brains over brawn, raised the return to formal education (college and beyond), and placed a new premium on willingness to work long hours. These forces have been amplified, at both the top and the bottom of the income distribution, by the rise of **globalization** over recent decades. Let's see how each of these have worked out.

Brains versus brawn: Although there was considerable technological change from the middle of the nineteenth century through the middle of the twentieth century, it offered new opportunities for those who worked with their hands and their backs just as much as it did for those who worked with their heads. Communications, transportation, manufacturing, and even agriculture all experienced rapid change, and people with all sorts of skills and abilities could prosper. Over the last half century, however, technological change has centered in computers and communications, creating jobs where minds, not muscles, are increasingly valued. Hence, pay for white collar, high-skilled jobs has risen rapidly relative to that for blue collar, low-skilled positions.

Formal education: Riding a horse, wielding a hammer, or operating a tractor or train all require the acquisition of skills. But these skills are best learned on the job, rather than in the classroom. Data management and analysis, computer programming, and network engineering are all best learned initially in an intensive, intellectually challenging classroom environment. To be sure, all of these modern tasks require considerable future skill acquisition on the job. But that subsequent training can be acquired *only* by those people who have the intellectual abilities to first succeed in the classroom. People without those abilities are left behind— and drift downward in the income distribution.

Hours of work: The modern systems of computer networks and communications infrastructure have stitched together the businesses and consumers of the world like never before. This global integration has created massive new gains from trade. But when a problem develops in one location, it can spread with frightening speed throughout a giant corporation and around the world. There is immense value in solving such problems exceptionally quickly, which means a premium is placed on those people who will come in early, stay late, work weekends—indeed, who will show up on the job *whenever* the need arises. As a result, pay now grows disproportionately with hours of work. One simple statistic helps make this clear: People who work 44 hours per week receive more than *double* the pay of those who work 34 hours a week. Those long hours thus translate into rapid advancement up the rungs of the income distribution.

Globalization: The good news of globalization (more integration of each national economy with the economies of other nations) has mostly been enjoyed at the top of the income distribution. The bad news has mostly arrived at the bottom. At the top, managers, problem solvers, athletes, and entertainers, who once reached audiences (or workforces) in the hundreds or thousands, now use modern computer and communications technologies to reach millions, even billions of people. The values of their skills have thus been vastly amplified by technological change, which has propelled their pay into the highest reaches of the income distribution. For unskilled individuals, however, globalization has mostly meant increased competition from lower-paid workers in far-off countries. To be sure, that low-cost foreign labor has brought dramatic reductions in the prices of many consumer goods. But for unskilled workers, this often has not been enough to offset the reduced employment and pay opportunities they have endured.

A LOOK AT THE OTHER DEMOGRAPHIC CHANGES

We noted earlier that senior citizens have fared particularly well over the last fifty years, that blacks have done much better than whites, and that women have done slightly better than men. Senior citizens have benefitted from Medicare and also from the rapidly growing generosity of the Social Security system. They have also enjoyed the fruits of fifty years of investing in corporate stocks that have had an annual rate of return of roughly 10 percent per year (which implies a doubling in value every seven years).

In the case of blacks, civil rights have dramatically improved and affirmative action programs have spread throughout the economy. These developments have created economic opportunities that—imperfect though they may be—are vastly better than those open to their parents and grandparents. Operating against these new opportunities has been the nation's war on drugs, which has led to much higher incarceration rates for blacks, especially young black males. A criminal record is almost guaranteed to depress one's future earnings.

The average hourly pay of women has risen by well over 30 percent compared to the hourly pay of men in recent decades. Thus, it is a bit surprising that women have improved only modestly relative to men in the income distribution. The explanation may lie in hours of work. Although women have moved rapidly into higher-paying occupations (such as medicine, law, and management), they have mostly taken jobs within those occupations that require less than average hours of work each week. Thus, the much-increased pay per hour for women has resulted only in modest increases in their annual incomes.

What Will the Future Bring?

Although data for periods more than fifty years ago are not as rich as those we have today, it is possible to make some useful generalizations about recent history compared to the distant past. The first is that the shape of the income distribution seems to be in a continual state of flux. Early in America's history, for example, there really was no middle class. There were a few very wealthy individuals and a modest-sized group of prosperous merchants. Then there was the vast bulk of the populace, with incomes that varied very little from person to person. Only during the nineteenth century did a true middle class begin to emerge, with distinct upper and lower tails on both ends of the distribution. So in this sense, the dominance of the middle class is a relatively recent development. Indeed, there may not be any particular reason for the middle class to be the dominant economic group of the future.

The second observation is that times of peace and economic prosperity tend to be associated with widening spreads in the income distribution—more people in both tails compared to the middle. In contrast, years of economic turmoil (such as the Great Depression), wars, and other catastrophes (such as the Black Death of the fourteenth century), tend to compress the income distribution. In effect, the operation of chance or Lady Luck becomes more important in periods of turmoil. Luck cancels out the advantages of hard work and ability, as well as the disadvantages of sloth and ignorance, leaving many more people in the middle.

Thus, although the likely short-term consequences of today's technological changes may be relatively easy to predict, no one has any special knowledge of what cataclysm may lie around the corner. But at least now you know how to analyze its consequences for the distribution of income when it does arrive.

For Critical Analysis

Questions 1, 2, and 3 are based on the following information regarding three hypothetical regional groups: Westies, Rusties, and Easties. For each of two years, 1977 and 2017, we show the percentage of each group that falls into each of three income categories: upper, middle, and lower.

	1977			2017		
	Upper	*Middle*	*Lower*	*Upper*	*Middle*	*Lower*
Westies	30	50	20	45	35	20
Rusties	20	60	20	10	50	40
Easties	20	50	30	25	50	25

1. Which regional group of individuals is the most prosperous in 1977? Which is the least prosperous? How do your answers change for 2017? That is, which are the most and least prosperous regional groups in the later year? Explain your reasoning.

2. Which regional group experienced the most favorable changes in income from 1977 to 2017? Which did the worst? Show your calculations, worked in the same manner that these calculations were done in the text.

3. Consider now the Westies and the Rusties. In light of the discussion in the text regarding likely sources of changes in the income distribution, explain what systematic differences you think there might be between the people in these two regions. Consider, at the very least, their education levels, hours of work, occupational choices, and types of goods or services produced by the industries in which they work.

4. Some people have argued that when the distribution of income becomes less equal, the government should impose higher taxes on high-income people and give the proceeds of those taxes to low-income people. How would such a policy affect incentives throughout the income distribution? In particular, how would this policy affect the incentive to become a high-income person? How would it affect the incentive to become a low-income person? What are the likely consequences for *total* income? (*Hint:* How does income reflect productivity?)

5. Salaries earned by professional athletes vary enormously and, within a given sport, appear to do so on the basis of performance: Top performers are paid much more than bottom performers. How would performance levels in sports be affected if all athletes were paid the same, regardless of performance?

6. One famous aphorism is that "birds of a feather flock together." Another aphorism is that "opposites attract." Let's suppose that

single individuals are distributed among lower, middle, and upper incomes. Now consider two different states of the world. In the "flock together" world, single people tend to marry other single people whose incomes are close to theirs. In the "opposites attract" world, single people tend to marry other single people whose incomes are much different from their own. How would the distribution of family income in each of these two worlds tend to differ? Construct a numerical example to illustrate your conclusion.

CHAPTER 10

Capital, Wealth, and Inequality

In 1867, German intellectual Karl Marx wrote *Das Kapital*, the full title of which in English is *Capital: Critique of Political Economy*. A central theme of this work was that in a **capitalist system,** the motivating force was the exploitation of labor. In his view, workers were never paid the full value of their services, which left what he called a surplus value from which employers obtain their profits. Marx predicted that "The worker becomes all the poorer the more wealth he produces. . . ."

Sounds pretty grim, doesn't it? So how have things turned out since Marx made his predictions? Well, as we note in Chapter 1, the average standard of living since 1867 has risen the most in—you guessed it—capitalist economies. But maybe averages are fooling us. At least that is what some anticapitalists argue.

THE RICH GET RICHER AND THE POOR GET POORER?

In recent years, there has been an increased interest in the topic of **income inequality.** Are Karl Marx's predictions finally coming true? Some politicians in America, many politicians in Europe, and at least a few economists believe so. Before we tackle the actual statistics on inequality in the United States, let's first look at the modern-day version of the reasoning in *Das Kapital*.

The core claim of those who argue that Marx's predictions are (finally) coming true goes something like this. People who invest in **capital**—plant, equipment, research and development, and the like—obtain a return on their investment that exceeds the rate of economic growth. The result, it is argued, is an ever-increasing inequality of **wealth** and income. Supposedly, then, capitalism inevitably results in wealth concentrated in fewer and fewer hands. To prevent this, it is claimed, we must raise the **marginal tax rate**—on income, on wealth, indeed on most anything and everything that might possibly be taxable.

THE EBB AND FLOW OF INEQUALITY

If we look back over the decades since World War II, or indeed over the past two centuries, there has been remarkably little substantive change in the inequality of either income or wealth. Why, then, is there rising concern over inequality today? It is because the inequality of both wealth and income appear to have risen substantially since about 1980. Thus, it is claimed, unless there is government intervention in this process, the distribution of income and wealth will continue to become less equal.

Thirty or even forty years is a blink of time in the sweep of world, or even American, history. One could easily select other periods of such length from the past and reach very different conclusions about the trend in inequality. The reason is simple: The ebb and flow of prosperity and depression, innovation and stagnation, and war and peace routinely change economic outcomes unevenly and unpredictably for people at all points in the economic stratum.

Thus, three questions arise. First, just what *has* happened to measures of economic inequality over the past few decades? Second, how much should we rely on these measures? And third, should we be concerned at the prospect of more economic inequality?

INCOME INEQUALITY IS RISING

As a report by the Congressional Budget Office (CBO) makes clear, government transfer payments (most importantly Social Security and heavily subsidized Medicare benefits) are an important source of income for many low- and middle-income individuals. These programs have had a significant impact on one form of inequality that used to be prevalent in America. Until about 1960 or so, older Americans typically had the lowest incomes and highest poverty rates of all age groups. But as the CBO (and other researchers) demonstrate, people over sixty-five have the *lowest* poverty rate of all age groups today, importantly because of Social Security and Medicare.

Based on the CBO and other readily available data, a number of economists have now re-examined the changing distribution of income over the past few decades. They have found two striking facts. First, people at all income levels have experienced rising incomes. As is conventionally done, the researchers divided people up into income "quintiles," ranked from top to bottom, with 20 percent of the population in each group. For every single quintile, average inflation-adjusted incomes have risen over this period. Income has risen the fastest in the top quintile over this period, and within this top group, incomes rose the fastest at the very top. But it is also worthy of note that people in the *bottom* quintile have experienced the second fastest rate of growth of income. It is in the middle of the income distribution where, although income has grown, it has done so sluggishly.

The conclusion from this research is that **real income** is rising across the income spectrum. The rich are getting richer, but so too are the poor. They are just not getting richer as quickly as the people at the top of the economic spectrum.

INCOME MOBILITY

In thinking about the distribution of income, it is important to remember that in America, most people exhibit a great deal of **income mobility**—individuals move around within the income distribution over time. The most important source of income mobility is the "life-cycle" pattern of earnings: Incomes are lowest for people when they are young, rising to a maximum at about age fifty-five, and then declining slowly until retirement. Earnings at the end of one's career are generally well above those at the beginning. Thus, a snapshot of the current distribution of earnings will find most individuals on the way up, toward a higher position in the income distribution. People who have low earnings now are likely, on average, to have higher earnings in the future.

There is also a life cycle pattern for the **net assets** (assets minus debt) of people. Based on the latest data, for example, families headed by thirty-year-olds have net assets of less than $20,000. Their assets of $98,000 are almost overwhelmed by debts of $81,000. For families headed by fifty-year-olds, however, net asset positions have improved to about $500,000. The peak occurs in families headed by someone who is age sixty-two, where the average net asset position has grown to about $830,000. After this, net assets begin to shrink as families use their accumulated assets to fund retirement spending.

Lady Luck is another source of income and asset mobility. At any point in time, the income of high-income people is likely to be abnormally high (relative to their average income) due to recent good fortune—they may have just won the lottery or received a long-awaited bonus. Conversely, the incomes of people who currently have low incomes are likely to be abnormally low due to recent bad luck, perhaps because they are laid up after an automobile accident or have become temporarily unemployed. Over time, the effects of Lady Luck tend to average out across the population. Accordingly, people with high incomes today will tend to have lower incomes in the future, while people with low incomes today will tend to have higher future incomes. The same patterns hold true for measures of net asset positions.

The effects of the forces that produce income mobility are strikingly revealed in studies examining the incomes of individuals over time. Over any given decade, almost half of the people in the bottom quintile will move to a higher quintile. Similarly, almost half of the people in the top quintile will have moved to a lower quintile. Just as importantly, in recent decades, there has been *no* tendency for the amount of income mobility in America to diminish. As the authors of one major study concluded, "the rungs on the income ladder have grown farther apart," but "children's chances of climbing from lower to high rungs have not changed."

THINGS AREN'T ALWAYS WHAT THEY SEEM

We noted earlier that government transfer programs help improve the lives of people at the bottom of the income distribution. These programs, plus **progressive tax** policies at the federal and state levels, drive a sharp wedge between what people earn and what they can consume. Because it is presumably consumption that is the key in determining material well-being, it is important to see how this works.

Federal and state tax and transfer programs tend to take income from high-earners and distribute it to low-earners. This happens at all points in the age distribution of the population, but let's focus on the consequences specifically for people in the forty- to forty-nine-year-old age bracket. According to recent research by Professors Alan Auerbach and Lawrence Kotlikoff, the top earners in this age group face a **net tax** (taxes paid minus income transfers received) of 45 percent. This means that their spending power is reduced by the tax and transfer system to only 55 percent of their resources. For those people at the bottom of the income distribution, the net tax rate is *minus* 34 percent. That is, they are able to spend 34 percent more than they have, thanks to a combination of government taxes and transfers.

Thus, spending power is much more evenly distributed than are incomes or assets. Ignoring the effects of taxes and transfers, it looks like people in the top 20 percent have about 14 times the spending power of people in the bottom 20 percent. Once we correct for taxes and transfers, spending power at the top is only about seven times that at the bottom—the differential is cut in half. The difference is big, but much smaller than it seems.

IS ECONOMIC EQUALITY IMPORTANT?

Having said all this, it remains a fact that income and wealth are unequally distributed, and this inequality seems to be rising in recent decades. But we must put this fact in the context of another fact we noted earlier: The overall standard of living is rising in America, at the top, the middle, and the bottom of the economic spectrum. Given this, does it matter that the rich are getting richer faster than the rest of us are getting richer?

Envy, of course, is one reason we might object, although most of us would not like to admit that we are guilty of this example of one of the "seven deadly sins." There might also be a moral reason why everyone should get richer at the same rate, although economics can offer little insight on this rationale. Politics is another reason we might be concerned. After all, the wealthy have more resources that can be used to influence the outcomes of elections. But in America, at least, wealth has never been concentrated just among liberals or just among conservatives. Democrats and Republicans have both prospered, even in the rarified world of billionaires. Moreover, as long as the government does not restrict political contributions, then wealthy people across all political persuasions are free to invest in issues and candidates as they like. Competition is beneficial in the marketplace, and there is no reason to think it is otherwise in the political spectrum.

THE SOURCES OF INEQUALITY

From an economic perspective, perhaps the most important reason we want to understand the facts of economic inequality is to help us understand the *sources* of inequality. In broad terms, there is no doubt that income and wealth are predominantly determined by the value of what people produce. This is easy to see in sports and entertainment—the superstars get rich while the second-stringers, has-beens, and never-weres struggle to make a living. But it is just as true in *all* walks of life: People are paid predominantly on the basis of what they produce.

But notice our use of the word *predominantly*, for it is certainly the case that factors other than productivity come into play. For example, wealthy people tend to leave more assets to their heirs than do lower-income individuals, which helps the children of the rich to be richer than otherwise. But asset inheritance accounts for only a very small part of the observed distribution of wealth. Moreover, heirs of the wealthy have shown a remarkable ability to spend their inheritances fast enough that their own heirs can expect relatively little to be left.

More important than inheritance is the possibility that the "rules of the game" might be skewed to favor the rich and disfavor the poor. Under these circumstances, rewards would not be distributed wholly in accord with production, and, thus, economic incentives would deviate from those that yield the highest possible level of output. That is, *total* real income and wealth in society would be lower. This scenario—the prospect that the rich might use the government to manipulate the rules in their favor—seems to be the one that is most troubling for many observers. But if this is so, then a "solution" that consists of higher taxes on the rich hardly makes sense. After all, if the rich can manipulate the government so expertly, then they will surely manipulate it to spend those extra tax proceeds on programs that benefit *them*, not the poor. It also makes one wonder, given our earlier discussion, why it is that the rich have permitted the tax and transfer system to cut their spending power in half compared to people at the bottom.

The key question, it might be argued, is not who is richer than whom or why either is wealthy. The question instead is why so many low-income individuals *don't* exhibit the upward income mobility that has been a hallmark of American history. As we noted above, about half of the people in the bottom quintile move upward within a decade. But this implies that about half *don't*. Understanding why this is so seems vastly more significant than worrying about whether someone's yacht is too big. America rose to greatness on the basis of opportunity for all, and maintaining that greatness requires that the promise of opportunity be real. So, despite the flaws of much of the data and many of the arguments, if the discussion of inequality gets us to focus on this issue, it has been a success.

FOR CRITICAL ANALYSIS

1. Does envy of those who are rich depend on the source of that wealth? For example, consider two people who are both equally rich. One of them worked eighty hours a week year after year to accumulate her wealth, while the other won the lottery. Would the envy felt by others toward each of these people differ?

2. When the capital gains tax rate was reduced from 28 to 20 percent in 1997 and especially when it was cut again to 15 percent in 2003, many people believed that these reductions would be temporary.

How did this belief affect the incentives to sell assets when the tax rates were cut, compared to a situation in which taxes were cut permanently? How would the belief that the cuts were temporary alter the choice between selling assets that had experienced large capital gains versus those that had experienced only small capital gains?

3. In 1984, individual balances in private retirement plans were $865 billion. By thirty years later, they had risen to almost $25 trillion. In general, balances in private retirement plans are not included in the statistics that show rising income or wealth inequality. How might such an oversight affect our conclusions about inequality?

4. Today, usually at little or no cost, you can Skype with your friends and family, no matter where they are located. Are you both psychologically and economically richer? Why or why not? Similarly, you can follow the lives of the rich and famous via their Twitter feeds, their blogs, or their Facebook pages. Are you better or worse off because you have this option?

5. If you play poker with a group of friends, you are playing what is called a zero-sum game. What you win, they lose, and vice versa. The sum of the funds that you start with together does not change. All that changes is who owns more or less of that sum at the end of your poker game. Many commentators (and politicians, too) believe that wealth creation is a zero-sum game. Is this a correct analogy? Why or why not?

6. Some observers have proposed higher income and wealth taxes on the wealthy. Given that one's wealth generally depends primarily on how much output one produces, how do these taxes affect the incentives of people who are the most productive? Assume that the proceeds from the taxes are given out to the poor. How does this affect *their* incentives? Overall, what do you predict will happen to the total income and wealth of society as a result of higher taxes such as these?

CHAPTER 11

The Great Stagnation

From December 2007 until June 2009, the U.S. economy experienced an economic downturn of historic proportions. **Real gross domestic product (real GDP)** fell sharply, housing foreclosures soared, and millions of people lost their jobs.

When the recession ended, however, many people were optimistic about the years ahead. After all, in the United States and elsewhere, major recessions are generally followed by robust economic recoveries. But the recovery that followed the recession of 2007–2009 was anything but robust. In fact, the first four years of recovery were so weak that some observers began referring to that period as the Great Stagnation. It took seven years to return to full employment, and even then, signs of stagnation littered the economic landscape. Our mission is to see why the recovery from the recession of 2007–2009 was so dismal for so long.[1]

THE GREAT RECESSION

The recession of 2007–2009, sometimes referred to as the Great Recession, was arguably worse than any other we have had since World War II. It also likely ranks among the half dozen or so worst recessions we've had in our history. For example, total employment fell 6 percent, compared to a mere 2 percent in the 2000–2001 recession, and 5 percent in 1948–1949, which had previously been the largest postwar drop. Similarly, total output in the economy fell 4.8 percent in 2007–2009. The

---

1 We explain in Chapter 6 how an aging population is reducing economic growth. Our focus in the present chapter is on the role of economic policies in slowing growth.

largest prior decline in a postwar recession was the 3.2 percent fall in 1973–1974. In addition, although the unemployment rate (10 percent) did not get as high as it had in the 1981–1982 recession (10.8 percent), the jump in the unemployment rate was similar in both recessions—just over five percentage points.

Of course, while the recession of 2007–2009 was large compared to other postwar recessions, it was minor compared to the Great Depression (1929–1933) and modest compared to the recessions of 1919–1920 and 1937–1938. Nonetheless, the latest recession will likely stick with the American people for a long time, for two well-deserved reasons. First, most economists agree that if the Federal Reserve had not stepped in aggressively to end the financial panic of 2008, the consequences could have rivaled those experienced in 1929–1933 when output fell 30 percent and the unemployment rate hit 25 percent. Second, the housing market was utterly devastated in the recession of 2007–2009, to a degree not seen since the 1930s. Housing prices fell over 30 percent, and millions of families lost their homes. The number of housing starts, which had previously peaked at 2 million per year, plunged to under 500,000. In many communities, housing construction ground to a complete halt, often with houses simply left behind, vacant and unfinished. All in all, there is no doubt that the recession of 2007–2009 was severe.

RECESSION AND RECOVERY

A recession is a time when the economy is, by definition, not in long-run equilibrium. Business in all markets is disrupted—meaning there are plenty of mutually beneficial exchanges that should be occurring, but are not. Workers and business owners all have strong incentives to get back to work and back to business as usual, and the farther they have been pushed away from equilibrium, the greater are those incentives. As a result, there is a general rule that applies to recessions and the recoveries that follow them: The deeper the recession, the stronger the recovery.

If we look at the relatively mild recessions of 1990–1991 and 2001, we see that during their subsequent recoveries, real GDP grew at an average pace of about 3 percent per year. During the four years after the much deeper recession of 1981–1982, real GDP roared back at an average rate of 4.5 percent per year. If we go back to the worst of all, the Great Depression, the results are even more dramatic. During the recovery after the Great Depression ended, real GDP grew at a torrid 9.0 percent per year.

Based on these numbers, we would surely expect that the Great Recession would have been followed by a robust recovery, perhaps similar to the strong recovery after the recession of 1981–1982. Some observers even hoped that the performance would rival that of the 1949–1953 recovery, when real GDP growth averaged 7.5 percent per year. In fact, this did *not* happen. Indeed, over the recovery years 2009 to 2017, real GDP grew barely more than 2 percent per year. This was not merely significantly slower than the typical economic recovery. It did not even reach the 3.1 percent average growth in GDP that the United States has experienced since World War II. (And remember, this 3.1 percent rate includes both recessions and recoveries.) In short, the recovery from the Great Recession fell flat.

THE GREAT STAGNATION

While there is no universally agreed-upon definition of economic stagnation, most economists take it to mean a period of lackluster performance in the overall economy. The fact that real GDP growth during 2009–2017 failed to match up with average post–World War II performance is part of the story. But there are other macroeconomic measures that also suggest that recovery from the 2007–2009 recession was weak. It took more than three years, for example, for the unemployment rate to inch down from 10 to 8 percent, and it took fully seven years to reach full employment. Investment spending, which is normally a big force in economic recoveries, grew far more slowly than it normally does. Consumer confidence, which leapt by more than 50 percent in the twelve months after the end of the 1981–1982 recession, spent the first three *years* going sideways after the Great Recession. Seven years after the end of the recession, inflation-adjusted house prices were still almost 20 percent below their prior peak. By the time voters selected Donald Trump to replace Barack Obama, it was clear to all that recovery was anemic.

HOUSING

Normally, new home construction is one of the first economic activities that accelerate in the aftermath of recession. Typically, interest rates have fallen during the recession, and when the downturn ends, consumer confidence normally rises rapidly. The combination normally spurs a surge in the demand for new homes. Not so in the aftermath of 2007–2009, for reasons that go back to the period preceding the recession.

During the years 2001–2006, a variety of federal policies encouraged substantial overbuilding, particularly of single-family houses and condominiums. Home ownership soared to record levels. This seemed like a good thing, until the recession hit and the housing market collapsed. Federal policies, it turned out, had encouraged people to buy houses even if their incomes did not justify those purchases. When the economy soured, many of those people simply walked away from their homes, and many more struggled to stay in them in the face of daunting mortgage payments.

Foreclosures swept across the country, and in Arizona, Florida, Nevada, and parts of California, some neighborhoods became virtual ghost towns as people were forced out of their homes—or moved out shortly before the bank showed up to evict them. Simply put, at existing prices, housing in the United States was overbuilt—there was an **excess supply** of housing. The market response was just what you would expect: House prices plunged by more than 30 percent nationwide and 50 percent or more in some of the hardest-hit areas. Gradually, the excess supply cleared, but the adjustment process was measured in years, not months.

New home construction, which had reached two million units in 2005, plunged to barely one-quarter of that by 2009. But instead of recovering sharply at the end of the recession, home construction edged up only slowly and slightly. By 2016, housing starts were still down 40 percent from 2005 levels. Potential new homes were competing with millions of empty existing homes across the country. Moreover, some home prices were still falling, even as the overall price level was rising. So builders did not build, did not hire workers, and did not buy construction materials. Thus, the unemployed former construction workers did not spend much on goods and services, nor did the people who used to work for companies that made construction equipment and materials. Instead of buoying the economy, housing was weighing it down.

THE ECONOMIC SAFETY NET

Government programs that comprise the so-called **economic safety net** include unemployment insurance, welfare, and food stamps. Spending on these programs rises automatically during recessions, as unemployment rises and people's reliance on **cash and noncash transfers** goes up. Normally, these programs help bolster consumer spending in downturns and thus help moderate recessions. Although such transfers performed this function in 2007–2009, changes in these programs actually *impeded* the recovery from the recession.

To see how, let's consider the following changes:

- *Unemployment benefits*—These payments by the federal and state governments to the unemployed normally can be collected for a maximum of twenty-six weeks (about six months). During this recession, however, Congress increased the maximum collection period to ninety-nine weeks (that is, almost two full years). This surely helped ease the pain of unemployment. Nevertheless, it is well known that unemployment benefits slow people's transition from unemployment to employment. (For example, the single best predictor of when an unemployed person will return to work is the expiration of his or her unemployment benefits.) By lengthening the eligibility period for benefits to a record duration, Congress reduced incentives for people to find new jobs. This helped keep the unemployment rate high for a longer-than-normal period. It also likely dampened overall spending during the recovery phase, because people's unemployment benefits were lower than the wages they would have earned once reemployed.

The extended eligibility for unemployment benefits was accompanied by an increase in the dollar amount of those benefits. In addition, for the first time, many people who were unemployed could have most of their health insurance premiums paid by the federal government. Whatever the merits of these higher benefits and insurance subsidies, there is little doubt that they reduced incentives for people to get back to work promptly and thereby helped slow recovery from the recession.

- *Welfare*—Officially called Temporary Assistance to Needy Families (TANF), this program provides for cash payments to low-income families, especially when one or more adults in a family are unemployed. In 1997 President Clinton strengthened the incentives for TANF recipients to return to work quickly. Under President Obama, however, these incentives were weakened. Once the recession ended in June 2009, Obama's policy change helped keep the unemployment rate higher than it would have been. It also likely dampened overall spending, because people's welfare benefits were lower than the wages they would have earned once reemployed.

- *Food stamps*—These are government-issued **vouchers** that can be used by low-income people to pay for eligible food items. (They got their name because they used to be issued in booklets much like postage stamps. Today people typically receive electronic transfers to debit cards.) Under President Obama, eligibility rules for the receipt of benefits were loosened considerably, and monthly benefits increased. Combined with the recession, these changes caused the number of people on food stamps to soar. There were particularly large increases in the number of able-bodied adults on food stamps. Just as with unemployment benefits and welfare, such policy changes prolong unemployment, because food stamp recipients can lose their benefits if they get jobs. The benefits make them better off, but their incomes are lower than if they worked, which has likely reduced post-recession economic growth.

GOVERNMENT SPENDING AND THE SPECTER OF HIGHER TAXES

Under both President Bush and President Obama, federal spending rose sharply during the recession. In Chapter 19 we discuss the extent to which this spending might have stimulated the economy. Here we focus on the dark side of that spending—the fact that it must be paid for with taxes.

These new taxes may come sooner or they may come later, but come they must, and the specter of these taxes must invariably dampen both business and consumer spending. Corporate profit taxes reduce the after-tax return to investment and thus cause investment spending to fall. Personal income taxes reduce disposable income and also the incentive for people to work. On both counts, personal income and consumption spending will be lower. The combined decline in investment and consumption spending reduces **aggregate demand** and employment, thereby slowing economic recovery.

As we note in Chapter 19, the "stimulus" spending that preceded these taxes may well have softened the recession. Nonetheless, as soon as the piper must be paid—that is, after the recession—the specter and reality of higher taxes kick in. The result is a less robust recovery. During the presidency of Barack Obama (2009–2017), this problem was likely made worse because of the inability of Congress and the president to agree on exactly *who* would pay the higher taxes. This heightened uncertainty made investment by both firms and individuals riskier than it would have been had tax bills been known. This, in turn, surely reduced investment even further and thus prolonged economic stagnation.

REGULATION AND MORE REGULATION

It is usually police and military actions that grab the headlines in both the war on drugs and the war on terror, but both wars have been accompanied by a barrage of new regulations over the last dozen years or so. Under President Bush and President Obama, regulations on financial institutions, the transportation industry, and education have imposed serious and costly new burdens across the economy. And since the Panic of 2008, an entirely new layer of financial regulations is now being termed the "war on borrowing," because the regulations have made it so difficult for anyone to borrow funds for any purpose. As a result, the home ownership rate in America plunged from 69 percent to 63 percent, the lowest seen since the 1960s.

During the strong economic times of 2001–2007, the costs and rigidities associated with the new regulations were largely masked by the healthy economy, but once the recession hit, their adverse effects became clear. This burden has recently intensified due to large-scale new environmental and health care regulations, which the Obama administration deferred until after the election of 2012. Costs and uncertainty have risen, and investment and consumption spending have suffered. The result has been a drag on the economy.

THE FUTURE

Some of the policies we have discussed in this chapter helped ease the blow of the Great Recession. Others surely yielded benefits by reducing drug smuggling or by protecting Americans from terrorists, pollution, or inadequate health care insurance. But there is no free lunch. There is a cost to every action, and for the policies discussed here, part of those costs have come in the form of prolonged high unemployment, sluggish real growth, and economic stagnation. It is a lesson we ignore at our peril.

FOR CRITICAL ANALYSIS

1. Spending on the food stamp program doubled during the first Obama administration, reaching $82 billion per year. People who received additional aid under the program surely benefitted from it, but people who had to pay for the program just as surely were made worse off. On what basis would you decide how much we should spend on food stamps? Why don't we simply have food stamps for everyone?

2. Under President Clinton's added work requirements, many long-term welfare recipients got jobs. Moreover, there is evidence that the educational performance of the children of these parents improved substantially. Why do you suppose that President Obama decided to effectively dismantle the reforms that President Clinton had worked so hard to achieve?

3. In this question, consider only the eighteen months for which the 2007–2009 recession lasted. Suppose that the liberalization of unemployment benefits tended to *raise* the unemployment rate because

it reduced the incentive of the unemployed to return to work. How would you decide whether the liberalization of benefits was good or bad for the economy?

4. Now consider the years *after* the recession and again answer the query posed in question 3. Is the impact on the unemployment rate the only factor to consider? (If you think other factors should be considered, make sure that you take into account both the disadvantages and the advantages of liberalized benefits.)

5. If higher federal spending reduces the unemployment rate, why don't we increase federal spending until the unemployment rate is 4 percent or even 3 percent?

6. When Congress created the Environmental Protection Agency (EPA), it effectively required the agency to *ignore* economic costs when deciding what regulations to issue. Analyze how this requirement changes the likelihood that the EPA issues regulations that make life better for Americans.

CHAPTER 12

The Case of the Missing Workers

Every month, the Bureau of Labor Statistics (BLS) goes out into the labor market to determine how many unemployed people there are in the United States. With the data it acquires, the BLS calculates the **unemployment rate.** This number is a key indication of how well the economy is doing. The unemployment rate is calculated in a seemingly straightforward way: It is the percentage of the total **labor force** that is (i) aged sixteen and older but not institutionalized or in school, and (ii) actively seeking employment but has not found it.

The reelection chances of incumbent presidents often hinge on the estimated rate of unemployment. Historically, when the unemployment rate is rising, the president's chances of reelection have been far worse than when the rate is stable or falling. As the old saying goes, "people vote their pocketbooks" (or in this case, their pay stubs).

For this and a variety of other reasons, understanding how the unemployment rate is measured is important for politicians and ordinary citizens alike. Remarkably, however, there is little consensus about the accuracy of unemployment statistics in the United States. First, consider the period when the United States had its highest measured rate of unemployment—the Great Depression, which started in 1929 and did not fully end until a decade later.

TWENTY-FIVE PERCENT UNEMPLOYMENT—HARD TO IMAGINE

If you look at statistics on the unemployment rate during the Great Depression, you will find that the rate hit 25 percent—meaning that one of every four Americans who were part of the labor force could not find a job during the depth of the depression. That high unemployment rate, of course, makes any **recession** since then seem insignificant in terms of the proportion of people adversely affected.

Some economists, though, are not so sure that one-fourth of the labor force was actually unemployed during the Great Depression. The reason is simple: At that time, the federal government had instituted numerous programs to "put people back to work." These included the Works Progress Administration (WPA), the Civilian Conservation Corps (CCC), and various lesser programs. Government statisticians decided that everyone working in these federally sponsored "make-work" programs would have been unemployed otherwise. Consequently, they decided to count these millions of Americans as unemployed. Michael Darby, an economist at UCLA, subsequently recalculated unemployment statistics for the depth of the Great Depression. After adjusting for people who were actually working but were counted as unemployed, he found a maximum unemployment rate of 17 percent. This number is still the highest we have had in modern times, but it is certainly not one-fourth of the labor force.

How much sense does Darby's adjustment make? The argument against the official government statistics is straightforward: The federal government taxed individuals and businesses to pay workers at the WPA and CCC. Had the federal government not levied the taxes to pay these new government employees, the private sector would have had more disposable income, more spending, and higher employment. Whether all of those people would have gotten private-sector jobs is impossible to know, but it is clear that the official numbers greatly overstated the true unemployment rate during the Great Depression.

DISCOURAGED WORKERS: A COVER FOR A HIGHER "TRUE" UNEMPLOYMENT RATE?

Certain individuals, after spending some time in the pool of the unemployed, may become discouraged about their future job prospects. They may leave the labor market to go back to school, to retire, to work full time at home without pay, or just to take some time off. Whichever path they choose, when interviewers from the BLS ask these individuals whether they are "actively looking for a job," they say no. Individuals such as these are often referred to as **discouraged workers.** They might seek work if labor market conditions were better and potential wages were higher, but they have decided that such is not the case, so they have left the labor market. For years, some critics of the officially measured unemployment rate have argued that during recessions, the rising numbers of discouraged workers cause the government to grossly underestimate the actual rate of unemployment.

To get a feel for the labor market numbers, let's look at the 1990s, perhaps one of the greatest periods of rising employment in U.S. history. During that decade, an additional 18 million people became employed, while the unemployment rate fell to 4 percent. Moreover, far fewer workers settled for part-time jobs. Many who had been retired came back to work, and many of those about to retire continued to work. There were even large numbers of students who left school to take high-paying jobs in the technology sector.

The onset of the 2001 recession produced a turnaround in all of those statistics. The number of unemployed rose by about three million individuals. The number of part-time workers who indicated that they would like to work full time rose by over a million, and the proportion of those out of work for more than half a year increased by over 50 percent.

According to some economists, another two million workers dropped out of the labor force due to that recession—the so-called discouraged-worker problem. For example, University of Chicago economist Robert Topel claimed, "The unemployment rate does not mean what it did twenty years ago." He argued that employment opportunities for the least skilled workers no longer exist in today's labor market, so such individuals simply left the labor force, discouraged and forgotten by the statisticians who compile the official numbers.

ARE DISCOURAGED WORKERS A PROBLEM?

Other economists argue differently. They note that the labor market is no different from any other market, so we can analyze it just as we analyze the market for any other good or service. The **labor supply curve** is upward-sloping. That means that as overall wages rise (corrected for inflation, of course), the quantity of labor supplied would be expected to increase. After all, when the inflation-corrected price of just about anything else goes up, we observe that the quantity supplied goes up, too. Therefore, argue these economists, the concept of discouraged workers is basically flawed. They say it makes no more sense to talk of discouraged workers than it would to talk of "discouraged apples" that are no longer offered for sale when the price of apples falls.

Because of the upward-sloping supply curve of labor, when **real wages** rise economy-wide, we expect that retirees and those about to retire will return to or remain in the labor market. We expect students to quit school early if the wages they can earn are relatively high. The opposite must occur when we go into a recession or the economy stagnates. That is, with reduced wage growth (or even declines in economy-wide real wages) and reduced employment opportunities, we expect more young people to stay in school longer, retirees to stay retired, and those about to retire to actually do so. In other words, we expect the same behavior in response to incentives that we observe in all other markets.

AMERICA'S UNWORKING MEN

There is no doubt about one development in America's labor markets: Men have never been less engaged. During the last fifty years the labor force participation rate for prime age men has plunged, with perhaps one-quarter of the drop coming in the last decade. There is now a huge army of men who are neither working nor looking for work, roughly seven million of them between the ages of twenty-five and fifty-four, the traditional prime of working life.

Who are these men? On average, they are unmarried, less educated, and born in America, and they are disproportionately African American. But there are crosscurrents in this army. Unmarried white men are less likely to be in the labor force than married black men. Native-born men, regardless of their races, are less likely to be working or looking for work than are immigrants. Indeed, native-born college graduates are more likely to be in the idle army of the unworking than are immigrants who are high school dropouts.

If we ask the question, "What are they doing?" the answer is "Not much." About 10 percent are students, but the rest are what the British call NEET: "neither employed nor in education or training." In a nutshell, they are simply idle. They don't help out around the house, they don't care for other family members, they don't even volunteer to help others. And when they are at home, they spend their time at home predominantly (about sixty hours a week) in front of television or computer screens.

How did they arrive in this state? Some are ex-prisoners, who have found that their market value in traditional jobs has been irreparably damaged by their time in jail. So they turn to untraditional activities in the underground economy, unmeasured by the government statisticians, until, perhaps, they return to crime and thus to jail. Others, as we'll see below, are disabled, at least in the eyes of the people who hand out government disability checks. Still others have simply found a parent, a partner, a sibling, or even a child who is willing to support them in the style to which they have become accustomed.

DISABILITY INSURANCE AND LABOR FORCE PARTICIPATION

As we just suggested, certain government programs have prompted some, perhaps many, of the departures from the labor force by low-skill individuals. We refer here to a portion of the Social Security program that has expanded dramatically over the past twenty years. It involves **disability payments.** Originally established in 1956 as a program to help individuals under age sixty-five who are truly disabled, Social Security Disability Insurance (SSDI) has become the federal government's second fastest growing program (after Medicare). The real value of benefits has steadily risen and the Social Security Administration (SSA) has gradually made it easier for individuals to meet the legal criteria for "disabled" status. SSDI now accounts for $150 billion in federal spending per year. Under SSDI, even individuals who are not truly disabled can receive payments from the government when they do not work.

In addition, because Social Security also offers Supplemental Security Income (SSI) payments for disabled people who have little or no track record in the labor force, some people are calling disability insurance the centerpiece of a new U.S. welfare state. Since 1990, the number of people receiving disability payments from the SSA has soared to over fourteen million—perhaps not surprising when you consider that the real value of the monthly benefits a person can collect has risen 60 percent in the past thirty-five years. The federal government now spends more on disability payments than on food stamps or unemployment benefits.

What does this mean? Simply that people who might have worked through chronic pain or temporary injuries—particularly those without extensive training and education—have chosen to receive a government disability benefit instead. The average Social Security disability payment is about $14,000 per year, tax-free. For many on the lower rungs of the job ladder, $14,000 per year tax-free seems pretty good. Indeed, those receiving disability payments make up the largest group of the two million or so who left the labor force during the 2001–2002 recession.

During and after the recession of 2007–2009, almost five million people departed the labor force, as the **labor force participation rate** fell from over 66 percent to under 63 percent. Early retirements by aging baby boomers fueled perhaps one-quarter of this shrinkage. Nevertheless, over this same period, the number of people receiving disability payments soared by more than two million, leading economists to conclude that the disability system played a significant role in the workers' disappearing act. And because people respond to incentives, we can be confident of one thing: Whatever happens to the economy in the future, if the real value of disability payments keeps rising, so will the number of people with disabilities.

FOR CRITICAL ANALYSIS

1. To what extent do you believe that the existence of unemployment benefits increases the duration of unemployment and consequently the unemployment rate? (*Hint:* Use demand analysis and **opportunity cost.**)

2. Is it possible for the unemployment rate to be "too low"? In other words, can you conceive of a situation in which the economy would be worse off in the long run because there is not enough unemployment?

3. It is believed that much of the increase in the number of people collecting SSDI has resulted from decisions by workers at the SSA to make it easier to qualify for benefits. How are the disability rules set by SSA workers likely to change depending on (i) whether the SSA budget is held constant or expands when the number of SSDI recipients rises, (ii) the overall state of the economy, especially the unemployment rate, and (iii) the likelihood that individuals with disabilities will be discriminated against in the workplace?

4. What would happen to the number of disabled people if Social Security disability payments were made subject to income taxes? Explain.

5. During the latest recession Congress increased the length of time people could receive unemployment benefits to ninety-nine weeks (almost two years) from its previous level of twenty-six weeks (about six months). Analyze the impact of this change on (i) the unemployment rate and (ii) the average duration of unemployment.

6. Imagine that at two different times—late 1933 (when the economy was struggling out of the depths of the Depression) and late 1939 (when the economy was expanding rapidly)—there were a million people on make-work government jobs who were officially classified as "unemployed." In which year (1933 or 1939) were these make-work employees more likely to have been displaced from private-sector jobs and in which were they more likely to have been displaced from the ranks of the unemployed? Explain. How would this distinction factor into your thinking about whether such people should be officially classed as "employed" or "unemployed"?

CHAPTER 13

The Gig Economy

During the Jazz Age in the 1920s, U.S. musicians and bands were always striving for ways to find and showcase their new sound. As they did so, jazz players also developed a new set of slang words. One such word was *gig* (short for the word *engagement*). So when jazz musicians of the time were looking for jobs or musical engagements, they were "trying to get a gig."

Today the word **gig** has expanded beyond the music world to describe a single task or project for which a worker is hired—often through an online marketplace. Thus, nearly a century after the Jazz Age, when looking for work, we often say we are doing so in a gig economy. A **gig economy** is one in which many workers find temporary employment or companies hire independent contractors for short-term engagements. The reasons behind this evolving economy include the rise of digitalization and increased mobility within our society. Is the gig economy here to stay? Will it continue to grow in importance? Will it change the way labor is perceived and used? We will answer these questions and more in this chapter.

ENTER THE HOLLYWOOD MODEL

To get a better sense of what exactly a gig economy entails, think about what it's like on a Hollywood movie set. If you are behind the scenes, you will see many different individuals engaged in lots of activity. There are, of course, the actors, but then there are also the director, set designers and builders, lighting engineers, makeup artists, sound-recording engineers, and stunt coordinators, to name a few. Almost always, each of these players is a **freelancer**—that is, an individual who is temporarily working on the movie set as long as her or his services are needed. When freelancers are no longer needed, they move on to another movie project.

Each freelancer and **independent contractor** is hired for a specific job for a specific fee. This Hollywood model has been refined over the years so well that each person on the movie set seems to be guided as if by an invisible hand to do the necessary work when needed. The Hollywood model is the ultimate version of a gig economy. Almost no one on the set is a full-time employee of a company.

THE AMERICAN DREAM

For decades, the American Dream has been relatively easy to describe. Most importantly, it has meant a house of your own (usually financed by a big **mortgage** loan). This house often has a two-car garage with one or more late-model cars parked inside. Walk in the front door, and you see the latest consumer goods, such as large-screen smart TVs, personal computers, and designer furniture and fixtures. Of course, the only way to attain this American Dream has been to find a steady, full-time job with employer-provided benefits, including health insurance and a retirement plan. In the past, Americans without full-time jobs considered themselves stranded on the fringes of the labor market—observing, rather than living, the American Dream. That is, traditionally, success has been defined as working for one company long enough to climb the corporate ladder, and in the process, accumulate enough wealth to buy a house and eventually retire to a life of ease.

Consider, though, that in the new gig economy, if a consultant or freelancer has gigs with five businesses at the same time, that person is proud to say so, because it shows how valuable he or she is to those businesses. Consequently, the gig workers of today are beginning to redefine our idea of how to achieve the American Dream.

HOW BIG IS THE GIG ECONOMY, REALLY?

Some observers believe that the size of the gig economy (and its importance) is grossly overestimated. To back this claim, they point to data from the federal government that does not show much of an increase in the number of U.S. freelance workers. The problem with that argument, though, is that until recently official government statisticians have not had a good way to estimate the size of the gig labor force. Typically, labor statistics come from surveys during which people are asked about their employment status. Most survey respondents usually only indicate their traditional permanent employer status. If they sign on with Uber or do a one-time design project for someone, however, they often don't realize that those short-term services should be considered employment, too.

So rather than relying on survey interviews, the U.S. Bureau of Labor Statistics (BLS) is now looking at Internal Revenue Service (IRS) data to better gauge the gig economy's size and impact. These data include detailed information on what are now called **non-employer firms,** meaning self-employed individuals operating unincorporated businesses with no paid employees. The IRS data show more than twenty-five million of these types of "businesses" nationwide. They mostly provide **on-demand services,** such as pet sitting and appliance repair. Here are some of the areas in which the BLS found the most non-employer businesses:

- Arts and design
- Computer and information technology
- Construction
- Media and communications
- Transportation and material moving

These non-employer firms are at the heart of the gig economy. According to the New York City-based Freelancers Union and digital freelancing platform Upwork, current estimates of the gig economy show that in the United States alone, more than fifty million people worked on a freelance basis in 2016. Additionally, this study found that more than 60 percent of freelancers are working independently by choice rather than by necessity, thereby contributing more than a trillion dollars a year to the U.S. economy.

In terms of the gig economy's broader impact, a recent report by McKinsey Global Institute estimates that up to 162 million people in America and Europe work outside normal employment (representing 20–30 percent of the working-age population). More than half of these individuals rely on such freelance work for their primary income.

Platforms and the Rise of the Gig Economy

One of the major reasons that the gig economy has become so important is due to the spread of platforms, which are based on the power of the Internet, and are channeling our economic and social lives. A **platform firm** provides the platform—usually the Web site and all the programming and digital storage behind it—for two groups that wish to be linked together. For example, platforms are available for purchasing and selling all types of tickets, finding a date or a mate, listening to music, and buying items via online auctions.

Perhaps the fastest-growing part of the gig economy involves platform firms for freelancers. Examples of such firms include the following:

- *Upwork*—a Web site that has more than 1.5 million clients. It accommodates both short- and long-term projects. Payment is hourly or per-project.
- *Freelancer*—a Web site that offers millions of projects. Freelance workers can prove their skills via contests.
- *Guru*—a Web site on which you can showcase your past work experience. It offers daily job-matching features.
- *College Recruiter*—a Web site designed for college students or recent graduates who are looking for freelance jobs of any kind.
- *SimplyHired*—a Web site that allows individuals such as construction workers, salespeople, administrative assistants, and drivers to search for freelance work.

UBER—THE SUCCESS STORY OF THE CENTURY?

Do not doubt the power of the gig economy, which is importantly driven by some very successful platform firms. One of the early platform firm success stories is Uber—the world's most valuable start-up and a leader in the race to transform the future of transportation. Launched in 2010, Uber attracted almost $20 billion in **start-up capital.** Today, its implicit **market valuation** is more than $50 billion. No technology firm in history has raised more money from private investors before going public. Its online ridesharing service is so popular that the company name has even become a verb: "I'll Uber home."

Uber now operates in more than 600 cities in 80 countries. In excess of forty million people worldwide use its services each year. Uber does not own cars. It does not directly employ drivers. Instead, it's a platform in a **two-sided market.** On the one side are individuals who have cars and want to offer their services as drivers. On the other side are individuals who need rides and want alternatives to taxis, buses, and subways. To be sure, Uber has competitors—such as Lyft in America, OLA in India, and Grab in Southeast Asia—but regardless, Uber stands out as the dominant platform firm in its ridesharing service industry.

Another highly valued platform firm is Airbnb, which is transforming another part of the service industry—temporary stays away from home. Like Uber, Airbnb has been met with serious political opposition to its services. Taxi firms have battled, via the political process, the invasion of Uber throughout the world. Some cities and countries have outlawed Uber. Others have tried to regulate it to death. Airbnb has seen the same political and regulatory response, driven by hotel owners, everywhere. Whenever there is a disruption in an industry, the first line of defense appears to be complaining to local politicians that such new competition is "unfair." Yet despite the objections from competitors, Uber, Airbnb, and other successful platform firms are proving that the gig economy is transforming the way we perceive employment, business, and even success.

THE GIG ECONOMY AND THE DECISION-MAKING PROCESS

The gig economy has already changed the decision-making process for both individuals and firms. For individual gig workers, rather than receiving hourly wages or monthly salaries with full employer-provided (and employer-decided) benefits, they receive multiple contractual payments with no benefits. As a result, gig workers must decide how to allocate their income to obtain healthcare services and plan for their pensions.

On the flip side, firms have much broader choices now than just deciding how much to spend on wage and salary payments. They can decide, in contrast, how many funds should be devoted to staffing short-term projects, rather than keeping full-time workers on hand. Resources that previously had been devoted to the management of full-time employees can now be shifted to the coordination of tasks that freelancers provide.

Not every individual wants to become part of the gig economy and not every firm wants to follow the Hollywood model. Nonetheless, the lure of a gig economy is such that at least over the next few years, its share of the total economy will continue to grow at double-digit rates.

FOR CRITICAL ANALYSIS

1. There has been worldwide backlash against Uber and other online-based platform-transportation services. From whom has this backlash originated, and why?

2. The provision of short-term housing rentals has proliferated, especially with the rising popularity of Airbnb. Are those who provide rooms for rent through Airbnb part of the labor force? Why or why not? What if they hire house cleaners and repair persons? Does their "work" then make them part of the labor force?

3. Long before there were jazz musicians, there were migrant farm workers, who moved from farm to farm from early spring to late fall, doing whatever needed to be done, and getting paid for exactly what they produced. In what sense were these migrant workers members of a gig economy?

4. What are the disadvantages for individuals who chose to be part of the gig economy rather than engage in full-time work paid for by a corporate employer?

5. Many individuals have highly marketable skills and training in occupations in competitive fields. These include engineers and coders. Nonetheless, a certain percentage of these individuals choose to be freelancers. What are some of the reasons that they do not wish to work full time for a corporate employer?

6. Most transactions in the gig economy pass through the banking system in such a way (for example, through credit card systems) that the Internal Revenue System can monitor them. Nonetheless, many gig economy transactions are done with cash. Why do such cash transactions make the collection of both information about and taxes from workers in the gig economy more difficult?

CHAPTER 14

Mobility in America

America has long been known as the "land of opportunity." This notion—that no matter where you start in life, where you end up depends on *your* effort and ability—is deeply embedded in our history. The Declaration of Independence expresses it in the proclamation that "all men are created equal." Giants of American literature, such as Mark Twain and F. Scott Fitzgerald, have fashioned enduring works on its premise. And politicians, entrepreneurs, and civic leaders who have risen from obscurity and poverty to wealth and prominence are held out as examples of its truth.

But not everyone is convinced that opportunity is available to all. The distribution of income in America is far from equal, the wages paid men and women differ for reasons that seem to have little to do with ability, and segregation and racial discrimination have yet to be abolished. To many people, equality of opportunity may be the American Dream, but the American Reality is far different.

LIFE AT THE BOTTOM

If we look at people at the bottom of the economic ladder, the promise of opportunity surely seems false. For example, in 1960 the poorest 20 percent of households in the United States received only about 4 percent of total money income. Today, despite decades of economic growth and more than half a century of government antipoverty programs, the bottom 20 percent still receive only about 4 percent of total money income. Almost forty million Americans officially lived in poverty in 1960. More than forty million U.S. citizens officially live in poverty today.

Nevertheless, even though the *absolute* number of Americans living in poverty has not diminished over the past half-century, because population is now much greater, there has been a large reduction in the *proportion* of Americans who are impoverished. As conventionally measured, more than 22 percent of Americans lived in poverty in 1960. Today, about 13 percent of the population is below the official poverty line.

In addition, over the past fifty years, the **poverty line** has been adjusted upward faster than the cost of living has risen. Hence, the *real* standard of living of a family at the poverty line has risen by 50 percent. In contrast, the real standard of living of a family in the middle of the income distribution has risen only 20 percent over these years. Thus, the people who are counted as poor today are much better off compared to the middle class than they were fifty years ago.

Finally, the government measure of poverty may be misleading because it focuses only on the *cash incomes* of individuals. Major parts of the federal government's antipoverty efforts come in the form of **in-kind transfers** (transfers of goods and services, rather than cash), such as Medicare, Medicaid, subsidized housing, food stamps, and school lunches. There is disagreement over exactly how much of these in-kind transfers should be included in measures of income. Nevertheless, as we noted in Chapter 10, these transfers, plus the **earned income tax credit** (which gives special **tax rebates** to low-income individuals), are major sources of income for people at the bottom of the income distribution. Adjusting for these transfers and tax credits, it seems likely that over the past fifty years, the proportion of Americans living below the poverty line has been cut in half. Just as important, the real standard of living for the poorest 20 percent of the population has doubled since the mid-1960s.

IS UP AN OPTION?

Despite the foregoing, to someone whose income is mired at the bottom, the relevant question may be: What are the chances of moving up? Obviously, the answer depends chiefly on the individual and his or her circumstances. But an examination of some key concepts and the experience of a broad cross-section of people may give us some insights.

However we measure income, there is a large body of evidence that an individual's income is likely to change considerably over her or his lifetime, both in absolute terms and relative to the incomes of others. For example, as we noted in Chapter 1, in those nations with secure systems of property rights, economy-wide real per capita income tends to rise over time. In the United States over the last 150 years or so, the standard of living has grown at about 2 percent per year. This may not sound like much, but over the course of about thirty-five years, it is enough to *double* the real income of the average person.

There is also a great deal of **income mobility** in all countries. That is, people tend to move around in the distribution of income, as their incomes change relative to the incomes of others. During the 1970s and 1980s, for example, among the people in the top 20 percent (quintile) of income earners at the beginning of the decade, fewer than half were in the top quintile by the end of the decade. Similarly, among the people who were in the bottom quintile at the beginning of the decade, almost half had moved out of that bracket by the end of the decade.

Income mobility remains robust. In each of the last two decades, about half of the people who were in the bottom quintile at the start of the decade had moved out of that bracket by the end of the decade. In addition, about 30 percent of the people in the top 20 percent at the start of each ten-year period had moved (down) out of that bracket by the end of that decade.

IS IT BETTER TO BE YOUNG OR LUCKY?

The most important source of income mobility is the "life cycle" pattern of earnings. New entrants to the workforce tend to have lower incomes at first, but most workers enjoy rising incomes as they gain experience on the job. Typically, annual earnings for an individual reach a maximum at about age fifty-five. Because peak earnings occur well beyond the **median age** of the population (now thirty-nine in the United States), a "snapshot" of the current distribution of earnings will find most individuals "on the way up" toward a higher position in the income distribution. Thus, people who have low earnings now are likely, on average, to have higher earnings in the future.

Another major source of income mobility is Lady Luck. At any point in time, the income of high-income people is likely to be abnormally high (relative to what they can expect on average) due to recent good luck—say, because they just won the lottery or received a bonus at work. Conversely, the income of people who currently have low incomes is likely to be abnormally low due to recent bad luck—perhaps because they are laid up after an automobile accident or have become temporarily unemployed. Over time, the effects of Lady Luck tend to average out across the population. Accordingly, people with high income today will tend to have lower income in the future, while people with low income today will tend to have higher future income. Equivalently, many people living below the poverty line are there temporarily rather than permanently.

WHAT MATTERS TO YOU?

If we look across America, there are distinctive geographic patterns of income mobility. Economist Raj Chetty and his colleagues have examined upward income mobility among people who start in the bottom half of the income distribution. They have found that upward mobility is lowest in three areas: the Southeast (from North Carolina around to Louisiana), the Southwest (Arizona, New Mexico, and southern Nevada), and a large portion of the "Rust Belt" (including Ohio, Indiana, and Michigan). In contrast, upward mobility is greatest in the middle part of the country: the Midwest (including Nebraska, Iowa, Minnesota, and much of the Dakotas) and the Rocky Mountain region (including Utah, Wyoming, and parts of Idaho, Montana, and Colorado).

Of course, there is nothing inherent about the geography of Nebraska or North Carolina that determines income mobility. As Chetty and his co-authors note, it is the characteristics of people who live there and their social environment that are important. The researchers identified several observable factors that are important in whether a person is likely to "move up" in life, that is, reach levels of economic prosperity exceeding those in which they grew up.

- *Family structure*—Growing up in a single-parent household appears to be the most damaging to a person's prospects of upward mobility. Moreover, even just growing up in a neighborhood in which a large fraction of households have only one parent at home is a significant impediment to moving up the economic ladder.
- *Social capital*—Upward mobility is higher in those communities with strong social networks and community involvement. For example, communities with high upward mobility tend to have higher fractions of religious individuals and more participation in local civic organizations.
- *School*—Communities where standardized test scores are higher, dropout rates are lower, and class sizes are smaller exhibit higher levels of upward mobility. Education matters, it seems.
- *Inequality*—Individuals who grow up in communities where income is distributed relatively equally have a better chance of moving up than do people who grow up where there is substantial inequality of income.

- *Segregation*—Even controlling for the other factors on the list, upward mobility for individuals is lower in areas with larger African American populations. But this effect is present for both black *and* white individuals who live in predominantly black communities. So there appears to be something about segregation *per se* that is linked to reduced upward mobility.

THE GREAT GATSBY—OR NOT

Other researchers have also found that upward mobility is lower in areas with large income inequality. Indeed, if one plots measures of upward mobility against measures of inequality, the resulting curve is downward sloping: More inequality is associated with less mobility. Indeed, such a plot has come to be known as the "Great Gatsby curve," named after one of author F. Scott Fitzgerald's most famous fictional characters.[1] Some economists have argued that this negative association implies that inequality inhibits income mobility. Other economists, including Greg Mankiw of Harvard, have noted that there may be less to the Gatsby curve than it seems.

Return to our earlier discussion of the role of Lady Luck, or chance. Imagine that economic outcomes in each year for each person result from two forces: ability (however measured) and luck. Also suppose that the effects of luck are pretty much the same everywhere. Now consider two specific communities. In community "L," there is large variation across people in their abilities, while in "S," the variation in abilities across people is small.

In community L, income will be very unequally distributed, because abilities differ widely. Moreover, the effects of luck in any given year will be unlikely to move people from the top of the income distribution to the bottom, or vice versa. Thus, low-income people will tend to remain poor and high-income people will tend to stay rich.

In community S, income will tend to be equally distributed, because ability is equally distributed. But now, the effects of luck will play a large role in one's place in the income distribution. Indeed, in the extreme case, whether you are high-income or low-income in any given year might be entirely determined by chance, simply because all abilities are equal. Thus, from one year to the other, people will exhibit lots of

---

1 Ironically, the effect's fictional namesake, Jay Gatsby, rose from poverty to wealth in a time and place of great economic inequality, exactly the *opposite* of the phenomenon labeled for him.

movement up and down the income distribution. So, in a community of equally distributed ability (and average income), we will also see lots of income mobility.

One implication of this argument is that in a nation such as the United States, where there is enormous diversity, we are likely to see much more income inequality than we observe in a homogeneous nation, such as Denmark. We are also likely to see less income mobility in America than in Denmark. And this is true even though in both countries, the long-term economic outcomes for all persons are based on their abilities.

So far, researchers have not yet found conclusive evidence on the true source of the Gatsby curve. But interest in this issue is high, so you can be sure they are working on it.

THE NEXT GENERATION

We noted in Chapter 10 that income inequality has been rising in America in recent years, even if not as fast as some people have argued. This raises the question of whether or not people of today have as much opportunity to move up as their parents did. Chetty and his colleagues address this question specifically, and the answer is "yes." Over the half-century studied by the researchers, economic mobility in America has *not* diminished. Now, depending on where you start in the income distribution, this might be good news or bad news. If you are starting near the bottom, moving up remains as much of a possibility as it has been in the past. Of course, if you are starting at the top, it also means that the chances of moving *down* the income distribution are also unchanged.

We cannot choose our parents, and we had little control over the circumstances and community in which we grew up. But the work of Chetty and many other researchers implies that education is one key to upward mobility. Moreover, there is plenty of evidence that hard work is also rewarded in the marketplace. So if your aspiration is to move up rather than down the economic ladder, our suggestion is simple. Study hard—and keep your fingers crossed.

FOR CRITICAL ANALYSIS

1. Why do most modern societies try to reduce poverty? Why don't they do so by simply passing a law that requires everybody to have the same income?

2. How do the "rules of the game" help determine the degree of income mobility? (*Hint:* How did the Civil Rights Act of 1964, which forbade discrimination on the basis of race, likely affect the economic

mobility of African Americans compared to that of white Americans?) Explain your answer.

3. Which of the following possible in-kind transfers do you think raises the "true" incomes of recipients the most: (i) free golf lessons, (ii) free transportation on public buses, or (iii) free food? Why?

4. Consider three alternative ways of helping people at the bottom of the income distribution to obtain better housing: (i) government-subsidized housing that costs $6,000 per year, (ii) a housing **voucher** worth $6,000 per year toward rent on an apartment or a house, or (iii) $6,000 per year in cash. Which would you prefer if you were poor? On what grounds might you make your decision?

5. Many government "safety net" programs (such as food stamps and unemployment insurance) are intended in part to soften the blow caused by adverse circumstances beyond the power of the individual (such as economic downturns). How do such programs also affect people's incentives to work hard to improve their economic outcomes? Taking into account all aspects of these programs, how are they likely to affect the degree of economic mobility?

6. One effect of the **minimum wage** is to reduce employment opportunities for minority teenagers. What effect do you think this has on the long-run economic mobility of minorities? Explain.

CHAPTER 15

Inflation and the Debt Bomb

When George W. Bush took office as president of the United States on January 20, 2001, the federal government was $5.7 trillion in debt. Over the next eight years, President Bush (with the help of Congress, of course) managed to rack up an *additional* $4.9 trillion in debt on your behalf. Many people were stunned that so much debt could be accumulated so fast. As it turns out, President Bush's spending habits were modest compared to those of President Obama, who took only three years and two months to pile up this much extra debt for you to pay off. By the time Obama left office on January 20, 2017, America's national debt was almost exactly $20 billion. Put somewhat differently, more than 70 percent of *all* of the debt incurred by the U.S. government since George Washington first took office has been incurred since George W. Bush first took office. The result, as one commentator has put it, is a "debt bomb."

THE DEBT MUST BE PAID

You might say, "What's the big deal?" Indeed, many people think that the government can simply pay off the **national debt** by borrowing more. But it cannot. As we saw in Chapter 5, the ability to borrow does not change the fundamental **budget constraint** facing our society. What is spent today must be paid for now or in the future. And when it is government doing the spending, that higher spending today *must* eventually be matched with higher taxes. Because the record-breaking spending by the federal government over the years 2001–2017 was not matched by higher taxes at the time of the spending, the result was the huge increase in the national debt. But all of that debt means higher taxes (and lower private spending) for you and everyone else who earns income in the United States.

Now, this does not settle what form those higher taxes will take. They might be higher personal income taxes, or higher payroll taxes, or higher corporate taxes, or even higher taxes on estates—the wealth that people leave to their heirs. In fact, almost surely *all* of these taxes will be higher in the future. But there is one other tax that is equally sure to rise in the future. It is called the **inflation tax.**

THE INFLATION TAX

Inflation is a rise in the average level of the prices of goods and services, as measured in terms of a country's **unit of account.** In the United States, the unit of account—that is, the unit in which we express prices—is the dollar. In much of Europe, the unit of account is the euro. In Japan, it is the yen. In China, it is the renminbi, and so forth. But whatever the unit in which prices are measured is, when the average level of those prices rises, we call that inflation.

Now, suppose you have a $100 bill stashed in your drawer for emergencies. Further suppose that there is inflation of 10 percent. That is, the price level rises by 10 percent this year. That $100 will buy fewer goods and services than before, because their dollar prices are higher. In this example, the $100 will now buy what it used to take only $90 to acquire. What happened to the other $10? Well, it went to the U.S. government, because it has the ultimate responsibility for the currency it issues. When the purchasing power of the $100 fell by 10 percent, so did the government's responsibility to you. The 10 percent inflation was a tax of $10 that was just as effective as any other tax would be in transferring wealth from you to the federal government.

ASSETS SUBJECT TO THE INFLATION TAX

The 10 percent tax that was applied to your $100 was at the same time applied to every other piece of currency issued by the U.S. government. Given that there is over $1.5 trillion in U.S. currency in circulation, a 10 percent inflation during the year would effectively impose a tax of $150 billion (= 10 percent × $1.5 trillion) on the holders of currency. Note that these extra taxes would be imposed and collected without the president having to ask for higher taxes and without members of Congress having to vote for those higher taxes. Hence, neither the president nor the Congress has to take responsibility for the new taxes.

It is not just currency that is subject to the inflation tax. Every I.O.U., or debt, of the federal government that is fixed in nominal (or dollar) terms is equally at risk of having this tax applied to it. Thus, mostly as a result of the huge budget deficits racked up by George W. Bush and Barack Obama, the national debt of the United States is today approximately $20 trillion. Of this amount, about $14 trillion is specified in dollar terms and is owned by the "public"—a term that includes not only Aunt Millie (who owns a few savings bonds) but also China (which owns almost $1.2 trillion in federal debt).[1] In our example, a 10 percent rise in the price level would constitute a tax of $1.4 *trillion* on the holders of those $14 trillion in bonds. By anyone's standards, this is a fairly sizable chunk of tax revenues—all collected without the Internal Revenue Service having to lift a finger.

The Temptation of Inflation

At this point, you should begin to see something that just about every government since the beginning of recorded time has seen: When a government has liabilities (such as currency or government bonds) that are fixed in **nominal** terms, inflation is a simple way to increase taxes. Consider, for example, the squabbles among politicians during 2012 about whether federal income taxes on the wealthiest Americans should be raised. At stake were proposed tax hikes that would generate $50 billion a year in extra tax revenue. The battle went on for months, dominating headlines. It played a significant role in the 2012 election and then resumed as soon as the election was over. In January 2013, Congress actually ended up hitting only the upper echelon of the rich with higher income taxes. The result was extra annual tax revenues of no more than $30 billion—which amounts to a few *days'* worth of federal spending.

This same $30 billion per year in additional tax revenues could have been raised, quietly and with no legislation required, if the federal government had been able to engineer—for just twelve months—inflation that was higher by about one-quarter of one percentage point. To put things slightly differently, because the inflation rate in 2012 was about

---

1 What happened to the other $6 trillion ($20 trillion total, minus $14 trillion owned by the public)? About $1 trillion or so is in the form of Treasury Inflation Protected Securities (TIPS). These debts have the special provision that if inflation reduces their real value, the federal government must make extra payments to the owners of the debts to compensate them. Thus, TIPS are protected from the inflation tax. The other $5 trillion is owned by the federal government itself, so what it collects in taxes from itself is exactly canceled out by the decline in the value of the dollar-denominated assets it holds.

2.5 percent, the federal government collected just about $300 billion in tax revenues that did not have to be voted on by Congress. Had the inflation rate been just over 2.7 percent that year, the government would also have gotten the extra $30 billion in taxes, without all the drama.

Some Historical Examples

From Rome in ancient times to Zimbabwe and Venezuela in recent times, governments around the world have succumbed to the temptation to use inflation to implicitly enhance their tax revenues. Sometimes the results have been catastrophic. After World War I, for example, Germany was required to provide **reparations** to the nations that had defeated it. Some of these reparations were in the form of gold or other physical assets.

Some reparations, however, were to be in the form of foreign currency—money issued by other nations. Germany did not have the foreign currency to make the payments, nor the conventional tax revenues to buy the foreign currency. So the German government simply started printing money to buy foreign currency to repay its debts. This caused inflation, which meant the government had to print even more money, which created more inflation, and so forth. Eventually, the price level in Germany was *doubling* every other day. The economy finally collapsed when people effectively refused to hold any German marks, forcing most voluntary trade within the country to a halt.

Although the German case is quite famous, there were more than fifty other hyperinflations during the twentieth century. In each case, the government involved printed money to pay for expenditures. The ensuing inflation effectively taxed those individuals and businesses that were either holding money or government debts denominated in money. Many of these hyperinflations came at the end of World Wars I or II, or after the Soviet Union broke up in 1991, although the Zimbabwean and Venezuelan hyperinflation of the early twenty-first century involved neither. In each instance, however, the source of the inflation was fundamentally the same: The government involved wanted to spend more than it could collect in other tax revenues. The revenue from the inflation tax made up the difference.

The American Experience

Although the United States is unlikely to have a hyperinflation in the foreseeable future, our government has routinely shown a willingness to use inflation as a source of tax revenue. Most of the Revolutionary War was financed with an inflation tax, and both the Union and (especially) the Confederacy used the inflation tax to help finance the Civil War. In the twentieth century, all the significant wars in which the United States fought were financed in some part by the inflation tax, as were the more recent wars in Iraq and Afghanistan.

Although the mechanics for engineering the inflations have varied over time, the typical pattern since the founding of the Federal Reserve System (the Fed) in 1913 is simple. The U.S. Treasury issues bonds (borrows funds) equal to the difference between what Congress spends and conventional tax revenues. These bonds are then sold directly or indirectly to the Fed. The Fed pays for the bonds by creating deposits that the Treasury can use to pay its bills. As soon as the Treasury spends the funds, they become part of the money supply and begin putting upward pressure on the inflation rate. And as inflation rises, so too does the tax on people who hold currency (just about all of us) and the people who own federal government bonds whose values are fixed in dollar terms. Thus, although the Treasury is not physically "printing money," the consequences (on a smaller scale, of course) are just as they were when the German government printed money after World War I: more inflation and a higher inflation tax.

THE RECENT EXPERIENCE

Since January 20, 2009, the Treasury has issued an additional $14 trillion in bonds to finance its multitrillion dollar spending splurge. This has produced rapid growth in the money supply, but not as much as would normally have been expected. Typically, banks would have lent out the extra reserves created by the Fed to finance the Treasury spending. Such lending creates new **demand deposits** and thus new money in circulation. But the Fed policy now pays interest on the reserves of **depository institutions** (such as banks). These interest payments give the institutions an incentive to hold on to more of the reserves created by the Fed, rather than lending the funds out to people and businesses. Thus, compared to what would have happened without the Fed interest payments, there has been less growth in the money supply and so a lower inflation rate.

Nevertheless, the reserves are there in the banking system, ready to become new money, money that will fuel inflation. It would be possible for the Fed to "sterilize" these reserves by either (i) selling some of its enormous asset holdings to the banks, or (ii) asking the Treasury to pay off the debt held by the Fed. Neither seems likely. And because it also appears unlikely that the federal government will cut spending enough to match receipts from conventional taxes, this leaves only two possibilities: default or inflation.

THE LESSER OF TWO EVILS?

Technically, the federal government could eliminate some or all of our national debt by simply refusing to pay the debt when it is due: We could **default.** Over the centuries, this is a course that some nations have taken. But this is not just embarrassing. It is also costly and inconvenient. After all, if a nation refuses to pay its debts, people will be reluctant to lend to it in the future.

A politically more palatable solution is inflation. The Fed will simply fail to fully sterilize the reserves of the banking system. Hence, bank lending will grow more rapidly over time, causing the money supply to grow more rapidly, thereby ultimately causing a higher inflation rate. Money balances and federal bonds that are fixed in dollar terms will gradually shrink in **real value,** and the burden of the national debt will gradually be reduced. There will be no ugly default. Instead the debt will be fully "repaid"—although, of course, it will be with dollars that are worth much less than those that were borrowed. And even though the inflation tax will add to the total tax burden, Congress will not have to go through the pain of voting this added tax into existence. The Fed will implement the higher taxes gradually and quietly over time, as it allows the inflation rate to rise. It is a solution that warms the heart of any talented politician.

FOR CRITICAL ANALYSIS

1. If Congress manages to agree on higher income taxes, what do you predict will be true about the size of the inflation tax, compared to a scenario in which Congress fails to agree to raise income taxes?

2. Suppose a nation has $100 billion in currency outstanding and $1 trillion in bonds, 30 percent of which are owned by agencies of the government. Assume that all the bonds are payable in the country's unit of account. Calculate how much revenue the government would collect in the form of an inflation tax if the inflation rate in the country were 2 percent. How much *extra* revenue from the inflation tax would be collected if the inflation rate were 5 percent instead? Show your calculations.

3. Analyze why many hyperinflations have been associated with wars or widespread civil unrest (or revolution). (*Hint*: Are wars expensive?)

4. The rule of 70 states that if something is growing at a rate of R percent per year, its value will double in 70/R years. Suppose the

inflation rate becomes 5 percent per year in the United States. How long will it take for the price level to double? How long will it take for the real value of the current stock of federal debt to be cut in half? Show your calculations.

5. A hyperinflation is sometimes defined as one in which the inflation rate is at least 50 percent per month. Use the rule of 70 to calculate how many days it takes for the price level to double in a nation experiencing inflation of 50 percent per month.

6. Average inflation rates tend to be higher in nations that have relatively weak judicial systems and property rights of the sort discussed in Chapter 1. Suggest some reasons why this pattern is observed.

CHAPTER 16

Is It Real, or Is It Nominal?

Every few years, some important commodity, such as gasoline, electricity, or food, experiences a spike in prices. Reporters examine such price spikes and plaster newspapers, magazines, and Web sites with the appropriate headlines—sometimes relentlessly, day after day. Television commentators interview frustrated and worried Americans who spout the expected negative reactions to the higher prices of essential items in their budgets. The world, it would seem, is coming to an end.

Was Gas Really Expensive?

Let's just take one often-in-the-press example: gasoline prices. The authors of the book you are reading are old enough to remember the television interviews that ensued when the price of gas first hit the unprecedented level of $1 per gallon, back in 1980. The same type of interviews occurred when the price of a gallon of gas broke the $2 barrier early in 2005, and lodged above $3 in 2007. Not surprisingly, virtually the same interviews occurred when the price of a gallon of gas rose above $4 in the summer of 2008. At each point in time, everyone interviewed had the same response, even though years had passed between the different price spikes: "I guess I'll just have to stop driving." "I'm going to get a bike." "I'm selling my big car and getting a small one." And of course, each time there was an accompanying story about how record numbers of people were (or soon would be) flocking to their neighborhood e-bike or moped dealerships.

If we wish to sensibly analyze the effects of higher prices on the quantity demanded and the quantity supplied of any good or service in this world, we can rely neither on what journalists report nor on what Americans say when they are interviewed. After all, what is important is not what people say but what they do. As economists, we best understand consumers by their **revealed preferences.** Similarly, business owners are best understood by their actions, not their words. What people do is reflected in how much they actually buy of any good or service after its price changes, not by their complaints to a television reporter or what they post on Facebook.

RELATIVE PRICES, NOMINAL PRICES, AND INFLATION

For economic analysis, the relevant price is the price *relative to* all other prices because people's decisions are based on **relative prices,** not **nominal prices.** The latter simply tells us the number of pieces of paper (dollar bills) you must hand over for a good. Nominal prices tell us nothing about the real sacrifice (measured in terms of other goods or of labor services) that one must make to obtain those goods. Relative prices reflect the real sacrifice involved in acquiring a good because they tell us the price of a good or service relative to the price of another good or service or to the average of all other prices. Relative prices tell us how much of other goods we must sacrifice.

Said another way, we have to separate out the rise in the general price level, called **inflation,** and the rise in the nominal price of a *particular* good or service. If *all* nominal prices went up exactly 3 percent, there would be no change in relative prices. This inflation of 3 percent would not change the real sacrifice entailed in acquiring any particular good. In the real world, even during periods of inflation, some prices go up faster than others and some prices even go down—witness the price of computing power and LED televisions. Nevertheless, if we want to predict people's behavior, we must know what has happened to the *relative* price of a good, and to determine this, we must adjust for inflation.

GAS PRICES REVISITED

Now let's get back to our example of gasoline prices. Your grandparents might be able to talk about buying gas for 30 cents a gallon (its average nominal price most of the time between 1956 and 1964). Today, what you pay in dollars per gallon is many times that level. People still drive nonetheless—indeed, the use of gasoline for cars and trucks in the United States is roughly triple what it was when the nominal price of gas was only 30 cents. Something must have happened. The most important "something" is a general rise in *all* prices, including gasoline prices.

In the summer of 2008, the price of gasoline spiked over $4 per gallon. One presidential candidate argued that the government should intervene on gas prices to "give families some relief." Two-thirds of American voters at that time said they thought that the price of gas was "an extremely important political issue." (Of course, when gas prices started tumbling in the fall of 2008, there were not many front-page articles or television interviews with happy consumers, and the politicians simply became silent on this subject.) Consider, though, that at its nominal price at the beginning of 2009, the *relative* price of gas was back down to about what it had been in 1960—after correcting for overall inflation. For many people, this is a shocking revelation. But correcting for inflation is absolutely essential if you want to sensibly analyze the price of anything over time. Often we talk about the **real price** of a good or service. This refers specifically to subtracting the rate of inflation from the change in a nominal price over time. Not surprisingly, we also do the same exercise when we want to go from **nominal income** to **real income** over time.

THE IMPORTANCE OF HIGHER DISPOSABLE INCOME

Another fact is particularly relevant when thinking about the real burden of gasoline. People are becoming more productive over time because they are getting better educated and because ongoing technological change enables us to produce more with a given input of our time. As a result of this higher **productivity,** U.S. consumers' **disposable incomes** generally rise from one year to the next—and certainly rise on average over longer periods of time. As Americans become richer on average, they are financially able to handle even higher relative prices of those items they wish to purchase, gasoline included.

To help us understand this point better, researchers Indur Goklany and Jerry Taylor came up with an "affordability index." They compared family income to the price of gas from 1949 to 2008. They arbitrarily set 1960 at an affordability index of 1. Relative to this, a higher affordability index number means that something is more affordable. Even when gas was $4.15 per gallon, the affordability gas index was 1.35. In other words, the ratio of the average person's disposable income to the price of gasoline was higher by about 35 percent in 2008 than it was in 1960—gasoline was *more* affordable than it had been back in 1960, when your grandparents were filling up their tanks at 30 cents a gallon. That is hard to believe for some of us but true nonetheless. And once gas prices turned down at the end of 2008, the gas affordability index rose even more, passing 2, meaning that gasoline was more than twice as affordable at the beginning of 2009 as it had been in 1960. Affordability declined from 2009 to 2012, but then rose once more. By early 2017, gasoline was again more than twice as affordable as it had been in 1960.

Product Quality Changes

The quality of gasoline typically does not change much over time. But the quality of many other products often changes significantly over time, usually for the better. Often we forget about this crucial aspect when we start comparing prices of a good or service over time. If you ask senior citizens today how much they paid for their first car, you might get prices in the range of $2,000–$5,000. The average new car today costs around $34,000 (in nominal dollars). By now, of course, you know that if you want to compare these numbers, you have to first account for the inflation that has occurred over whatever time period you are examining. In this instance, adjusting for inflation still means that the relative price of a car appears to be about 20 percent higher than it was, say, fifty years ago.

Does that necessarily mean that a car is really 20 percent more expensive than it was a half-century ago? Probably not. We must take into account improved quality features of cars today compared to those of the past. Today (unlike fifty years ago), the average car has the following:

- Antilock computer-controlled power brakes
- Power steering
- Digital radio with Bluetooth
- Air-conditioning
- Steel-belted radial tires
- Cruise control
- Power windows and locks
- Air bags
- Seventy percent better fuel economy

The list of improved and new features is actually much longer. Today, the average car is safer, breaks down less often, needs fewer tune-ups, has a host of amenities that were not even dreamed of fifty years ago, and almost certainly lasts for at least twice as many miles. If you correct not only for inflation but also for these quality increases, the relative price of cars today has almost certainly *fallen* appreciably in the past fifty years, in spite of the "sticker shock" that you may experience when you go shopping for a new car. That is, appearances to the contrary, the inflation-corrected **constant-quality price** of automobiles is actually lower today than it was five decades ago.

DECLINING NOMINAL PRICES

The necessity of adjusting for inflation and quality changes continues to apply even when we examine goods whose nominal prices have declined over time. A good example is computing power. The nominal price of the average personal computer has gone down in spite of general inflation over the past several decades. These days, a Windows-based desktop computer has an average price of about $500. For a laptop, the average price is about $600. A decade ago, the average machines in each category would have had nominal prices of twice as much. You might be tempted to conclude, then, that the price of personal computing has fallen by 50 percent. You would be wrong: The price has actually fallen by *more* than 50 percent.

Why? There are two reasons. First, over the past ten years, the average dollar prices of all goods increased by 20 percent. That is how much overall inflation there has been. That means that the *relative* price of the average computer has fallen by two-thirds, which, of course, is greater than 50 percent. But even here we are missing something extremely important: The quality of what you are buying—computing power—has skyrocketed. The processor speed of the average computer today is at least ten times greater than it was ten years ago and is increasing exponentially. Moreover, hard drives are bigger, monitors are flat-screen LCDs instead of bulky old cathode ray tubes, laptops are lighter, RAM is larger—the list of improvements goes on and on. And despite people's frustrations with both the hardware and software of the personal computer today, long-time users can tell you that both are vastly more reliable than they were a decade ago. Thus, if you look only at the inflation-corrected decrease in computer prices, you will be underestimating the *true* decrease in the relative price of computers.

The moral of our story is simple. At some point in your education, you learned that "what goes up must come down." Now you know that when it comes to prices, it is often the case that "what goes up has actually gone down." It is a lesson worth keeping in mind if you really want to understand the behavior of consumers and businesses alike.

FOR CRITICAL ANALYSIS

1. Create a list of goods (or services) whose quality has improved over time in such a way that the current prices of these commodities do not accurately reflect their real prices, even after adjusting for inflation. Now see if you can come up with a list of items whose quality has systematically *decreased* over time. Can you suggest why it is easier to find examples of the former than the latter?

2. The demand for small-engine motor scooters jumped when the price of gasoline started moving up in the summer of 2008. Make a prediction about the demand for this form of transportation, say, two years from today. Explain your answer.

3. Explain why you will make more accurate predictions if you focus on the changing incentives people face rather than listening to what they say they are going to do.

4. When the price of gasoline rose to $4 from $2 per gallon, media commentators spoke as though people were headed to the poor house as a result. But here are some other facts: The average car is driven about 12,000 miles per year and gets about 24 miles per gallon. Even if people did not drive less when the price rose, by how much did the average driver's "real" income fall due to the $2 per gallon rise in the price of gas? Given that per capita income is about $56,000 per year, what is this income change in percentage terms? Show all calculations.

5. One implication of the **law of demand** is that the pain to a consumer of a price increase is always *less* than suggested by multiplying the price increase by the amount of the product consumed before the price increase. Explain why.

6. The law of demand also implies that the pleasure that comes from a fall in the price of a good is always *more* than implied by simply multiplying the price cut by the amount of the good consumed before the change. Explain why.

PART THREE

Fiscal Policy

CHAPTER 17

Can We Afford the Affordable Care Act?

The Affordable Care Act (ACA), sometimes referred to as Obamacare, was signed into law by President Obama in 2010. By the time Obama left office in January 2017, the law was in trouble—deep trouble. Insurance premiums under the ACA were skyrocketing and consumer choices were shrinking, as major insurers dropped out of the market across the country. Plans available under Obamacare had gotten so expensive that millions of healthy individuals were paying fines rather than buying the insurance. In hundreds of counties, including all counties in five states, there was no choice among insurers when purchasing an ACA plan— only one firm was left in the market.

Before we can understand the crisis of Obamacare and why President Trump vowed to repeal it, we'll need to first see how we got here. By the time you read this, Obamacare may have been replaced, but we'll talk in this chapter as though it is still with us.

INSURANCE COVERAGE

At the time of the ACA's passage, almost fifty million Americans were without healthcare insurance. There is no doubt the law has increased the number of Americans with health insurance. By 2017, about twenty million people had gained coverage due to the ACA. Roughly 40 percent of these people purchased private insurance policies, while the other 60 percent became eligible for Medicaid, the federal-state health insurance program for low-income individuals. Nevertheless, this left almost thirty million adults uninsured, and most knowledgeable observers now predict that over the next decade the number of uninsured adults is unlikely to decrease much more.

Originally, the ACA was forecast to have a much greater impact on the number of uninsured people. After all, the law is quite specific. You are required to have health insurance, and if you don't have it, you are fined each year—a fine that, depending on your circumstances, is now either $695 or 2.5 percent of your income. The requirement to purchase insurance is called the **individual mandate.**

THE FAILURE OF THE MANDATE

The original purpose of the individual mandate was to ensure that younger, healthier individuals would buy medical insurance. When the insurance pool does not contain significant numbers of the young and the healthy, the high healthcare costs of older, sicker individuals can send insurance premiums skyrocketing. Moreover, because taxpayers are paying for Medicaid and subsidizing the private insurance obtained under the ACA, without the young and healthy, the burden on taxpayers is also rising.

To see how this works—or has failed to work under Obamacare—consider the fact that the average sixty-four-year-old consumes six times as much healthcare as the average twenty-one-year-old. Under open market conditions, the older individual would thus be expected to pay about six times as much for health insurance as the younger person—just as teens pay more for their auto insurance, due to their high accident rates. But under Obamacare, insurers are not allowed to charge older customers more than three times as much as they bill the young. In our example, the law requires that the price to the young person be 75 percent *more* than her actual costs, while the older person would be charged 13 percent *less* than her costs. The sensible response of consumers is quite obvious. Older, costlier consumers sign up for insurance, while young people "just say no," declining to purchase the overpriced insurance. Even plenty of healthy people in their thirties, forties, and fifties have chosen to pay the fine rather than buy insurance. In 2016, eight million people paid fines rather than purchased insurance, leaving the insured population much sicker, and much more expensive.

YOU'RE SICK BUT HAVE NO HEALTH INSURANCE—NOT TO WORRY

The Affordable Care Act directs that you may not be turned down for health insurance due to a preexisting ailment. The purpose of this rule was to ensure that people who had serious health problems could get insurance. But the rule has also had two other effects. First, people *without* serious problems are declining to buy insurance, knowing that when problems crop up, they are guaranteed insurance no matter how sick they are. This problem, known as **adverse selection,** drives up costs for everybody else—including both taxpayers and the relatively healthy insured population. Second, people with newly acquired insurance suddenly seem to develop health problems they never knew they had before, a phenomenon known as **moral hazard.** This, too, drives up costs for taxpayers and for others in the insured pool.

The combination of these forces began showing up quickly in the healthcare spending data. For example, during the first part of 2014, serious health problems were more than twice as prevalent among newly insured individuals, compared to those who had previously had insurance. Now, these high health costs were not totally a surprise. After all, one problem the law was designed to address was the inability of sick people to get insurance. But the *magnitude* of the high costs has exceeded all forecasts. With each passing year, costs have risen even faster. The jump in insurance rates from 2016 to 2017 exceeded 40 percent in five states, with rates rising nearly 150 percent in Arizona. Moreover, in all fifty states the number of firms offering insurance plans under the ACA has dropped sharply, because firms have found it too difficult to predict their costs. For example, the ACA was supposed to encourage people to obtain primary care physicians and to use them instead of emergency rooms for their health care. And while some of the newly insured are doing this, the fact is that emergency rooms visits are *up* sharply under Obamacare, the opposite of what was predicted by its backers.

THE HAZARDS OF PRE-EXISTING CONDITIONS

All insurers must concern themselves with potential adverse selection and moral hazard. But the challenges facing insurers operating under the ACA are amplified. This is because the law forbids insurers from denying coverage (or charging higher premiums) to people with costly-to-treat pre-existing medical conditions, such as diabetes or heart disease. You cannot purchase fire insurance on your house after a fire has started, just as you cannot buy auto insurance to cover the repairs from a previous accident. The health insurance market used to work the same way. If you had a known pre-existing medical condition, whether it was a broken arm or cancer, you could not buy health insurance to cover the costs of treating that condition. Under Obamacare, firms are *required* to sell you a policy that will cover those pre-existing ailments, and they must charge the same price to you that they charge to people without those conditions. This feature of the law has produced some innovative behavior.

Insurers are finding under the ACA that up to 20 percent of their costs are caused by people who purchase insurance and immediately have a major medical procedure (such as a $40,000 hip replacement or $100,000 heart bypass operation). Then they drop the insurance as soon as the bills are paid.[1] In a slightly different twist, companies that perform kidney dialysis are paying the insurance premiums for people with end-stage kidney disease to ensure that their dialysis (at a cost of $80,000 per year) will be covered. This is a great deal for these patients, of course, as well as for the dialysis providers. But because the premiums only cover about 5 percent of the cost of the treatment, the *other* people buying insurance are the ones who pay for the remaining 95 percent.

Many Hospitals Have Hit the Jackpot

Thus far, there is little doubt that the ACA has caused an increase in the demand for health care. Partly this is because many previously uninsurable people now have coverage. Plus, there are people who are now buying policies simply because they are eligible for government subsidies offered under the ACA to low-income individuals. Both groups are consuming more health care: more emergency room visits, more elective surgeries, more prescription drugs. And this additional health care has no doubt had substantial benefits for these consumers—which was, after all, the point of the law.

But there is another group of beneficiaries, the suppliers of health-care services, most notably hospitals and pharmaceutical companies. *Uninsured* in-patient admissions have fallen at most hospitals throughout the United States, at the same time that *insured* admissions have risen even more, yielding a substantial net increase. Hospitals, therefore, benefit in two ways. They have more patients, and the revenue they collect per patient is higher than before. Pharmaceutical companies have also seen a sharp rise in demand for their products as new enrollees are taking advantage of their insurance coverage. Between 2010 (when the law was passed) and 2017, the stock prices of healthcare companies rose by roughly 50 percent compared to the average of all stock prices, due to the upsurge in healthcare profits.

---

1 Under the ACA, people cannot simply purchase insurance any time they wish. But everyone is allowed to buy during the three months from November 1 to January 31, and many people qualify to purchase at other times during the year under special arrangements. For example, if you move across a state line (and in many cases just across a county line), you qualify to buy insurance immediately.

The Continuation of a Two-Tier Healthcare System

One thing the ACA will not do is eliminate the two-tier healthcare system in the United States. Newly insured individuals fall into two broad groups—those who have purchased their own insurance policies on the exchanges and those whom the law has made newly eligible for Medicaid (the federal-state healthcare program for the poor). Although there are a variety of insurance plans available in the exchanges, their typical provisions are much more modest than employer-offered plans or even individual plans offered outside the exchanges. The amounts that people have to pay out of their own pocket for services ($6,000 to $10,000) are thus higher with exchange policies, and enrollees have sharply limited choices of doctors and especially hospitals. In short, none of these plans come close to the "Cadillac" plans commonly available to unionized employees, or even to the "Chevrolet" plans purchased outside the exchanges.

The situation is even worse for Medicaid enrollees. The federal and state governments place significant restrictions on what types of care Medicaid can provide and how much doctors and hospitals will be paid for this care. As a result, healthcare outcomes tend to be worse for Medicaid patients than for persons with their own health insurance. Moreover, because of the low reimbursement rates under Medicaid, about one-third of primary-care physicians and one-fourth of specialists have completely closed their practices to new Medicaid patients. The bottom line is that the newly insured are better off than they were, but the care they are getting is still significantly below average.

The Impact on the Previously Insured

Written into the ACA were many items that Congress and the president thought should be covered by all insurance plans, regardless of whether those plans were purchased through the exchanges. Thus, the law mandated that all policies offer maternity care, contraceptives, annual checkups, and so forth.

Almost 80 percent of individual plans in place when Obamacare became effective did not contain one or more of these provisions. Hence, insurers were required to *cancel* tens of millions of policies, which were no longer in compliance with federal law. Eventually people were able to purchase new coverage, but it typically cost more (sometimes much more) than their previous policies. In pushing for the law's passage back in 2010, the president had promised that "if you like your insurance, you can keep it." It was a promise not kept for many Americans.

THE RISE OF THE 49ERS

No, we are not talking about the football team. Rather, we are talking about companies that refuse to hire their fiftieth employee. Businesses with fewer than fifty employees are exempt from the most costly ACA requirements that larger employers incur under the healthcare law. Indeed, firms with fewer than fifty employees may lawfully offer no health insurance at all and avoid paying the penalties that apply to large companies that don't offer insurance. Thus, some firms have been reorganizing themselves, or simply firing employees, to get down to forty-nine or fewer employees. Others are shelving their company expansion strategies, which have now become uneconomical in light of the law's costly insurance requirements.

Firms with fifty or more employees do have options to avoid the law, however. They can make sure that many more of their employees are "29ers." That is, they can limit their employees to working twenty-nine or fewer hours a week because thirty hours or more per week is Obamacare's definition of full-time employment. Employers are not required to offer health insurance to part-time employees, so firms can save thousands of dollars per employee by utilizing this tactic. There are now about twenty-eight million part-time workers in America. Most would be working reduced hours even without the ACA, but observers generally agree that the health insurance law is contributing to the numbers.

THE BOTTOM LINE

The ACA has conferred substantial benefits on a narrow segment of the American population. Indeed, for people at the bottom of the income spectrum, it has been estimated that the law has added about 6 percent to their real income, by improving their health care or reducing their out-of-pocket healthcare costs. And for some of those people who were previously uninsurable, the law literally has been a lifesaver.

For many more individuals, the ACA has raised the cost of insurance and compelled some of them to pay for items of insurance coverage against their will. Some have had their policies cancelled and found the replacement policies offered them to be too expensive. Taxpayers can also expect their bill to go up, both to pay for the expansion in Medicaid and to cover the subsidies on those policies sold on the insurance exchanges.

Overall, the law has contributed to an increase in the demand for health care, which has increased prices for healthcare services. The law has a number of provisions that are supposed to reduce healthcare costs by encouraging people to seek routine treatment before their health deteriorates. So far there is little evidence that people are doing this. Of course, Medicare and Medicaid (both enacted in the 1960s) were supposed to reduce costs in some of the same ways, but actually ended up drastically *raising* healthcare costs because of the sharp increase in demand for healthcare that they induced.

Not all of the uncertainties that have developed under the Affordable Care Act have resolved themselves, and they may not for quite some time. One thing does seem certain, however. Given the importance of health care to everyone and the high costs of consuming it, this is an issue that will not go away.

For Critical Analysis

1. Under what circumstances would you try to avoid purchasing health insurance?

2. Do the increased physician and hospital treatments for serious illnesses among the newly insured tell you anything about the price elasticity of demand for medical care? If so, what?

3. When an employer chooses to reduce the hours worked by many of its employees to fewer than thirty per week, what might be some of the negative consequences to the business? What damages might the affected employees suffer?

4. People over the age of sixty-five are eligible for Medicare, which offers subsidized health care—as long as the doctor involved agrees to accept the relatively lower fees paid by Medicare. Some people over sixty-five choose instead to pay out-of-pocket for so-called "concierge" physicians, who provide medical services on a cash or credit card only basis. Can you explain why patients would turn their backs on Medicare and instead pay out of their own pockets?

5. In Britain, everyone has the right to health care provided by the National Health Service, paid for out of tax revenues. Nevertheless, two-thirds of British citizens earning more than $80,000 per year currently purchase private health insurance. Why would these people opt to "pay twice" for healthcare services? (*Hint:* Think of Americans who pay to send their children to private schools.)

6. Under what circumstances would an employer be willing to pay an annual fine for not providing legally required employee health insurance?

CHAPTER 18

Who *Really* Pays Taxes?

During (and even after) the last election campaign, politicians had plenty to say about taxes. Some of the discussion focused on whether taxes should go up or down. But much of the talk was about who does—or does not—pay taxes. Some politicians (usually Democrats) claimed that high-income individuals ("the rich") do not pay their "fair share." Others (usually Republicans) claimed that the rich pay *more* than their "fair share." Regardless of party affiliation, most of the politicians had their own anecdotes to illustrate why their claims were correct. Let's see if some systematic data will illuminate this debate.

BURDENS AND FAIR SHARES

Economists have some well-defined and widely accepted ways to think about the "burden" of taxes (also called tax "incidence"). The simplest way to measure tax incidence (or burden) is to examine the share of taxes paid by different taxpayers. Thus, if $100 in taxes is collected and Alicia pays $60 while Roberto pays $40, we say that Alicia bears 60 percent of the burden. This measure of tax burden (or incidence) is just the proportion of the tax bill paid by people. (All taxpayers are people in this discussion, because only people can pay taxes, whether they do so as workers, business owners, or whatever.)

Many commentators feel that this way of thinking about the burden of taxes is inadequate or misleading. Suppose, for example, that Alicia earns 80 percent of the income and Roberto earns the other 20 percent. One might argue that the relevant burden of taxes is *higher* for Roberto than for Alicia, because his share of taxes (40 percent) is so much higher than his share of income (20 percent). When looking across individuals or groups of individuals then, we might compare shares of total taxes paid with shares of total income earned.

A variant of this view is that it is useful to examine the share of each person's income that goes to paying taxes. Continuing with our example, suppose that Alicia's income is $240 and Roberto's is $60. Then 25 percent (= $60/$240) of Alicia's income goes to taxes, while approximately 67 percent (= $40/$60) of Roberto's income goes to taxes. This measure of the tax burden is called the **average tax rate.**

We cannot tell you which view of the tax burden is "better." What we *can* do is show you what these measures look like in the United States. Then you can decide which you think is best—and perhaps even decide whether or not various people are paying their "fair share."

In what follows, we shall be referring to all federal taxes, not just one portion or another of those taxes. We shall include federal income taxes, social insurance (Social Security and Medicare) taxes, corporate taxes, and even federal excise taxes (imposed on gasoline, alcohol, and cigarettes). We will also compare tax burdens across broad groups of people, so that we do not fall into the trap of thinking that the tax burden that happens to be borne by one or a few people is the relevant number to look at when deciding on national tax policy.

THE SHARE OF TAXES PAID

Let's look first at the simplest measure of the tax burden: What share of total federal taxes is paid by people at various income levels? First, we'll divide people up into "income quintiles." That is, we select the 20 percent of the people who earn the highest incomes and call this the top income quintile. Then we take the 20 percent of the population who earn the next highest incomes and call this the second income quintile. We continue this process until we reach the 20 percent of the population that earns the lowest incomes, which we call the bottom income quintile. Then we ask the simple question: What share of total federal taxes is paid by each quintile? The answer is in column (1) of Table 18–1.

This comparison in column (1) is exactly like our initial comparison of the share of taxes paid by Alicia and Roberto. We see that the distribution of the tax burden is almost as striking as in our hypothetical example. The top quintile of income earners in the United States pays more than two-thirds of all federal taxes, even though only 20 percent of the population is in this group. When you hear people saying that "the rich" pay *more* than their fair share of federal taxes, this is the set of numbers that often are being referenced.

Table 18 –1   Incomes, Taxes, and Tax Rates (by income group)

Income Quintile	(1) Share of Federal Taxes (percent)	(2) Share of Income (percent)	(3) Average Tax Rate (percent)
Top quintile	69.0	52.6	26.3
Second quintile	17.1	20.2	17.0
Middle quintile	8.9	13.9	12.8
Fourth quintile	3.9	9.3	8.4
Bottom quintile	0.8	5.1	3.3

Source: Congressional Budget Office

Although not shown explicitly in Table 18–1, the distribution of taxes paid is even more skewed toward the top income earners if we break the highest quintile into smaller units. For example, the top 1 percent of earners pays 25.4 percent—more than one-quarter—of all federal taxes. Another way to think about this is that the top 20 percent of earners pay more than double what the *combined* bottom four quintiles pay (30.9 percent), while the top 1 percent pays almost double what the combined bottom three quintiles pay (13.6 percent).

INCOMES VERSUS TAXES

Of course, the comparison in column (1) takes no account of the fact that people's incomes vary widely from top to bottom. Many people would argue that people with higher incomes have a greater ability to pay taxes, and thus they should be expected to pay more taxes. So, in column (2) we examine the share of total (before-tax) income that goes to each quintile. People in the top 20 percent of all income earners earn fully *half* of all income in the United States. Meanwhile, those in the bottom 20 percent earn only about 5 percent of all income. Equivalently, although people at the top pay much more in federal taxes than anyone else, the contrast between top and bottom is not nearly so dramatic if we take into account differences in income.

We come to similar conclusions if we take a closer look among those people at the very top. Thus, the top 1 percent of income earners pull in 15 percent of all income in the United States. Top earners fork over much more taxes than anyone else, but one key reason they do so is because they make much higher incomes.

AVERAGE TAX RATES

Our final point of comparison of federal tax burdens comes in column (3) of Table 18–1. Here we see the average tax rate paid by people in different income quintiles. These numbers are calculated by adding up all federal taxes, adding up all incomes, and then dividing total federal taxes by total income. In the top quintile, people pay about $1 in taxes for each $4 of income, on average. In the middle quintile, people pay about $1 in tax for each $8 of income. At the bottom, taxpayers hand over $1 in taxes for each $30 in income.

These numbers seem to confirm our conclusions in the previous section regarding the burden of federal taxes. Although people at the top garner plenty of income, the taxes they pay rise even faster than their incomes do. Thus, the average tax rate rises rapidly as we move up the income ladder. Whether this is "fair" or not, we cannot say.

THE 91 PERCENT FANTASY

In recent years, some commentators have argued that since the decade of the 1950s, the burden of taxes on the rich had actually *fallen*. The centerpiece of this claim is based on the **marginal tax rate** over time. The marginal tax rate is simply the proportion of an *additional* dollar of income that goes to taxes. Thus, if a person pays $100 in taxes on the first $1,000 in income and $200 in taxes on the second $1,000 in income, we say that the marginal tax rate on the first $1,000 is 10 percent, while the marginal tax rate on the second $1,000 is 20 percent. (Note a person making $2,000 would pay a total of $300 in taxes and so pay an *average* tax rate of 15 percent.)

It is true that the marginal federal tax rate for top income earners is about 40 percent today, depending on exactly the form in which their income is earned. It is also true that in, say, 1958, the marginal tax rate at the top was 91 percent. But there was a key difference between then and now: Large numbers of high-income earners today are actually *paying* the top marginal tax rate. Almost *no one* was paying the top marginal tax rate back in 1958, even the richest of the rich. In fact, so few people paid it that the Internal Revenue Service (IRS) will not reveal the exact number, because that number is so small you might be able to figure out who was paying it—which would violate IRS rules on taxpayer confidentiality. (We do know that 236 out of 45.6 million taxpayers were paying rates of 81 percent or higher, so the 91 percent tax rate must have applied to an even smaller number of people.)

Sixty years ago, people at the top earned much more than the average amount of income and paid much more than the average amount in federal taxes. To illustrate, in 1958 the average tax rate on people in the top 5 percent of the income distribution was almost double the average tax rate in the middle of the distribution—just as it is today. Thus, although the marginal tax rate at the top may have come down dramatically, the average tax rate has not. Whether this is fair or not, we cannot say.

FACTS VERSUS ...

Elections tend to bring out the best and the worst in humans. The rhetoric can be magnificent, but the disregard for facts (and worse, the venture into fantasy) can be just as striking. Over the century or so that income taxes have been levied in the United States, two facts have been true. First, incomes have been distributed unequally. Second, taxes have been distributed even more unequally, with people's tax bills rising even faster than their incomes as they move up the income distribution. Reasonable people can disagree over whether or not—in their opinion—the rich should pay more (or less) than they do in fact pay. But for there to be any hope that these disagreements will lead to sensible public policy, the rhetoric should at least be based on facts rather than fantasy or falsehood.

FOR CRITICAL ANALYSIS

1. Suppose that on the first $10,000 of income people must pay 10 percent of their income in taxes. Also suppose that for the next $10,000 in income, they must pay 20 percent in taxes, and for the next $10,000, they must pay 30 percent in taxes. Compute the average and marginal tax rates for each of three people who earn (respectively) $5,000, $15,000, or $25,000.

2. Referring back to the previous question, suppose that each of these people is paid the same before-tax hourly wage, but they work 500 hours per year, 1,500 hours per year, and 2,500 hours per year, respectively. Calculate the after-tax hourly wage that each is earning. Comparing these people, who would you say likes leisure the most (compared to work)? Who likes leisure the least compared to work?

3. When comparing the share of income going to various quintiles in this chapter, we used before-tax income. Suppose, instead, we had used after-tax income. Given what you've learned about the taxes people pay, would the difference in shares of "income" between top and bottom be larger or smaller? Explain, briefly.

4. If you were a politician who wanted to make the case that the rich are taxed "too heavily," which column in Table 18–1 would you feature in your speeches?

5. President Obama once said that when it comes to taxes "for some time now, when compared to the middle class, [the rich] haven't been asked to do their fair share." For this question, assume that people in the middle-income quintile are the middle class and that the people in the highest-income quintile are the "rich." Based on what you've learned in this chapter, would you agree with the president? Does your answer change if the "rich" are those people in the top 1 percent? (*Hint*: Be sure to do what the president did not do: Define what you mean by "fair share.")

6. Although just about everyone who works pays Social Security and Medicare taxes, roughly 45 percent of such people pay either *zero* federal income taxes or *negative* federal income taxes. What do you suppose the attitude of these people is when a politician proposes an increase in federal income tax rates? Would their attitude likely be different if the politician proposed raising Social Security and Medicare tax rates?

CHAPTER 19

Are You Stimulated Yet?

George Bush supported one. Barack Obama proposed one too. And Republicans and Democrats in both houses of Congress ended up passing one for each president. Then, within days after his election, Donald Trump claimed he was planning on the biggest stimulus package yet. With all of this backing, surely economic stimulus packages must be good for the economy, right? Well, maybe not. Let's see why.

STIMULUS PACKAGES

As implemented by the U.S. (or a foreign) government, so-called economic stimulus packages generally contain some combination of two elements: higher government spending and lower government taxes. One consequence of such packages is that the size of the government **deficit** grows, implying that the **national debt** must get larger. Higher debt is merely a side effect of a stimulus package, however. The *objective* of such packages is to increase total spending in the economy, raise employment, and reduce the unemployment rate.

Trump's proposal was made after more than seven years of economic expansion. Nonetheless, proposals for stimulus packages usually come during economic recessions, when **gross domestic product (GDP)** is depressed and the unemployment rate is elevated. At first blush, it seems like a government stimulus is exactly what we need at such times. After all, government spending is part of the GDP, so more government spending seemingly must, as a matter of definition, generate more GDP. And because the items the government buys (such as cement for new highways) are produced using labor, it seems pretty clear that more people will be hired, thereby cutting the unemployment rate. Alternatively, to the extent that part of the stimulus comes in the form of a tax cut, this puts more **disposable income** in the hands of consumers, some or all of which will presumably be spent by them. Again, production of goods and services rises and the unemployment rate falls. Either way, it seems, a government stimulus package is the sure-fire way out of a recession, and perhaps will even put the economy in overdrive. Before we jump to this conclusion, however, it will be wise to take a closer look.

Tax Cuts

Let's look first at the tax cuts that are often components of stimulus packages. To do so, imagine for the moment that we keep government spending at current levels and simply cut the taxes we are collecting from people during the current period. Such an action is what people have in mind when they refer to a "tax cut." To fully appreciate the effects of a tax cut, however, we must carefully specify how it is conducted. For example, in the Economic Stimulus Act of 2008 the tax cut consisted of **lump sum tax rebates.** Each eligible person received $300, regardless of income, with another $300 for each dependent child.[1] In contrast, tax cuts pushed by President Kennedy in the 1960s, President Reagan in the 1980s, or President Bush in the early 2000s reduced the **marginal tax rate** for many taxpayers. That is, the taxes taken out of additional dollars of earned income were reduced. This not only lowered the individual's **tax liability** (total taxes owed), it also *increased* the incentive to work more, produce more, and thus earn more, because taxpayers could keep more of what they earned.

However the tax cut is implemented, it is clear that if the government is going to pay for its spending, at least initially it must borrow, that is, run a budget deficit. Unless potential lenders are convinced they will be repaid, they will not lend, and the only way for the government to repay its loans is to collect *more* taxes in the future. Indeed, future taxes must rise by enough to repay both the principal and the interest on the loan.

Now we see the problem with trying to stimulate the economy by cutting taxes: A reduction in *current* taxes must be met by an even larger increase in *future* taxes. For a given level of government spending, taxes *cannot* actually be reduced. They can at best only be moved around in

---

1 For individuals earning over $75,000 or couples earning over $150,000, the rebate was gradually phased out to zero and thus technically not a lump sum. This phase-out feature discouraged work effort among these high-income individuals, which acted to reduce real GDP. This effect was likely tiny, however, because the dollar amounts were quite small.

time. Thus, although a "tax cut" puts more current disposable spending in the hands of consumers, it also loads them up with an added debt burden. In the case of tax cuts of the rebate variety, this is the end of the story. The higher debt burden will weigh on the spending decisions of consumers, so there is no particular reason to think that consumers will spend more today. They may just save most or all of the increase in disposable income so they'll be ready in the future when their bigger tax bills come due.

Of course, consumers may not *think* this way about their taxes at all. But the key point is how they *behave*. And the fact is that many consumers act *as though* they are quite conscious of the added burden of future taxes they bear when current taxes are cut. Now, not all consumers act this way. Some have incomes so low that they spend 100 percent of what they have each year, whether it is high or low. Thus, a tax cut brings an uptick in their spending, and when the tax cut ends, so too does the extra spending. Ultimately, then, how *total* consumer spending reacts to tax cuts is an empirical question. Stanford researchers led by John B. Taylor have examined the impact on consumer spending of both the Economic Stimulus Act of 2008 and the American Recovery and Reinvestment Act of 2009. The researchers found that neither the tax rebates of 2008 nor the cash transfers and tax rebates of 2009 had any measurable impact on consumer spending, despite all the predictions by the politicians. In the words of Taylor and his colleagues: "The stimulus didn't work."

Reductions in marginal tax rates offer hope of something more. Again, we cannot expect people to go on a spending spree just because taxes have been moved around in time. But there is an added feature with lower marginal tax rates. People have an incentive to work more, produce more, and thus earn more, because they get to keep a larger share of what they earn. This feature of this type of tax cut does indeed stimulate the economy, although it does so from the supply side (labor supply rises) rather than from the demand side. Indeed, many researchers attribute much of the prosperity of the 1960s and the 1980s to the cuts in marginal tax rates implemented by President Kennedy and President Reagan in those decades.

Spending Increases

Now, what about the other half of stimulus packages—higher spending by the government? To sort this out, we will first have to distinguish between two broad types of government spending: that which is a substitute for private spending and that which is not. For example, although the government spends plenty on education (primary, secondary, and college), so do private citizens. The government spending is a substitute for private spending, and when the government spends more on education, private spending on education falls. This offsetting change in private spending clearly reduces the potential stimulus effect of the government. Indeed, in some cases, education included, it appears that the reduction in private spending offsets *all* of the higher government spending. The stimulus effect in this instance is obviously zero.

Of course, plenty of government programs do not compete directly with private spending. For example, most defense spending (such as expenditures on the war in Afghanistan) does not compete with private spending. Also, some so-called infrastructure spending, such as on highways and bridges, competes little with private spending. Thus, when government defense or infrastructure spending goes up, there is no direct dollar-for-dollar cut in private spending, as there can be with items like education. Nevertheless, there are generally substantial *indirect* impacts on private spending—impacts that can markedly reduce the stimulating effects of the government spending. Let's see why.

INDIRECT OFFSETS IN PRIVATE SPENDING

As we suggested above, the real burden of the government is its spending. Taxes are simply the means of deciding who shall bear that burden. Thus, for a given level of other expenditures, when defense or infrastructure spending rises, taxes *must* rise at some point now or in the future. And because consumers know this, many of them will make some provision for it, by reducing their own spending. This clearly dampens the overall stimulus effect of the higher government spending.

There is another potential offset when government spending rises. If the government "finances" this spending by borrowing rather than raising current taxes, the result can be upward pressure on interest rates. Higher interest rates in turn reduce the attractiveness of consumer durable goods (such as houses and cars) and also reduce the profitability of business investment spending. Thus, when larger government deficits push up interest rates, private consumption and investment spending will decline, again dampening any hoped-for stimulus.

DELAYS IN SPENDING

As amazing as this may seem, there is yet one more obstacle in the path of stimulus spending—time. Despite all the headlines about so-called "shovel ready" projects and "immediate action," there are usually long delays in implementing the spending portion of stimulus packages. Let's consider one simple example. As part of the 2009 stimulus pushed by President Obama and passed by Congress early in that year, more than a dozen states were supposed to get federal funds for building or expanding light rail commuter systems. Ultimately, two of the states (Wisconsin and Ohio) decided that, for them, the benefits of this spending failed to outweigh the costs. Hence, these states declined to accept the money for light rail systems, hoping the federal government would let them keep the money and use it to repair and expand their roads and bridges. In fact, late in 2010 (nearly two years after the stimulus package was passed) President Obama ordered that the rejected funds be redirected to the dozen states that had accepted the rail funding. Well into 2011, most of these funds were still unspent, as were many billions of dollars of other funds included in the 2009 stimulus package.

Not all spending is delayed this much, of course (although some can be delayed even more). But the key point is simple. Despite all of the claims politicians make about taking "immediate action," it just does not work out this way. In fact, over the span of the last fifty years or so, much of the government spending supposedly designed to help pull us out of recessions was not actually spent until after these recessions were over and recovery was well underway.

The Stimulus That Mostly Was Not

The 2009 American Recovery and Reinvestment Act (ARRA), President Obama's first major piece of legislation, received lots of media attention, in no small part because of its size—$862 billion. But its impact on aggregate demand appears to have been minimal. One reason is that a large portion of the legislation called for grants to state and local governments. The law's backers argued that these funds immediately would be spent by the recipients on all sorts of new programs, thereby stimulating the economy. In fact, the state and local governments used almost *all* of these transfers to reduce their borrowing. Thus, the mechanics went like this: The federal government borrowed funds (about $120 billion per year during each of the first two years), distributed those funds to the states, which then borrowed $120 billion less. Net effect: Federal debt went up, state and local debt went down, and aggregate spending remained unchanged.

The ARRA was also touted as being big on infrastructure—roads, bridges, and so forth. In fact, the legislation itself never called for more than about 10 percent of its funds to be used in this way, and by two years after its passage, only a small fraction of this sum had been spent. Indeed, by 2010, government purchases of goods and services had risen only $24 billion, and infrastructure spending had risen only $3 billion. In a $14 trillion economy, these sums were trivial. It is perhaps little surprise then, that Robert Barro of Harvard found that the ARRA had only a tiny stimulus effect during the recession itself. Barro also estimates that once the need for subsequent tax hikes is factored in, the overall impact of President Obama's "stimulus" bill will be a *reduction* in the GDP.

IS STIMULUS POSSIBLE?

As you may have gathered, our overall conclusion is that unless marginal tax rates are reduced, we should typically not expect government stimulus packages to actually stimulate the economy very much. Lump sum tax cuts are not really tax cuts at all, and higher government spending levels are routinely offset in whole or in part by cuts in private spending. But notice our use of the word *typically*. There is in fact a set of circumstances in which stimulus packages have the potential to live up to their billing. Fortunately, these circumstances do not come around very often. Indeed, the only time they are likely to have been observed is during and immediately after the Great Depression (1929–1933).

A series of declines in aggregate demand over the period 1929 to 1933 ended up pushing economy-wide output down by 30 percent and raising the unemployment rate to an unprecedented 25 percent of the labor force. By the depths of 1933, many people had been unemployed for years, and they and their families were living hand to mouth. They were **cash-constrained.** Every time their income changed by a dollar, so too did their spending. Thus, when so-called "relief" spending by the federal government began, most people worried not a bit about the future tax liabilities that might be involved. Moreover, much of the federal spending was on items (such as the Hoover Dam, post offices, and other public buildings) that did not compete directly with private spending.

This set of circumstances meant that the government stimulus spending during the 1930s did help increase total spending and also helped get people back to work. Indeed, it was during this period that stimulus spending first gained credibility among both economists and politicians. But the circumstances of the 1930s were extreme. No recession since then has come remotely close to being as severe, not even the recessions of 1981–1982 and 2007–2009. Moreover, since the 1930s, credit markets have become much more developed. People have credit cards and lines of credit and thus the ability to continue spending even when their incomes decline. To be sure, a prolonged period of unemployment can eventually exhaust these reserves. Fortunately, the number of people who find themselves in such circumstances is generally small, even in recessions. As a result, we cannot expect a repeat of the stimulating effects observed for stimulus packages during the 1930s, unless of course the 1930s somehow repeat themselves.

So our moral is that if you have not felt stimulated by federal spending increases or tax cuts, do not feel left out. You have plenty of company.

For Critical Analysis

1. Why is it in the interest of politicians to promote the notion that unemployment can be lowered if federal spending is increased?

2. If the unemployment rate can be reduced by cutting taxes, why don't we cut taxes to zero, at least during recessions?

3. During World War II, federal spending rose to roughly 50 percent of total spending in the economy, from its prewar level of just under 10 percent. How was this possible—that is, what spending had to decline to make it feasible for the federal share of spending to rise by a factor of five?

4. Some people argue that unemployment benefits (i.e., cash payments by the government to people who are unemployed) help stimulate the economy. The reasoning is that without the benefits, the incomes of unemployed people would be lower, and thus their spending on goods and services would be lower. Keeping in mind that (i) to collect unemployment benefits one must be unemployed, and (ii) the benefits are generally no more than 40 to 50 percent as large as the typical earnings of people when working, answer these questions:

   i. How do unemployment benefits change the incentive to be *employed*? Explain.

   ii. Is it possible that a system of unemployment benefits could actually cause total spending in the economy to *fall*? Explain.

5. If current taxes are reduced by way of a lump sum rebate, does the consumer response likely depend on how long it will be before taxes are actually raised to pay off the debt incurred by the government? In answering, be sure to account for the fact that the longer the delay in raising taxes, the greater will be the interest debt that accrues.

6. Who is more likely to think of a cut in current taxes as being a true reduction in taxes: a young worker with several young children or an older retiree with no children? Explain.

CHAPTER 20

Higher Taxes Are in Your Future

"These road improvements of $241,000,000 were paid for:

86 percent from the Federal Highway Trust Fund

12 percent from state funds

2 percent from local funds."

Most of you have seen at least one sign similar to this while driving somewhere in the United States. If you have ever driven anywhere in Europe, you see comparable signs, but they usually have a longer list of "contributors." The parallel, though, is that the "contributors" are government agencies, not *you*. Now, it would be nice to think that funds for highway improvement projects come from the moon or Mars or even from the bank account of some foreign oil mogul. But they do not.

THOSE PESKY BUDGET CONSTRAINTS

Government does not exist independently of those who live, work, spend, and pay taxes in our society. As an economy, we face a **budget constraint.** Whatever is spent by government—federal, state, or local— is not and cannot be spent by individuals in the nation. Whatever government commands in terms of spending decisions, private individuals do not command. All of those dollars available for spending on final goods and services in the United States can be controlled by you, the private citizen, or by government. Otherwise stated, what the government spends, you do not spend. It is as simple as that, despite the periodic efforts of government (especially at the national level) to conceal the truth of this budget constraint.

Stimulus and Bailout

Early in 2008, as the recession of 2007–2009 worsened, President Bush proposed, and Congress enacted, an "economic stimulus" package said to cost $152 billion. Most of the package consisted of tax cuts that were supposed to raise disposable income and thus produce an increase in private spending. As we noted in Chapter 19, however, neither these tax cuts nor similar provisions in President Obama's 2009 stimulus package had *any* measureable impact on consumption spending.

Later in 2008, as the recession continued to worsen and financial panic hit, the president and Congress reacted by bailing out some of the biggest financial companies in the United States, including insurance giant AIG. The legislation implementing these bailouts called for up to $700 billion in taxpayer funds to be used to prop up the companies.

Just a few months later, newly elected President Obama successfully pushed Congress to pass yet another stimulus package, this one said by the Congressional Budget Office to cost $833 billion. This legislation provided additional money for extended unemployment benefits and also transferred hundreds of billions of dollars to state and local governments.

Not long afterward (ironically, just as the recession was officially ending), President Obama pushed for and got funds to bail out the major American automobile companies. Ford declined the funds, but both General Motors (GM) and Chrysler accepted the money, enough in the case of GM to make taxpayers of the United States majority shareholders in the company.

Taken together, the stimulus and bailout programs enacted over this eighteen-month period had a price tag of somewhere between $1.5 and $2 trillion. Remarkably, even though these programs were supposed to be temporary, federal spending continued at unprecedented levels through 2016. All in all, during his first term in office, President Obama managed to spend $6 trillion *more* than the federal government collected in tax revenues. (During his second term, spending exceeded taxes by "only" $3.5 trillion.) For Obama's terms in office, we thus had cumulative federal budget deficits that were almost as big as the cumulative deficits that had been incurred from 1789 to 2008. Because all of these new debts will have to be repaid, higher taxes are in your future—and President Trump's promises of higher spending mean still *more* taxes are in your future.

Increased Spending, Increased Taxes

When Congress passes legislation to spend more, whether it is for bailing out the financial sector, improving education and public infrastructure, or attempting to reduce poverty, there is ultimately only one place it can obtain the resources. That place is you and everyone else who earns income each year in the United States. As we noted in Chapters 15 and 19, having the ability to run a larger federal government deficit (and thus increase the net national debt) does not change the fundamental budget constraint facing our society.

What government spends, the rest of us do not spend. Perhaps without your realizing it, your **real tax rate** can rise long before the Internal Revenue Service (IRS) ever sends you a tax bill. How? All it takes is for federal government spending to increase as a share of **gross domestic product (GDP)**. Your real tax rate is easily calculated. It is the percentage of GDP controlled by the government. Back in 2000, that number was 18 percent of GDP and today is above 20 percent of GDP. You may not have felt the bite yet, but the observed taxes that you pay through automatic withholding of federal income taxes on your wages or salary will eventually catch up. The budget constraint guarantees that.

BUT WHAT ABOUT ALL THOSE TAX CUTS?

By the time the election of 2010 rolled around, taxpayers were finally starting to get nervous about all of this new federal spending. But the economy was still going sideways coming out of the recession of 2007–2009, so the first thing Congress did after the election was to extend tax cuts passed back in 2001 and 2003, during the Bush administration. Moreover, Congress extended unemployment benefits (even though the recession had ended eighteen months before) and even enacted a temporary cut in the payroll taxes used to finance Social Security. (The cut was supposed to last two months. It actually lasted two years.)

As we noted above and in Chapter 19, such "tax cuts" cannot be expected to increase aggregate demand—and in fact they did not. Because government spending was not reduced, the burden of the government was not reduced. The net effect was to raise the deficit relative to what it would have been and to make the necessary eventual tax increases even larger. No matter what the politicians promise, the budget constraint cannot be avoided. Hence, higher taxes are in your future.

There was one tiny bright spot. Because **marginal tax rates** were reduced as part of the 2010 package, people have likely worked more, produced more, and thus earned more in the years since, because they get to keep more of what they earned. This "supply side" effect of the lower tax rates probably helped the economy recover a bit faster from the recession of 2007–2009.

The flip side came in 2013, when Congress voted to return the payroll tax to its previous, higher, level. Congress also hiked federal income taxes on individuals making more than $400,000 per year. Taken together, these measures will likely generate about $60 billion a year in tax revenues. They also reduce the incentive to work—and so dampen the level of real economic activity.

WHO GETS THE BILL?

Although 150 million personal tax returns are filed with the Internal Revenue Service every year, many of these filers pay no federal income taxes at all. In fact, about 45 percent of "taxpayers" either pay no federal income taxes or actually pay *negative* federal income taxes because they receive **tax credits.** Under a tax credit, people who pay no federal income taxes effectively get a check from the federal government, which they can use to pay other federal taxes they might owe (such as Social Security) or to pay *future* federal tax liabilities should they arise. If there *are* no current or likely future tax liabilities, well, they get to keep the cash.

There may well be perfectly good reasons to effectively exempt some people from paying income taxes, perhaps because they are impoverished or have major medical bills. But it is important to recognize two implications of shielding large numbers of people from income taxes. First, this helps create the impression for many voters that federal spending is effectively "free"—because, after all, they will not be responsible when the bills come due. Thus, they are more likely to favor an expansion of government spending that does not confer benefits that exceed its costs. This reduces the overall wealth of society. Second, with large numbers of individuals exempt from federal income taxes, the burden on those who *do* pay taxes is that much greater. This will induce such people to work less, produce less, and earn less because they get to keep less of what they earn. This lower production means that the wealth of our society is reduced.

IS ARGENTINA SHOWING THE WAY?

Argentina was the sixth richest country in the world a hundred years ago. It has since slipped to about sixtieth on that list. Over the same period, government spending in Argentina has been growing relative to the overall size of the economy, as have taxes there. Not too long ago, Cristina Kirchner, the president of Argentina from 2007 to 2015, announced that the nation's private pension system was being taken over by the national government. While she claimed that it was for the "good of the people," because the market was too risky for retirement savings, in fact President Kirchner wanted to use those assets to fund more government spending. Technically, the government "borrows" from the retirement system. But because the Argentine government has a track record of defaulting on its borrowings, many people expect that they will get back few, if any, of their hard-earned retirement pesos.

As you might expect, contributions into the private pension plan plummeted as soon as the government announced its plan. Some Argentine citizens quietly began moving other **assets** out of the country, hoping to protect them from similar confiscation. Still others began making plans for moving *themselves* out of the country, on the grounds that emigration was the ultimate form of protection.

The Argentine government's nationalization of the private pension system is simply a once- and-for-all increase in taxes. While it is unlikely that the U.S. government would seek to take control of private pension plans here, the Argentine story illustrates the key point of this chapter: What the government spends, we must pay for. Sometimes the government must be creative in making that happen, but happen it will. Hence our prediction: Higher taxes are in your future.

FOR CRITICAL ANALYSIS

1. As a result of the federal bailouts of U.S. corporations, the government ended up owning shares of stock and warrants in many companies. (Warrants are rights to own future shares of stock.) How would subsequent changes (up or down) in the prices of these stocks affect the taxes owed by taxpayers for any given level of federal spending? Explain.

2. If you are a lower-income-earning individual and thus pay no income taxes, should you care about tax increases for other individuals? Explain.

3. Is it *possible* that in, say, ten years, the real tax rate paid by U.S. residents will be lower than it is today? What circumstances would have to change to make this occur? Explain.

4. Who, exactly, will be paying the higher future taxes implied by the stimulus packages, tax cuts, and bailouts of 2008–2012 and the continued deficits since then? (*Hint:* Look in the mirror.)

5. Why do most politicians love to spend money and hate to pay for their expenditures? Is this attitude different from the one you have

toward making purchases as opposed to paying for those purchases? What are the consequences for you if you spend more than your income? What happens if you try to avoid paying your debts?

6. Most states have laws or constitutional provisions that require them to quickly eliminate any budget deficits by either raising taxes or cutting spending. Can you suggest why states would have this rule, but the federal government would not?

CHAPTER **21**

The Myths of Social Security

You have probably heard politicians debate the need to reform Social Security. If you are under the age of thirty-five, this debate has been going on for your entire lifetime. Why has nothing been done? The reason is that the politicians are debating over "facts" that are not facts: Most of the claims made about Social Security are myths—urban legends, if you like. Sadly, the politicians have been repeating these myths so often for so long that they believe them and so do their constituents (perhaps including you). As long as these myths persist, nothing meaningful will be done about Social Security, and the problem will simply get worse. So let's see if we can cut through the fog by examining some of the worst Social Security myths.

MYTH 1: THE ELDERLY ARE POOR

The Social Security Act was passed in 1935 as the United States was emerging from the Great Depression. The **unemployment rate** at the time was the highest in our nation's history. **Bank runs** and the stock market crash of 1929 had wiped out the savings of millions of people. Many elderly people had few or no **resources** to draw on in retirement, and their extended families often had few resources with which to help them. In the midst of these conditions, Social Security was established to make sure that the elderly had access to some *minimum* level of income when they retired. It was never meant to be the sole source of retirement funds for senior citizens.

Given the circumstances of the program's founding, it is not surprising that many people associate Social Security with poverty among the elderly. The fact is that both the Social Security program and the financial condition of older people have changed dramatically over the years. For example, measured in inflation-adjusted dollars, initial Social Security payments were as little as $120 per month and reached a maximum of $500 per month, or about $6,000 per year. Today, however, many recipients are eligible for payments in excess of $30,000 per year. More important, people over age sixty-five are no longer among the poorest in our society.[1]

Despite the ravages of the recession of 2007–2009, today's elderly have accumulated literally *trillions* of dollars in **assets.** These assets include homes and substantial portfolios of **stocks** and **bonds.** In addition, millions of older Americans are drawing *private* pensions, built up over years of employment. Social Security payments, for example, now provide only about 40 percent of the income of the average retired person, with the rest coming about equally from private pensions, employment earnings, and investment income. Far from being the age group with the highest poverty rate, the elderly actually suffer about 25 percent *less* poverty than the average of all U.S. residents. To be sure, Social Security helps make this possible, but just as surely, only about 9 percent of the elderly are living in poverty. In contrast, the poverty rate among children is 20 percent.

MYTH 2: SOCIAL SECURITY IS FIXED INCOME

Most laypersons and economic and political commentators treat Social Security benefits as a source of fixed income for the elderly, one that supposedly falls in **real purchasing power** as the general **price level** rises. This myth, too, has its roots in the early days of Social Security, when payments were indeed fixed in dollar terms and thus were potentially subject to the ravages of **inflation.** But this is no longer true. In 1972, Congress decided to link Social Security payments to a measure of the overall price level in the economy. The avowed reason for this change was to protect Social Security payments from any decline in real value during inflation. In fact, because of the price level measure chosen by Congress, the real value of payments has actually *risen* each year there is inflation (which is almost every year).

---

1 The age of sixty-five is conventionally used to designate the onset of senior citizen status, because Medicare eligibility begins at that age, as once did eligibility for full Social Security retirement benefits. Today, eligibility for full benefits begins at ages from sixty-six to sixty-seven, depending on birth year, although people can choose to take reduced Social Security benefits as early as age sixty-two.

Although there are many potential measures of the average price of goods and services, Congress decided to tie Social Security payments to the **consumer price index (CPI).** The CPI is supposed to measure changes in the dollar cost of consuming a bundle of goods and services that is representative for the typical consumer. Thus, a 10 percent rise in the CPI is supposed to mean that the **cost of living** has gone up by 10 percent. Accordingly, the law provides that Social Security benefits are automatically increased by 10 percent.

In fact, the CPI actually overstates the true inflation rate: It is *biased upward* as a measure of inflation. This bias has several sources. For example, when the price of a good rises relative to other prices, people usually consume less of it, enabling them to avoid some of the added cost of the good. But the CPI does not take this into account. Similarly, although the average quality of goods and services generally rises over time, the CPI does not adequately account for this fact. Until a few years ago, the upward bias in the CPI amounted to about 1.1 percentage points per year on average. Revisions to the CPI have reduced this bias to about 0.8 percentage points per year. Thus, currently, if the CPI says prices have gone up, say, 1.8 percent, they have really gone up only 1.0 percent. Nevertheless, Social Security payments automatically increase by the full 1.8 percent.

Now, 0.8 or 1.1 percentage points do not sound like much, and if it happened only once or twice, there wouldn't be much of a problem. But almost every year for forty years, this extra amount has been added to benefits. Over a long period, even the small upward bias begins to amount to a real change in **purchasing power.** Indeed, this provision of the Social Security system has had the cumulative effect of raising real (inflation-adjusted) Social Security benefits by about 50 percent since the early 1970s. Therefore, despite the myth that Social Security is fixed income, in reality the benefits grow *faster* than inflation.

MYTH 3: THERE IS A SOCIAL SECURITY TRUST FUND

For the first few years of Social Security's existence, taxes were collected, but no monthly benefits were paid. The funds collected were used to purchase U.S. Treasury bonds, and that accumulation of bonds was called the Social Security Trust Fund. Until 2010, tax collections (called **payroll taxes**) exceeded benefits paid each year—so that the trust fund grew to about $2.5 trillion in Treasury bonds. Benefits now exceed tax revenues because retiring baby boomers are collecting more and paying less. The bonds will have to be sold to finance the difference. By around 2034, it is estimated that the trust fund will have a balance of zero.

The standard story told (by politicians at least) is that the bonds in the trust fund represent net assets, much like the assets owned by private pension plans. *This is false*. Congress has already spent the past excess of taxes over benefits and has simply given the trust fund I.O.Us. These I.O.Us are called U.S. Treasury bonds, and they are nothing more than promises by the U.S. Treasury to collect taxes from someone to pay benefits. As the trust fund sells the bonds over the coming years, Congress will have to raise taxes, cut spending on other programs, or borrow more to raise the funds. But this would be true even if there were *no* Treasury bonds in the trust fund: All Social Security benefits must ultimately be paid for out of taxes. Thus, whatever might have been intended for the trust fund, the only asset actually backing that fund is nothing more and nothing less than an obligation of Americans—you—to pay taxes in the future.

MYTH 4: SOCIAL SECURITY WILL BE THERE FOR YOU

Social Security was a great deal for Ida Mae Fuller, who in 1940 became the first person to receive a regular Social Security pension. She had paid a total of $24.75 in Social Security taxes before she retired. By the time she died in 1975 at the age of 100, she had received benefits totaling $22,888.92. And although Ida Mae did better than most recipients, the *average* annual real rate of return for those early retirees was an astounding 135 percent *per year*. (That is, after adjusting for inflation, every initial $100 in taxes paid yielded $135 *per year* during each and every year of that person's retirement.)

People retiring more recently have not done quite so well, but everyone who retired by about 1970 has received a far better return from Social Security than could likely have been obtained from any other investment. These higher benefits relative to contributions were made possible because at each point in time, *current retirees are paid benefits out of the taxes paid by current workers*. Social Security is a **pay-as-you-go system.** It is not like a true retirement plan in which participants pay into a fund and receive benefits according to what they have paid in and how much that fund has cumulatively earned from investments. Thus, as long as Social Security was pulling in enough new people each year, the system could offer benefits that were high relative to taxes paid. But the number of people paying Social Security taxes is no longer growing so fast, and the number of retirees is growing faster. Moreover, today's trickle of new retirees is becoming tomorrow's flood as the baby boom generation exits the workforce. The result is bad news all around.

One way to think about the problem facing us—which is chiefly a problem facing *you*—is to contemplate the number of retirees each worker must support. In 1945, forty-two workers shared the burden of each Social Security recipient. By 1960, nine workers had to pick up the tab for each person collecting Social Security. Today, the burden of a retiree is spread out among about four workers. By 2030 or so, fewer than three workers will be available to pay the Social Security benefits due each recipient.

The coming tax bill for all of this will be staggering. If we *immediately* raised Social Security (payroll) taxes from 15.3 percent to 20 percent—roughly a 30 percent increase—and kept them there for the next seventy-five years or so, the system's revenues would probably be large enough to meet its obligations. But this would be the largest tax increase in U.S. history, which makes it extremely unlikely that it will occur. Yet every day that Congress delays, the situation gets worse. If Congress waits until 2030 to raise taxes, they will have to be increased by more than 50 percent. Indeed, some commentators are predicting that without fundamental reforms to the system, payroll taxes *alone* will have to be hiked to 25 percent of wages—in addition to regular federal, state, and local income taxes, of course.

What are any reforms likely to be? Well, rules will specify that people must be older before they become eligible for Social Security benefits. Existing legislation has already scheduled a hike in the age for full benefits up to sixty-seven from its current sixty-six. This age threshold likely will be raised again, perhaps to seventy. It is also likely that all Social Security benefits (rather than just a portion) will eventually be subject to federal income taxes. It is even possible that some high-income individuals—you, perhaps—will be declared ineligible for benefits because their income from other sources is too high.

So, what does all this mean for you? Well, technically, a Social Security system will probably be in existence when you retire, although the retirement age will be higher than it is today and benefits will have been scaled back. Strictly speaking, something called the Social Security Trust Fund may even still be around when you hit the minimum age for benefits. But whatever else happens to the Social Security system between now and your retirement, you can be secure in your knowledge of one thing: You will be getting a much bigger tax bill from the federal government to pay for it.

FOR CRITICAL ANALYSIS

1. Where has all of the Social Security money gone?

2. People over the age of sixty-five have been highly successful in protecting and enhancing the real benefits they receive from Social Security. This has come at the expense of other people in society,

particularly young people. What do you think explains the ability of older people to win political battles with younger people?

3. Analyze how each of the following hypothetical policy changes would affect people's decision to retire. Would the change induce people to retire sooner or later? Explain your reasoning.

   a. An increase in the age at which one can receive full Social Security benefits (currently age sixty-six to sixty-seven, depending on the year in which a person was born)

   b. A decrease in the fraction (currently 75 percent) of full benefits that one can receive if retirement occurs at age sixty-two

   c. An increase in the Medicare eligibility age from its current level of sixty-five

   d. An increase to 100 percent from its current 85 percent in the maximum fraction of Social Security benefits that is subject to the federal income tax

4. If a person starts collecting Social Security benefits before full retirement age but also continues to work, then for each $2 in income earned (above a modest level), that person's benefits are reduced by $1. What is the effective **marginal tax rate** imposed by the Social Security system on such earnings from work? Explain.

5. For each year after full retirement age that a person delays collecting Social Security benefits, the annual benefits are raised by 8 percent. (This "bump" in benefits ceases at age seventy. Additional retirement delays do not cause benefits to rise any further.) How is the incentive to retire before age seventy affected by this provision for benefit increments, relative to a system in which benefits were not raised in this manner? Explain.

6. What does the existence of the Social Security system do to the incentive of a worker to save for his or her retirement? What does it do to the worker's incentive to save to provide an inheritance for his or her children? Explain.

PART FOUR

Monetary Policy and Financial Institutions

CHAPTER 22

The Fed and Financial Panics

The Panic of 1907 began after a failed attempt by Otto Heinze to "corner the market" on **shares of stock** in the United Copper Company. Heinze had expected the demand for United's shares to increase in the near term and thought that if he bought up enough shares quickly at low prices, he could turn around and sell them at a handsome **profit.** His judgment proved wrong, and Heinze had to sell out at devastatingly low prices. Not only did his stock brokerage firm go out of business, but more disastrously, the public's confidence in banks that had large holdings of United Copper shares evaporated. Confidence also plummeted regarding the financial health of several banks with whom Otto's brother Augustus was associated.

Both groups of banks suffered **bank runs,** in which large numbers of customers simultaneously withdrew their deposits, and some banks ultimately failed as a result. The banking panic soon spread more widely, threatening the security of the entire financial system. The panic was halted only when the famed financier J. P. Morgan eventually induced a large number of banks to join a consortium and mutually stand behind each other's financial obligations.

BIRTH OF THE FED

The Panic of 1907 achieved notoriety at the time by causing the recession of 1907–1908, but the panic's longer-term importance lies elsewhere. Hoping to avoid a repeat of 1907's financial meltdown, in 1913 Congress established the **Federal Reserve System,** commonly referred to as the **Fed.** The Fed is now the nation's monetary authority and, among other things, our first line of defense against financial panics.

As had been true in prior financial panics, the crux of many banks' woes in 1907 was their inability to convert their assets into the cash that panicked depositors desperately wanted. So the Fed was created to serve as "lender of last resort" to the nation's **commercial banks.** Congress empowered the Fed to lend funds to banks to meet whatever demands depositors put on the banks, regardless of how great those demands might be. The intention was that there would never be another financial panic in the United States, an objective that, if achieved, would significantly reduce the number and severity of the nation's economic **recessions.**

Opportunity and Failure

The Fed's first real chance to perform as lender of last resort—the function for which it was created—came in 1930 when several prominent New York banks got into financial difficulties. Customers of those and other banks started withdrawing funds, fearing that their banks might be weak. This spreading decline in confidence was exactly the scenario the Fed was created to defend against—yet it did nothing. The result was a banking panic and a worsening of the economic downturn already under way.

The next year, the Fed had two more opportunities to act as lender of last resort when confidence in banks sagged, yet in both cases it again failed to act. The results were recurring bank panics in 1931 and an intensification of what was by then an extremely severe recession. Early in 1933, eroding public confidence in the banking system gave the Fed yet another opportunity to step in as lender of last resort, and *again* it failed to do so. The resulting banking panic was disastrous and ushered in the deepest stages of what has come to be known as the Great Depression. It is little wonder that Herbert Hoover, who was then president of the United States, referred to the Fed as "a weak reed for a nation to lean on in time of trouble."

Lessons Learned

Thirty years after the end of the Great Depression, Nobel laureate Milton Friedman and Anna Schwartz published *A Monetary History of the United States.* Among other things, this book laid out in detail the story of the Fed's failings during the 1930s. The book's lessons were absorbed by at least two people who have since served as the head of the Fed— Alan Greenspan, who was chair of the Fed from 1987 to 2006, and Ben Bernanke, who chaired the Fed from 2006 to 2014.

Greenspan's opportunity to have the Fed serve as the banking system's lender of last resort came in September 2001, in the wake of the terrorist attacks on the World Trade Center towers. Banks found themselves in need of a quick infusion of funds as panicked depositors made large-scale withdrawals of cash. The Fed quickly stepped in to provide funds to banks, enabling them to meet the demands of depositors without having to sell off **assets** at depressed prices. The legislators who created the Fed surely had never contemplated a terrorist attack. Nevertheless, the Fed acted vigorously as a lender of last resort and thus achieved the objectives of its creators—prevention of financial panic.

THE PANIC OF 2008

Only two years after he replaced Greenspan as chair of the Fed, Ben Bernanke had an even bigger opportunity to put the Fed to work. Late in 2008, rapidly eroding confidence in the U.S. financial system led to the near or total collapse of several major financial firms. Many commercial banks, investment banks, and even insurance companies were suddenly in dire condition. Potential borrowers across the country found themselves unable to obtain funds from anyone, at any rate of interest. Although circumstances differed from 1907 in that commercial banks were not at the center of the panic, there was no doubt about one point: The Panic of 2008 was just as threatening to the U.S. economy as its century-old predecessor had been.

Mindful of the costs of inaction, the Fed moved swiftly to maintain and restore confidence in key components of the financial system. But its actions were considerably broader than ever before. Historically, for example, the Fed has lent funds to commercial banks and to the federal government itself. But in 2008, the Fed also lent hundreds of billions of dollars directly to nonbank corporations around the country, including tens of billions to insurance giant AIG. The Fed also began purchasing obligations of government-sponsored **mortgage** market giants **Fannie Mae** and **Freddie Mac**, hoping to bolster their solvency. And finally, the Fed agreed to the following trade with commercial banks: It would exchange billions of dollars of risk-free federal **bonds** it held for billions of dollars of high-risk private bonds that they held. In effect, the Fed helped the banks remove high-risk assets of questionable value from their **balance sheets,** thus reducing the chances that skittish depositors might suddenly make large-scale withdrawals of funds from commercial banks.

THE SURGE IN EXCESS RESERVES

For many of their deposits, commercial banks are required to keep a minimum amount of **reserves** on hand, either in their vaults or on deposit with the Fed. These are referred to as **required reserves.** Any reserves above these minimum required levels are called **excess reserves.** Over the past seventy years, bank holdings of excess reserves generally have been quite small, amounting to no more than $2 billion for the entire banking system. This is not surprising. In normal times, banks generally keep only enough excess reserves to handle day-to-day transactions with depositors, because they can earn interest on any funds they lend out.

By 2009, excess reserves had soared to more than $800 billion, hit $1.6 *trillion* in 2011, and soared to $2.7 trillion by 2014. Total reserves (required plus excess) were up sharply because the Fed was providing banks reserves in return for other assets. Among the purchases were commercial paper (debts issued by private companies), securities backed by credit card debt and home mortgages, and even home mortgages. But almost all of the Fed-provided reserves simply sat there—either in bank vaults or on deposit with the Fed—because banks lent almost none of them out.

Banks across the country held on to the excess reserves for four reasons. First, the sagging economy meant that borrowers were riskier and hence less profitable at any given interest rate. Second, depositors were greatly concerned about the financial condition of commercial banks. The banks therefore wanted plenty of funds on hand—in the form of excess reserves—in case they had to meet increased withdrawal demands by depositors. Third, the Dodd-Frank Act, which became law in 2010, imposed regulations on banks that sharply limited their ability to lend to any but the best credit risks. But oddly enough, the fourth reason for the failure of banks to lend out reserves was a new policy implemented by the Fed itself.

PAYING INTEREST ON RESERVES

In 2008, the Fed began paying interest on the reserves held by commercial banks, something it had never done before. And it was paying interest not just on required reserves but on *excess* reserves as well. This policy encouraged banks to hold excess reserves rather than to lend the funds to customers. Thus, the payment of interest on commercial bank reserves made it *more difficult* for companies and individuals to get loans.[1] (See Chapter 23 for more on this.)

On balance, it remains to be seen whether the Fed actions during the last recession lived up to the expectations that the Fed's founders had

---

1 European commercial banks are allowed to hold reserves with the Fed, and they too receive interest payments on their reserves. Indeed, as of 2016, about 40 percent of the Fed's interest payments on reserves were going to European banks, rather than to American banks.

more than a century ago. By providing funds to banks and other financial institutions, the Fed helped reduce the impact of the financial panic and helped prevent widespread runs on commercial banks. Nevertheless, the Fed decision to pay interest on reserves markedly discouraged banks from lending those reserves to companies and households across the land. This surely *slowed* recovery from the recession.

Moreover, recall that the Fed was founded to serve as a lender of last resort for *banks*. As we noted above, however, in 2008 it chose to serve also as a lender of last resort to major *non-bank* companies (such as AIG). It is likely that this Fed choice will encourage such firms to behave in a riskier fashion in the years ahead, confident that the Fed will save them if they get in trouble. Such risky behavior will tend to make the economy more subject to future financial panics. Thus, only time and further study will tell whether, on balance, the Fed's actions during the recession made us better off—or worse off.

FOR CRITICAL ANALYSIS

1. How did the Fed's long-standing policy of not paying interest on bank reserves act much like a tax on bank reserves?

2. If the Fed continued to pay interest on required reserves but stopped paying interest on excess reserves, how would the lending incentives of banks be changed?

3. If the Fed had not injected reserves into the banking system in 2008, what would have been the consequences for the banks and for **aggregate demand**?

4. By late 2010 concerns over bank solvency had faded. How did this change likely alter the incentives of banks to lend out excess reserves? What are the implications for aggregate demand? Explain.

5. In the long run, if the Fed fails to remove the excess reserves from the banking system, what will the banks do with them? What are the implications for inflation? Explain.

6. The Fed was given great power in 1913 to undertake potentially beneficial actions. Did this also give it great power to engage in potentially *harmful* actions? Explain why or why not.

CHAPTER 23

The Fed Feeding Frenzy

"QE1 didn't seem to work. QE2 fared little better. QE3 has been phased out."

If you have no idea what the above quote means, you are not alone. Here is the origin of the abbreviation "QE." Financial reporters decided a few years ago to accept a new term for what is largely an old concept. That term is **quantitative easing (QE).** Consequently, "QE1" is a reference to the Fed's expansionary monetary policy during the latest serious recession, in 2008 and 2009. QE2 refers to the Fed's expansionary monetary policy that started in November 2010. QE3—well, the Fed started that in September, 2012, with the economy still moving sideways.

MONETARY POLICY—THE WAY IT USED TO BE

Historically, the Fed's main tool for monetary policy has been the purchase and sale of U.S. government securities, usually **Treasury bills.** When the Fed has wanted to engage in expansionary monetary policy, it bought U.S. Treasuries in the **open market,** thereby increasing **reserves** in the banking system. **Excess reserves** (those over and above legally **required reserves**) were used by banks to expand loans. In the process, the **money supply** grew, which increased the aggregate demand. Contractionary monetary policy was just the opposite—the Fed sold U.S. government securities, thereby reducing the reserves. The end result was a decrease in the money supply in circulation and a decrease in aggregate demand.

That was then, but the Fed's ordinary monetary policy took on a new twist in response to the financial panic of 2008.

THE FED STARTED TO LIKE OTHER ASSETS

During the first ninety-five years of its existence, the Federal Reserve dealt with U.S. government securities only. All that changed in 2008 when the Fed decided to target specific sectors in our economy. So, instead of engaging in traditional expansionary monetary policy, the Fed started buying assets other than U.S. government securities. This had never been done before.

The assets purchased by the Fed included short-term corporate debt, short-term loans to banks, **mortgage-backed securities (MBS),** mostly issued by the government-sponsored corporations Fannie Mae and Freddie Mac, other debt issued by Fannie Mae and Freddie Mac, and preferred shares in the former investment bank Bear Stearns and in the insurance company American International Group (AIG). Oh, and let's not forget that for well over a year the Fed engaged in **foreign currency swaps** with other countries—perhaps that was considered the icing on the larger cake.

All of those purchases of all of those assets clearly increased the size and composition of the Fed's **balance sheet.** For much of its more recent existence, the Fed "owned" anywhere from several billion to several hundred billion dollars of U.S. Treasury securities. But by 2011, the Fed's assets totaled more than $2.5 trillion (including many hundreds of billions in "new" securities it had bought as part of its quantitative easing policy). Throughout 2012 and 2013, Fed assets remained in the range of $2.8 to $3.0 trillion. By the end of 2014 they had hit $4.5 trillion.

So, in a sentence, the Fed's traditional monetary policy abruptly changed in 2008. Rather than seeking to stimulate the entire economy in general, the Fed decided to provide credit to parts of financial markets (and even specific corporations) that it believed private lenders were abandoning. Never before in its history had the chair of the Fed and its board of directors used such discretionary policy to benefit specific sectors of the economy.

WHY DID INFLATION STAY TAME FOR SO LONG?

When the Fed aggressively adds to the money supply in circulation by buying U.S. government securities, the banking system suddenly has excess reserves. Not wanting to lose out on potential income from those excess reserves, depository institutions increase their loans, the money supply rises, and aggregate demand increases. At least that is the way economists used to tell the story.

While QE1, QE2, and so forth got the headlines, however, there was another revolution in central banking going on in the United States. Starting on October 1, 2008, the Fed began paying interest on reserves—*all* reserves, including excess reserves. While monetary economists for years had argued that interest should be paid on required reserves, none ever demanded that interest be paid on excess reserves, too. This policy change by the Fed converted excess reserves into an income-earning asset for banks and thus fundamentally altered the nature of the conduct of monetary policy.

If you are the manager of a bank and know that the Fed will pay interest on excess reserves, you are not so keen to loan out those reserves to businesses and individuals. After all, if you make loans to businesses and individuals, you run a risk. During the recession of 2007–2009, that risk soared far above historical norms. Why not just sit back, collect interest checks from the U.S. government on all of your reserves, and wait to see what happens?

Well, that is exactly what most banks have done over the past few years. The numbers tell the story. When they did not earn interest, excess reserves were a drag on bank profits and so banks kept them to a minimum. Typically, excess reserves for the entire banking system averaged under $2 billion. During 2011 they peaked at over $1.6 *trillion* and reached $2.7 trillion in 2014. Thus, most of the reserves injected into the banking system since 2008 ended up not in new loans, new money, and new spending. Instead, they ended up sitting around as excess reserves. That means that the "expansionary" quantitative easing of the Fed was almost completely offset by its decision to pay interest on excess reserves. The result was little increase in aggregate demand and little upward pressure on inflation—at least in the short run.

ON WANTING MORE INFLATION

For several years, the Fed has told reporters and experts alike that it was worried about **deflation.** Deflation has been associated with bad times—the Great Depression in the United States, for example, and the "lost decade" of the 1990s in the Japanese economy. In justification of its quantitative easing (QE2) in November 2010, the Fed pointed to the "need" for a little bit of inflation, to avoid a deflationary downward spiral.

Actually, as measured by the **personal consumption expenditures (PCE) price index,** there had been inflation running at about 1.2 percent annually, a number that was bumping up around 2 percent toward the end of 2010, when the Fed announced QE2. In other words, based on the Fed's historically preferred price index, there was no sign of deflation so it seemed strange that the Fed argued in favor of quantitative easing to avoid deflation. The source of the Fed's deflation worries is easily identified, though. Without much publicity, in 2010 the Fed began paying added attention to the consumer price index (CPI). The weight of housing prices in the CPI is almost double the weight in the personal consumption expenditure price index. Given that housing prices fell quite dramatically during the years 2006 to 2010, it is not surprising that the CPI showed some deflation, especially in 2008.

GETTING BACK TO QUANTITATIVE EASING

Even if the Fed's argument about deflation was based on no more than an interest in a different price index, its desire to prime the pump for the faltering U.S. economy has been genuine. The recession that started in December 2007 pushed the unemployment rate above 10 percent, and the rate was slow to come down. So the Fed argued that QE2 would lower long-term interest rates and thereby give the economy a boost. QE3 was similarly justified on the ground that the unemployment rate was still declining, only sluggishly. By 2016, however, the unemployment rate dropped below 5 percent (generally considered to be full employment) and inflation was rising, so the Fed was in a difficult position.

When the Fed buys up government and other debt obligations, it tends to push investors into stocks and corporate bonds—raising the latter's values and lowering interest rates. Lower borrowing costs help some homeowners refinance their mortgages. Some businesses are helped, too, because they have access to cheaper credit. Such an analysis is quite traditional and at times has worked—*in the short run*. In the long run, in contrast, large-scale purchases of debt, whether labeled quantitative easing or not, simply lead to more rapid growth in the money supply, a higher rate of inflation, and a return of interest rates to their previous and even higher levels.

So, by 2017 the Fed was on a tightrope of its own making. The huge infusion of reserves into the banking system helped moderate the recession of 2007–2009, but the payment of interest on reserves slowed the recovery from that recession. The presence of large excess reserves presents a huge potential threat of inflation down the road, but if the reserves are pulled out of the banking system too fast, the economy will surely sink back into recession. It is the classic case of the two-handed economic policy problem. On the one hand, the economy is threatened by severe inflation. On the other hand, it is threatened by a relapse into recession. Stay tuned, for this is one drama that will work itself out in front of your very eyes.

FOR CRITICAL ANALYSIS

1. Why do increases in the money supply in circulation ultimately lead to inflation?

2. Was the Fed justified in targeting specific sectors of the economy during the financial panic of 2008? Why or why not?

3. When the Fed buys U.S. government securities, how does it pay for them?

4. Is there any risk to the Fed in holding mortgage-backed securities and debt issued by Fannie Mae and Freddie Mac? If so, what is it?

5. Why did excess reserves increase so much in recent years?

6. Why have banks been so reluctant to loan funds to businesses in recent years?

CHAPTER 24

Deposit Insurance and Financial Markets

During the Panic of 2008, the federal government announced a key new policy: It was insuring against loss all bank deposits up to $250,000 per account. Thus, if your depository institution happened to be holding some toxic (possibly even worthless) **mortgage-backed securities (MBS),** you were home free. The bank could suffer terrible losses, even go out of business, and yet your accounts, up to $250,000 each, would be guaranteed by the full faith and credit of the U.S. government—which is to say, the U.S. taxpayer.

If you happened to notice the announcement of this policy, you may have wondered to yourself: Why would the government do this? For example, although the federal government bought **shares of stock** in numerous banks at the same time, it most assuredly does not guarantee the value of those shares. Why treat deposits differently? A subtler question is this: How do banks and other **depository institutions** behave differently because of this special deposit insurance? And you might even have wondered whether *your* behavior is likely to be any different because of this insurance. To get a handle on these and other questions, we must look back to the 1930s, before the notion of deposit insurance had even been conceived.

BANK RUNS

Bank runs are defined as the simultaneous rush of depositors to convert their deposits into **currency.** Until the federal government set up deposit insurance in 1933, runs on banks were an infrequent but seemingly unavoidable occurrence, sometimes becoming widespread during economic **recessions.** The largest number of bank runs in modern history occurred during the Great Depression. As a result of these runs, more than *nine thousand* banks failed during the 1930s—one-third of all that had been around in 1929.

Just put yourself in the shoes of the depositor in a typical bank in 1930 and remember that you are a **creditor** of the bank. That is to say, your deposits in the bank are its **liabilities.** Suppose a rumor develops that the **assets** of the bank are not sufficient to cover its liabilities. In other words, the bank is, or will soon be, **insolvent.** Presumably, you are worried that you will not get your deposits back in the form of currency. Knowing this, you are likely to rush to the bank. All other depositors who hear about the bank's supposedly weak financial condition are likely to do the same thing.

This is the essence of a bank run: Regardless of the true state of the bank's financial condition, rumors or fears that a bank is in trouble can cause depositors to suddenly attempt to withdraw all of their funds. But many assets of a bank are in the form of loans that cannot immediately be converted into cash. Even if **solvent,** the bank is said to be **illiquid** because it does not have enough cash on hand to meet the demands of fearful depositors. And when it attempts to get that cash by selling some assets, any resulting decline in the market value of those assets can quickly turn a solvent bank into an insolvent one.

Bank runs can be disastrous for the economy because when they occur, the nation's **money supply** shrinks as people pull cash out of banks and stuff it under their mattresses (or wherever they think it might be safe). This in turn causes **aggregate demand** to fall, leading to higher unemployment, business failures, and yet more concerns for the solvency of banks. Quickly enough, the result can be an economic recession and widespread hardship.

DEPOSIT INSURANCE

When four thousand banks failed in 1933 alone, the federal government decided on action to prevent further bank runs. That year, Congress passed, and the president signed into law, legislation creating the Federal Deposit Insurance Corporation (FDIC) and the next year created the Federal Savings and Loan Insurance Corporation (FSLIC). Many years later, in 1971, the National Credit Union Share Insurance Fund (NCUSIF) was created to insure credit union deposits, and in 1989, the FSLIC was replaced by the Savings Association Insurance Fund (SAIF). To make our discussion simple, we will focus only on the FDIC, but the general principles apply to all of these agencies.

When the FDIC was formed, it insured each account in a commercial bank against a loss of up to $2,500. That figure has been increased on seven different occasions, reaching $250,000 in 2008. The result of federal deposit insurance is that there has not been a widespread bank run in the United States since the Great Depression, despite numerous bank failures in the interim. Even during the Panic of 2008, when confidence in many financial institutions collapsed, federally insured depository institutions continued to operate. Indeed, total deposits in them actually *rose*. The good news about federal deposit insurance is that it has prevented bank runs. But this has come at a significant cost, arising largely from the unintended consequences of deposit insurance.

ADVERSE SELECTION

Suppose someone offers you what is claimed to be a great **investment** opportunity. That person tells you that if you invest $250,000, you will make a very high rate of return, much higher than the 3 percent your funds are currently earning elsewhere. No matter how much you trusted the person offering you this deal, you would probably do some serious investigation of the proposed investment before you handed over all of your hard-earned dollars. You, like other people, would carefully evaluate the risk factors involved in this potential opportunity.

For example, if you use part of your **savings** to buy a house, you will undoubtedly have the structural aspects of the house checked out by an inspector before you sign on the dotted line. Similarly, if you planned to purchase an expensive piece of art, you surely would have an independent expert verify that the artwork is authentic. Typically, the same is true every time you place your accumulated savings into any potential investment: You look before you leap. In circumstances such as these, there is initially **asymmetric information**—in this case, the seller knows much more than the potential buyer. But with diligence, the buyer can eliminate much of this knowledge gap and make a wise decision.

Now ask yourself, when is the last time you examined the financial condition or lending activities of the depository institution at which you have your checking or savings account? We predict that the answer is never. Indeed, why should you investigate? Because of federal deposit insurance, you are personally risking nothing, even if the depository institution that has your funds is taking huge risks. If that depository institution fails, the federal government will—with 100 percent certainty—make sure that you get 100 percent of your deposits back, up to the insurance limit.

So here we have it—the first unintended consequence of depository insurance. Depositors like you no longer have any substantial incentive to investigate the track record of the owners or managers of banks. You care little about whether they have a history of risky or imprudent behavior because at worst you may suffer some minor inconvenience if your bank fails. Thus, unlike in the days before deposit insurance, the marketplace today does little to monitor or punish past performance of owners or managers of depository institutions. As a result, we tend to get **adverse selection**—instead of banks owned and operated by individuals who are prudent at making careful decisions on behalf of depositors, many of them end up run by people who have a high tolerance for taking big risks with other people's money.

Moral Hazard

Now let's look at bank managers' incentives to act cautiously when making loans. You must first note that the riskier the loan, the higher the interest rate that a bank can charge. For example, if a developing country with a blemished track record in paying its debts wishes to borrow from a U.S. depository institution, that country will have to pay a much higher interest rate than a less risky debtor. The same is true when a risky company comes looking for a loan: If it gets one at all, it will be at a higher-than-average interest rate.

When trying to decide which loan applicants should receive funds, bank managers must weigh the trade-off between risk and return. Poor credit risks offer high **profits** if they actually pay off their debts, but good credit risks are more likely to pay off their debts. The right lending choice means higher profits for the bank and likely higher salaries and promotions for the managers. The wrong choice means losses and perhaps insolvency for the bank and new, less desirable careers for the managers.

To understand how bank managers' incentives are changed by deposit insurance—even for managers who otherwise would be prudent and conservative—consider two separate scenarios. In the first scenario, the bank manager is told to take $250,000 of depositors' funds to Las Vegas. The rules of the game are that the manager can bet however he or she wants, and the bank will *share* the winnings *and losses* equally with the deposit holders whose funds the manager has in trust. In the second scenario, the same bank manager with the same funds is given a different set of rules. In this case, the bank does not have to share in any of the losses but it will share in any of the gains when betting in Las Vegas.

Under which set of rules do you think the bank manager will take the higher risks while betting in Las Vegas? Clearly, the manager will take higher risks in the second scenario because the bank will not suffer at all if the manager loses the entire $250,000. Yet if the manager hits it big, say, by placing a successful bet on double zero in roulette, the bank will share the profits, and the manager is likely to get a raise and a promotion.

Well, the second scenario is exactly the one facing the managers of federally insured depository institutions. If they make risky loans, thereby earning, at least in the short run, higher profits, they share in the "winnings." The result for them is higher salaries. If, by contrast, some of these risky loans are not repaid, what is the likely outcome? The bank's losses are limited because the federal government (which is to say you, the taxpayer) will cover any shortfall between the bank's assets and its liabilities. Thus, federal deposit insurance means that banks get to enjoy all of the profits of risk without bearing all of the consequences of that risk.

So the second unintended consequence of deposit insurance is to encourage **moral hazard.** Specifically, bank managers of all types (risk lovers or not) have an incentive to take higher risks in their lending policies than they otherwise would. Indeed, when the economy turned downward in the early 1980s, we got to see the consequences of exactly this change in incentives. From 1985 to the beginning of 1993, a total of 1,065 depository institutions failed, at an average rate of more than ten times that for the preceding forty years. The losses from these failures totaled billions of dollars—paid for in large part by you, the taxpayer.

What, then, might be expected from the 2008 insurance hike to $250,000? Well, in the short run, confidence in banks was renewed and depositors were encouraged to keep more funds in banks. This was good news, for it helped the economy adjust to the financial shocks of 2008 and 2009. But the bad news will be forthcoming in the long run: The higher deposit insurance limits will encourage both adverse selection (more risk-loving bank managers) and moral hazard (more risk taking by bank managers of all stripes). Eventually, the lending standards of banks will deteriorate to the point that losses mount once again—paid for in part by you, the taxpayer.

Paying for Deposit Insurance

For the first sixty years or so of federal deposit insurance, all depository institutions were charged modest fees for their insurance coverage. Unfortunately, the fee that these depository institutions paid was completely unrelated to the riskiness of the loans they made. A bank that made loans to Microsoft was charged the same rate for deposit insurance as a bank that made loans to a start-up company with no track record whatsoever. Hence, not even the fees paid by banks for their insurance gave them any incentive to be prudent. This is completely unlike the case in private insurance markets, in which high-risk customers are charged higher premiums, giving them at least some incentive to become lower-risk customers.

In the early 1990s, the federal government made a feeble attempt to adjust fees for depository insurance to reflect the riskiness of their lending activities. But the political strength of the depository institutions prevented any fundamental change in the system. In 2008, the insurance fees paid by depository institutions were doubled, but even this was not enough to keep up with the added risks of the higher insurance limits. In 2009 and 2011, the insurance rules were changed again. There are now four basic risk categories for banks, with different insurance premiums charged in each category. In addition, there is a separate set of rules and premiums that apply to what the FDIC calls "large and highly complex institutions." Although this multitiered arrangement is an improvement on the past, most experts believe that it still does not adequately charge banks for the risks they impose on the insurance system. That is, the premiums are not nearly enough to cover the likely losses of the riskiest banks or enough to get them to change their risky behavior.[1]

So while your banker is headed to Vegas, you'd better plan on staying at home to work. Sooner or later, as a U.S. taxpayer, your bill for deposit insurance will come due.

FOR CRITICAL ANALYSIS

1. If premiums for federal deposit insurance were zero, who pays when an insured depository institution fails and its depositors are nonetheless reimbursed for the full amount of their deposits?

2. In a world without deposit insurance, what are some of the mechanisms that would arise to "punish" bank managers who acted irresponsibly? (*Hint:* There are similar types of mechanisms for consumer goods and in the stock market.)

---

1 In 2010 the Dodd-Frank Act became law. Among other things, the law imposes a host of new rules on banks to limit their ability to take risks. But banks have already devised ways around portions of the law. Moreover, many observers argue that Dodd-Frank is far too restrictive and intrusive, so by the time you read this, the law may well have been modified. For better or for worse, the result is likely to be riskier behavior by banks.

3. Explain how "experience rating" of insurance—charging higher premiums to higher-risk customers—affects the incidence of both adverse selection and moral hazard.

4. Why doesn't the federal government charge insurance premiums that fully account for bank failure risks?

5. How would the likelihood of a major economic depression change if federal deposit insurance were eliminated?

6. Why doesn't the federal government offer automobile accident insurance?

CHAPTER 25

Revolutionizing the Way We Pay

Dollars, quarters, dimes, nickels, pennies, credit cards, debit cards, and don't forget checks. Then there is something called wire transfers between banks. Everything just listed, in one way or another, makes up our **payments system.** Some of us find it rather quaint to use **currency**—bills and coins—for transactions. Indeed, it probably won't be long before we find it quaint to use credit cards. And for most young people, checks appear quite strange indeed, for the youth of today are used to debit cards. Massive computing power, the Internet, and the communications revolution, however, are about to change how all of us pay for what we buy.

CURRENCY AND COINS—A RELIC OF THE PAST?

For those who want to work "off the books" (to avoid paying income taxes) and those who are engaged in illegal drug trafficking, currency conveniently leaves no electronic trail. But currency also has lots of disadvantages, whoever uses it. If you lose your wallet or purse, you lose the currency in it. If you want to pay for something in cash, unless it involves a modest amount, currency is awkward (and can become heavy).

Using coins is even more of a bother. And certainly today in the United States and elsewhere, most coins cannot buy you much at all. Plus, it costs 1.7 cents to produce one U.S. penny and 8.1 cents to produce one nickel. In 2012, Canada finally got rid of its penny, which had been around since 1858. In Britain, the farthing was worth one-quarter of an old penny. Nonetheless, it remained **legal tender** for seven hundred years before it was retired from circulation in 1960. Although coins last fifty times as long as paper currency, they are heavy and awkward. Once a coin is no longer usable to buy an item, it is living on borrowed time. Once upon a time, a penny would get you an ice cream cone. Today, there is little reason to keep it in circulation.

Retailers often price goods at $9.99 or $14.99. That custom was started to avoid fraud. Employees are forced to open the cash register to provide change. Because most customers use debit or credit cards today, the .99 is now superfluous. But the major reason that coins and bills are going to disappear has to do with the move to electronic money.

THE IMPACT OF FALLING COMPUTING COSTS

Before we describe the coming electronic payments revolution, we need first to understand why it has become possible. The "why" of course involves the falling costs of computing. Consider that in 1991, a megabyte of memory was priced at $50. If nothing had changed since then, a typical 32-gigabyte smartphone would cost about $1,600,000. But the price of memory has fallen dramatically. Even ten years ago, a smartphone with 32 gigs would have cost $10,000. Since then, of course, the market for smartphones has exploded. Not only has the price of memory plunged, so too has the cost of producing smartphones. (Smartphone and tablet device manufacturers have been able to take advantage of **economies of scale.**)

Along with fast and cheap computing with smartphones and tablet devices, the spread of the Internet and its speed have improved, too. Dial-up Internet connections have gone the way of the horse and buggy. Just over the past decade, download times have been slashed by roughly 95 percent. Internet speeds and availability of networks have improved so much that we take fast access on our smartphones and tablet devices for granted. Oh, did we mention the millions of Wi-Fi hotspots throughout the world? A decade ago, such "necessities" would have been dreams of pure fantasy, but not today.

THE DIGITAL WALLET—IT'S HERE TO STAY

Big banks, big retailers, big credit card issuers, Google, Apple, and Microsoft all would like to see **digital wallets** succeed. A digital wallet acts as a real wallet, but is not a physical object. Rather, it is embedded in your smartphone, smartwatch, or other digital device. Just as you have currency in your physical wallet, you can have the equivalent of currency in a digital wallet.

For digital wallets to really be effective, they must be able to transmit to an e-cash register in a store. To do so requires **near-field communication (NFC)**. This is the technology that enables radio communication between smartphones and other devices that are close by—without actually touching the device. Most NFC systems involve common radio frequency identification (RFID) technology, which can be made quite secure.

In 2011, Google introduced the Google Wallet. That NFC-linked payment service has since been added to many smartphones that use Google's Android operating system. Few merchants, though, installed the necessary systems to read Google's digital wallet.

BIG CHANGES ARE HAPPENING NOW

Since Apple introduced its Apple Pay system in 2014 on its latest iPhones, iWatches, and iPads, the digital wallet revolution has advanced dramatically. Even though Apple takes a small per-transaction fee from credit card issuers, the major card companies have signed up—Visa, MasterCard, and American Express. In fact, credit card issuers that represent over 80 percent of credit card purchase volume in this country are now on board.

Apple is encouraging merchants to install the necessary software and hardware. McDonald's came on board immediately with its 14,000 U.S. locations, as did Macy's and Bloomingdale's. Many more retailers may decide to do so because of another recent change in U.S. credit card networks. In order to avoid being liable for credit card fraud, retailers now must have payment terminals that accept cards with embedded chips. Such cards are ubiquitous throughout Europe and much of the world. In the process of upgrading their terminals, many merchants have added near-field communication, hastening the spread of the digital wallet—and the demise of the credit card.

DIGITAL WALLETS AND SUBSTITUTE CURRENCIES

When most people think of using a digital wallet, they think of paying for something without presenting a physical credit card or currency. But there is more. Digital wallets, whether they are from Apple, Google, or elsewhere, can use airline miles, cell phone minutes, and even loyalty points. What we are talking about is the potential rise in numerous ways to use digital purchasing power.

Actually, there is a sense in which you are always using digital purchasing power, even when you use a credit card or currency. Dollars do not have value because the government says they do. Rather, it's the fact that you can exchange them for what you want to buy that gives them value. The same will be true with other forms of money. If you have, say, loyalty points in your digital wallet and you want to buy a pair of shoes at Nordstrom's, you will be able to use any combination of cash and loyalty points to make the purchase. You also may eventually be able to buy and sell loyalty points directly with other digital wallet owners. In exchange for their loyalty points, they will receive cash in their digital wallets. Money has always been whatever people decide works for them, and the digital revolution is making possible all sorts of new things that work. (See Chapter 26 for more on this.)

The Future of Coins and Even Currency Is Bleak

Consider the following statistics: Currency and coins constitute two-thirds of all transactions under $10. They account for almost 60 percent of transactions under $25. Digital wallets will probably reduce those percentages slowly, but eventually quite dramatically. Coins are costly to produce, and the risk of loss or theft is high with currency. We can thus expect that no tears will be shed for this improvement in **resource allocation** as we move into a future of digital wallets.

For Critical Analysis

1. Would it be a mistake to impose a uniform technology standard on today's payment systems?

2. What are the downsides of loading a digital wallet into your smartphone or tablet device?

3. What are the upsides for retailers of a smartphone payments system?

4. Will anyone be worse off with the rise in digital wallets? (*Hint:* Think armored trucks and Brinks.)

5. What is the downside, even with a fully functional digital wallet system in place, of never carrying any cash with you?

6. What is the difference between preloaded cash cards offered by, for example, American Express, and digital wallets?

CHAPTER 26

Cryptocurrencies

Whether it's the folded bills in our wallets or the jingling coins in our pockets, we traditionally think about money as something we can hold in our hands. When we wish to deposit, withdraw, or transfer funds, we most often go to the bank or to an automatic teller machine (ATM). Times are changing, however. Today, **cryptocurrencies**—that is, decentralized digital currencies that use encryption techniques for security—are on the rise. These **digital currencies** are created outside the banking system of any country in the world. Such currencies include Bitcoin, Zcash, and Litecoin. While it may seem that digital currencies are novelties, we actually are using them all the time.

MOST MONEY DOESN'T PHYSICALLY EXIST

It may surprise you to learn that in our **fractional reserve banking system,** banks and other **depository institutions** hold only tiny amounts of physical currency or coins to distribute to their customers. In other words, if you have an account in your local bank, that bank does not hold all the funds that belong to you in a vault in some part of the building. Rather, you have **property rights** to those funds in the amount of your bank balance. In turn, your bank has a **liability** to you in the equivalent amount. Because most of our transactions are not done with physical paper bills and coins, your demand for physical paper bills and coins is relatively limited.

So, then, what is your money, and where is it? In reality, almost all of your money consists of electronic entries in the bookkeeping ledgers of our banks, and this is true throughout the world. In that sense, all money is digital—except for the physical bills and coins that are out in the real world for everyday transactions. You access most of your money through debit card transactions, or by making online payments toward your credit card bills.

ENTER BITCOINS

Obviously, no one is going to be interested in a digital currency that anyone can copy or steal. That means some type of encryption system must be used to ensure the digital currency's security. Enter cryptography, which is the art of writing or solving codes. All transactions with digital money, whether they are debit card purchases at a gas station or massive funds transfers between banks, are protected by cryptography. If they weren't, criminals could easily steal the money, or even make their own money, not by printing it, but by writing computer code.

In 2008, however, the use of cryptography in protecting transactions entered an entirely new realm. In that year, a nine-page paper titled, "Bitcoin: A Peer-to-Peer Electronic-Cash System," went out to a cryptography newsgroup. In essence, this paper revealed that an unidentified programmer (using the pen name Satoshi Nakamoto) had created a new encryption-secured cryptocurrency—using units of account called "bitcoins." These bitcoins would enable digital transactions to occur between two users directly, with no bank or other third party involved.

In 2009, the first bitcoins were created online, and in the following year, the world's first bitcoin commercial transaction took place when a programmer in Florida used bitcoins to buy two pizzas.[1] Since then, the use (and occasional abuse) of bitcoins has grown dramatically. In addition, the bitcoin now has a host of competitors, including Litecoin, Darkcoin, Peercoin, Zcash, and Monero.

HOW DO CRYPTOCURRENCIES GET THEIR VALUE?

For centuries, gold (and sometimes silver) was the preferred money in circulation. Gold was heavy, durable, and pleasing to the eye. But the value of gold, and hence the "cash" that people held in their hand, fluctuated according to the **laws of supply and demand.** Essentially, the value of gold (cash) depended on how much was being mined throughout the

---

1   At the time, each bitcoin (denoted BTC) was worth well under a penny, so the purchase of the pizzas for 10,000 BTC cost the buyer about $25. In 2017, the price of a bitcoin hit $1500, making the value of 10,000 BTC equal to $15 million.

world. When there was a new gold discovery, for example, the value of gold declined (**inflation**) because of an increase in supply. Ultimately, the value of gold depended on the **marginal cost** of mining it, and on its use in non-monetary functions, such as jewelry. If the price went above mining costs, gold production rose and the price dropped. In the downward direction, the value of the gold as money could not drop below its use value in jewelry, because otherwise people would melt coins to convert the gold to rings and necklaces.

A cryptocurrency has no alternative use outside of functioning as a form of money. But its value does have some protection afforded to it because bitcoins and other such currencies are expensive to produce, just as gold is expensive to produce. Thus, even though this form of digital currency has no physical presence, it can still be valuable.

Blockchains, Mining, Miners, and All That

When you go to your bank or use a debit card to withdraw currency from your account, there is a recordkeeping procedure using a type of bookkeeping ledger that deducts an amount from your balance in that bank. Now imagine a set of ledgers similar to those in a bank that contain information on, say, bitcoin transactions. Let's assume that one hundred bitcoin users make transactions at about the same time. These one hundred transactions are put all together into a block. When this block of bitcoin transactions is verified by "bitcoin miners" (similar to gold miners), then the entire block of verified bitcoin transactions is added to all blocks of previous bitcoin transactions to become part of a **blockchain.**

All of the general information about the transactions is public. That means you can see any transaction you want. The blockchain keeps those records for you. Indeed, it creates a time-stamped record of receipts and expenditures among all bitcoin-system participants. Because of the blockchain technology and cryptography marriage, there is never a duplicate recording of the same transaction. Each successive block is protected by what is called a "hash," which is a unique fingerprint of the previous encryption code.

The blockchain can be thought of as a database. The difference is that the so-called header for each transaction is public. If you are a participant, however, you have a private key to gain access to the unique information related to your own transactions. Think of it in the same way as an online database of residents and addresses in your hometown. While the database of names and addresses is public, only you and your family have the specific key to enter your own house. In short, just because information regarding the physical location of your house is available to others, it does not mean that they can see inside your house. The privacy of bitcoin transactions is further enhanced because users employ pseudonyms.

Interestingly, Zcash, a competitor to Bitcoin, also offers a decentralized, open-source cryptocurrency, but with additional privacy features. In particular, Zcash users can fully shield their transactions. All that is publicly disclosed in their blockchain is that "something" happened at a particular point in time. In this sense, Zcash is being hailed as untraceable.

THE COSTS AND REVENUES OF MINING

Anyone can become a bitcoin miner. All it requires (in addition to some knowledge of computers and the software that runs them) is some expensive computer equipment, plus lots of electricity to run that equipment. It is this equipment that performs the work to certify and protect each block as it is added to the existing chain of blocks.

The protocol for the bitcoin system automatically does two things. First, it generates new bitcoins to pay the miners each time they verify a new block. This is the chief source of revenue for the miners. The protocol also adjusts the difficulty of certifying blocks over time, in such a way that the costs of mining increase exponentially. This will ultimately make it prohibitively expensive to produce a new bitcoin, and thus limit the ultimate number of coins to no more than 21 million. Once all of the bitcoins have been produced, people will still be compensated for certifying new blocks of transactions. But their fees will come directly from users of the system, and because no new bitcoins will be produced, the certifying individuals may no longer even be referred to as miners.

WHY ISN'T THE WORLD FLOODED WITH BITCOIN IMITATORS?

Cryptocurrencies provide security and privacy to their users, who are growing in number each year. So why, then, don't we see more cryptocurrencies in our everyday lives? The main reason is that the value of these currencies fluctuates too much to be a reliable source of "money" for everyone. In the early days of bitcoin, for example, there were fears that the system was not totally secure. And indeed, there was even one massive example of counterfeiting, but it was quickly discovered and undone. In another example from February 2014, the world's largest bitcoin exchange, Mt. Gox, declared bankruptcy because some smart computer experts had figured out a way to steal about 750,000 bitcoins.

As a result, the price of a bitcoin fell from a high of over $1,100 to about $400. Although the price eventually recovered, it continues to fluctuate substantially. Such value volatility must be resolved before cryptocurrencies become more routinely acceptable in transactions, and hence earn status as "money."

Blockchain Technology May Become Widespread

While you may never buy and sell bitcoins or Zcash, you may, in the not-too-distant future, implicitly end up using blockchain technology to conduct business. Today, for instance, when you buy a house or condominium, the transaction is complex. It often involves banks, insurers, attorneys, and regulators. Each participant in a house sale or purchase transaction maintains separate records. All of those records have to be verified and recorded each step of the way. Consequently, it usually takes at least a month and often two months or more to close a real estate transaction.

Consider what a blockchain system would offer in the same type of transaction. A digital, trusted ledger would be visible to all participants in the real estate transaction. Every element of the transaction would be known to each party quickly and easily, yet secured from fraud by cryptography. Not surprisingly, many banks are working on blockchain projects because of this unique and efficient feature. Blockchain technology will soon become a part of purchasing a car, too. In fact, one blockchain startup, La'zooz, is developing a ride-sharing app that allows drivers to connect directly with customers. No intermediary (or middleman) between driver and passenger, such as Lyft or Uber, will be required.

The Downside of Cryptocurrencies

While cryptocurrencies are definitely here to stay, they are not for everyone. Their value fluctuates, thereby negating some of their benefits as a substitute for a national currency. When you get paid in dollars, you know that when you spend them, their value will be about the same. That is not necessarily true if you get paid in bitcoins.[2]

Cryptocurrencies also have a dark side created by the secure privacy they offer. They can be used to hide illegal transactions, such as payments for prohibited drugs, or to move money among terrorists. They

---

2 Indeed, in 2017 a dispute over whether to increase the size of the blockchain used in bitcoins caused their value to drop by more than 10 percent in just three days. The dispute also led to the possibility that there may be two parallel bitcoin systems in existence by the time you read this.

may also allow individuals to engage in transactions that should otherwise be taxed. Bitcoins have even been used to facilitate a type of hacking in which an individual computer or entire computer system is taken over. Control is not returned unless the owner pays a ransom—in bitcoins.

If you are not interested in using bitcoins as money for transactions, you can simply think of them as an investment in an asset whose value fluctuates but may grow over time. In either case, cryptocurrencies and the systems on which they are based will be affecting our way of doing business for years to come. Indeed, by the time you read this, you may well be using the blockchain technology that lies behind cryptocurrencies, without even knowing it.

FOR CRITICAL ANALYSIS

1. Why don't we use gold or silver coins as a physical means to make payments for purchases of goods and services today?

2. Why are cryptocurrencies currently not used for many transactions throughout the world?

3. How are cryptocurrencies able to avoid using the current banking systems?

4. Banks use digital additions and subtractions for maintaining the account balances of their customers. Users of the bitcoin system also use a similar system in the sense that a blockchain is basically a set of ledgers showing additions and subtractions to individuals' bitcoin accounts. Are there any differences between the two systems? If so, what are they?

5. Explain why there were so many bitcoin transactions within China when the Chinese national currency lost value in terms of other currencies of the world. The Chinese government has restricted the ability of Chinese citizens to move financial assets out of China. What has this restriction done to the demand for bitcoins in China?

6. If cryptocurrencies make illegal hacking more profitable, facilitate trade in illegal drugs, and enable terrorists to move funds around the world more securely, is it possible that these new means of payment could actually make society as a whole worse off? Be sure to consider the offsetting benefits of cryptocurrencies when formulating your answer.

Globalization and International Finance

CHAPTER 27

The Value of the Dollar

When the euro was introduced in 1999, you could purchase one for $1.18. Three years later, when euro banknotes and coins began circulating as the monetary unit of most of the **European Union (EU),** the market price of the euro had fallen to $0.90. Since then, the euro's price has fluctuated between $0.86 and $1.70. This pattern of fluctuating prices is not unique to the euro. In a world of **flexible exchange rates,** the forces of **demand** and **supply** determine the prices at which different **currencies** trade for each other. Thus, if the demand for euros rises, its price will rise, and if the demand falls, so too will its price. And what is true for the euro is just as true for the British pound sterling, the Japanese yen, and our very own U.S. dollar. As we shall see, these changes in market forces, and the resulting changes in **exchange rates,** play a key role in determining patterns of international trade.

SOME TERMINOLOGY

Although we referred to the dollar price of the euro, we could just as well have talked of the euro price of the dollar. Thus, if it takes $1.10 to purchase a euro, it must also be true that a dollar buys less than a euro. In fact, it buys exactly 1/1.10 euros in this example. That is, the euro price of the dollar is €0.91 (where € is the symbol for the euro). The exchange rate between the two currencies can be expressed either way, although in the United States people usually refer to the exchange rate as the dollar price of foreign currency and so too shall we. In this example, the exchange rate between the dollar and the euro is thus $1.10.

177

You will also hear some people, especially journalists and politicians, talk about a "stronger" or "weaker" dollar, accompanied by pronouncements that one or the other condition is good for the United States. When people say the dollar has gotten "stronger," what they mean is that one dollar will buy more units of foreign currency than it used to. Hence, a reduction in the exchange rate from, say, $1.10 to $1.05 per euro amounts to a stronger dollar. Conversely, if the dollar price of the euro rises from $1.10 to $1.20, this would mean that the dollar was weaker because one dollar would buy fewer euros.

Good News or Bad?

Is a weaker dollar good news or bad? Like most value judgments (notice the words *good* and *bad*), the answer is in the eye of the beholder. Suppose the price of the euro rises from $1.10 to $1.25. We say that the dollar has gotten weaker relative to the euro because people must pay more dollars for each euro. Because American consumers must eventually come up with euros if they want to buy French wine or Italian pasta, when the euro becomes more expensive, European goods become more expensive for American consumers.[1] Thus, from the perspective of American consumers, a weak dollar is bad news.

But producers in the United States may have a different view of the world. For example, automobile manufacturers with plants in the United States compete with manufacturers that have European facilities. When the dollar price of the euro rises, so does the dollar price of cars made in Europe. This induces some American consumers to "buy American," which is surely good news for the companies that receive their business. Similarly, recall that the *rise* in the price of the euro is equivalent to a *fall* in the price of the dollar. Such a move in the exchange rate makes American-made goods cheaper abroad. As a result, foreign consumers are also more likely to "buy American," again good news for the companies from whom they purchase. Thus, a weaker dollar encourages exports and discourages imports, but whether that is "good" or "bad" news is clearly a matter on which people might reasonably disagree.

Now, what about the consequences of a "stronger" dollar? When the dollar can buy more euros, this means it can also buy more European goods. This clearly benefits American consumers, so we conclude that they like a strong dollar. American producers, however, will have a different take on matters. They will lose business from American customers,

---

1 Of course, consumers typically do not physically obtain the euros themselves, but the importers who bring the goods in on their behalf must certainly do so.

who are now more likely to "buy European." In addition, people in the EU will now find American goods more expensive because the dollar is now more expensive. So they will buy fewer American goods and make more purchases at home. Thus, we conclude that a stronger dollar will encourage imports into the United States and discourage exports from the United States. Presumably, American consumers and producers will have quite different opinions on whether this is good news or bad.

PURCHASING POWER PARITY

Of course, exchange rates do not move around without cause. There are four well-established forces that play key roles in making them what they are. The first of these, which is by far the most important long-run determinant of exchange rates, is called **purchasing power parity (PPP)**. This principle simply states that the relative values of different currencies must ultimately reflect their **purchasing power** in their home countries.

To see how this works, let's consider the exchange rate between the United States and Switzerland, which uses the Swiss franc as its currency. Over the past sixty years, the exchange rate between these two currencies has varied between roughly $0.23 and $1.38—that is, by a factor of six. In the 1960s, for example, the exchange rate was near the bottom end of that range, but it has followed a persistent rise until a few years ago, albeit with ups and downs along the way. The reason the Swiss franc has risen in value relative to the U.S. dollar is simple: Typically, the **inflation** rate in Switzerland has been much lower than that in the United States. The amount of goods that American dollars would buy generally has been shrinking, so the Swiss demand for dollars has fallen, even as Americans have tried to unload their depreciating dollars for Swiss francs. Together, these forces helped push the value of the Swiss franc up, and so the exchange rate rose, to $0.40, then $0.70, and then even above $1.00.

This process applies across all countries. When the **price level** rises in country A relative to the price level in country B, people in both nations will switch some of their purchases of goods from country A to country B. This will push down the value of A's currency and push up the value of B's currency. In fact, this tendency is so strong that it will continue until "parity" is reached. If A's price level *rises* 20 percent relative to B's price level, A's currency ultimately will *fall* in value by 20 percent relative to B's currency. It may take a while for this adjustment to work out, and it may be temporarily masked by some of the forces we shall talk about next, but eventually it will happen.

INTEREST RATES

One key reason for wishing to acquire the currency of another nation is that you want to acquire goods produced in that nation. But there is an added reason: You may wish to invest or to lend funds in that nation. For example, suppose you wanted to purchase **bonds** issued by a Canadian corporation. These would be denominated in Canadian dollars (C$), so you would first have to obtain those Canadian dollars before you could purchase the bonds. Given this, it should be apparent that one of the factors influencing your demand for Canadian dollars is the rate of return, or interest rate, on **investments** in Canada, compared to the interest rate on investments elsewhere. The simplest way of putting this is that if interest rates in Canada rise relative to interest rates in the United States, investors will want to move funds from the United States into Canada. That is, there will be a drop in the demand for U.S. dollars and a rise in the demand for Canadian dollars, and so the exchange rate will rise: You will have to give up more U.S. dollars to obtain one Canadian dollar. The U.S. dollar will have become "weaker" against the Canadian currency.

Note that the interest rates we speak of are **real interest rates,** that is, adjusted for any expected inflation. If interest rates rise in Canada because of an increase in the expected inflation rate there, this hardly makes them more attractive to American, European, or Chinese investors. It simply neutralizes the effects of the higher expected inflation. Similarly, we must be careful to compare interest rates on obligations that have the same **default risk.** If the interest rate is high on bonds issued by a Canadian company that is in danger of **bankruptcy,** that higher interest rate simply compensates **bondholders** for the added default risk they face. It does not make those bonds unusually attractive to investors in the United States or elsewhere.

But as long as we are careful to adjust for expected inflation and risk, interest rate differences can sometimes be quite useful in understanding events. For example, during the late nineteenth century, inflation- and risk-adjusted interest rates were higher in the United States than they were in Britain because the United States was rebuilding from the Civil War, settling the West, and industrializing at a rapid rate. All of these factors made the United States a productive place in which to invest. The higher rate of return in the United States made it attractive for British investors to lend funds to American firms, which in turn meant a higher demand for American dollars. As a result, the American dollar was more valuable on world markets than it otherwise would have been.

HARD CURRENCY

If you have ever visited a developing nation, you may have heard people refer to "hard currency." You may even have had them insist you pay for your purchases not with the local currency but with American dollars or euros or even Swiss francs. The reasoning behind this insistence is simple.

In such countries, whatever the *current* state of economic and political affairs, the *future* state of both is often filled with great uncertainty. Perhaps the current government's political support is not too secure. Or there may be the simmering threat of a military-backed coup. Or maybe there is a suspicion that the national government will not be able to finance its future spending with conventional taxes. Should any of these eventualities be realized, the likely result is that the government will resort to printing money as a means of financing its activities, causing future high inflation that will devastate the purchasing power of the local currency. And because the exact timing and magnitude of this outcome are highly uncertain, so is the expected future value of the local currency.

To reduce their risk, people thus try to hold currencies whose value is unlikely to be subject to political vagaries—and these are currencies issued by strong democratic governments, such as those in the United States and the EU. This increases the demand for such currencies and thus tends to set their values in world markets higher than they otherwise would be. The reference to "hard currency" stems from the notion that the purchasing power of such currencies is as stable as a rock—which it is, compared to the local monies that people are trying to avoid holding.

BOEING AND THE BEATLES

The final key factor that helps determine exchange rates is quite simply the relative attractiveness of the goods produced in various nations. Consider the Boeing Corporation, long regarded as the maker of some of the best commercial jet planes in existence. Airlines all over the world purchase billions of dollars' worth of Boeing aircraft every year. To do this, they must acquire U.S. dollars, and their demand for dollars makes the value of the dollar on world markets higher than it otherwise would be.

Of course, the residents of foreign countries have been known to produce some nice products themselves. Many people feel that the best wines come from France, the best ties from Italy, and so forth. And then there are the Beatles, perhaps the most prolific and popular rock group ever, at least measured by worldwide sales of music. When the Beatles hit the music scene in the 1960s, millions of Americans wanted to acquire recordings of their songs. To do so, they first had to acquire pounds sterling (the money used in Britain). This increased the demand for pounds sterling and thus caused the dollar price of the pound to rise in foreign exchange markets. Thus, the next time you pay to download music of the British rock group Coldplay, you will know that your decision to buy their music has pushed the dollar price of the pound sterling up, even if just by the tiniest of amounts.

For Critical Analysis

1. Although Denmark is a member of the EU, it does not use the euro as its monetary unit. Instead it uses the krone. If Denmark decided to switch from the krone to the euro, how might this decision affect the value of the euro in foreign exchange markets?

2. In an effort to discourage drug smugglers from using U.S. currency in major drug deals, the U.S. government refuses to issue currency in denominations greater than $100. How does this policy decision affect the demand for dollars and thus the exchange rate between the dollar and other currencies, such as the euro (which comes in denominations as big as €500, the equivalent of over $500)?

3. Sometimes national governments decide that they want their currencies to be more valuable than they currently are. Explain how, if a country wants to raise the value of its currency in foreign exchange markets, it might use the following tools to do so:

   a. Altering the rate of growth in its money supply, thus changing the current and expected inflation rate

   b. Limiting the ability of citizens to invest in foreign nations

   c. Imposing **tariffs** or **quotas** on imports

   d. Subsidizing exports by domestic firms

4. From shortly after World War II to the early 1970s, the United States (like many countries) was on a system of fixed exchange rates. That is, the U.S. government pledged to take whatever actions were necessary to keep the value of the dollar fixed relative to other currencies. Consider the emergence of the Beatles in the 1960s. What would the U.S. government have to do to prevent the value of the

dollar from changing as a result of "Beatlemania" in America? Alternatively, consider the introduction of the popular Boeing 707 in the 1950s. What would the U.S. government have to do to prevent the value of the dollar from changing as a result?

5. Why do politicians worry about whether the dollar is "strong" or "weak"?

6. What do you think happened to the value of the U.S. dollar when BMW (a German company) moved an important part of its manufacturing facilities to the United States some years ago? Explain.

CHAPTER 28

The Eurozone after Brexit

Here is a fictitious story about the United States. Assume that until twenty years ago, all fifty states were separate countries with their own separate currencies and their own **central banks.** Assume further that there were no trade restrictions so that goods and services could be exchanged between any two state-countries. Next assume that all fifty got together and agreed to use one currency—the dollar—controlled by one central bank in Washington, D.C. Further assume that all the states signed a formal agreement in which they established that there would be no government transfers of income from one state to another. They also agreed that none of them would run much of a government deficit.

Flash forward twenty years. Certain states did not "follow the rules." They ended up with huge government deficits because of generous welfare spending, generous pay and pension packages for their government employees, and lavish state building projects. What to do? Just ask all of the other states to help them out because of the **debt crisis** they faced. And why would other states likely help them out? There are two reasons. First, if the states with debt crises do not get help, they will go bankrupt. This will reduce the demand for goods from other states, tending to raise unemployment and lower economic growth. Second, bankruptcies in some states will likely cause people in other nations around the world to fear even more defaults by other states. This will cause a loss of confidence in the dollar and might even force all of the states to abandon the dollar as their common currency.

MOVE FROM FANTASY INTO EUROPEAN REALITY

Of course, the situation just described did not actually happen twenty years ago in the United States. Rather, it happened in the so-called **Eurozone** in Europe. The **European Union (EU)** started decades ago and now has twenty-eight member countries. Nineteen of those countries all use one currency—the **euro.**

When the euro was created at the very end of the twentieth century, all the participating countries signed agreements. They pledged that the creation of the Eurozone was not the creation of a welfare system in which richer countries would transfer wealth to poorer countries. There was also an agreement that participating countries' **budget deficits** would not exceed 3 percent of **gross domestic product (GDP)** in any one country.

It took less than a decade for this system to face a series of crises. Some politicians figured out that if their nation got into financial trouble, other Eurozone countries would answer their cries for help. After all, no one would want to see the demise of the euro, and therefore no one would want to see any Eurozone country collapse and pull out of the one-currency system.

GREECE PAVED THE WAY

Greece has never been a rich country. Apart from its antiquities, Greece has been best known for corruption. For years, the average Greek family has paid about $2,000 annually in "official" bribes. The simple fact is that if you want anything done in Greece, you better grease the skids (no pun intended). Greece was not allowed to join the Eurozone at first, but then was accepted because it showed it had a budget deficit of only 4 percent of GDP. Six months after its acceptance, Greek government officials admitted that the numbers were a little off—its deficit had actually been 12 percent of GDP, triple what it originally had claimed. Eurozone leaders said "tsk, tsk" and asked Greece to behave like a proper member of the one-currency area. After this bit of scolding, Greece disappeared from the financial news headlines.

Then Greece (population: 11.3 million) successfully bid on the 2004 summer Olympics. Conservative estimates place the cost to that small country of at least $15 billion, but the reality is probably much more. Soon after the glow of the XXVIII Olympiad wore off, Greece started having trouble paying its bills. It turned out that government spending was rising much faster than government revenues. Lenders got nervous, so when Greece went to finance those deficits, its borrowing costs started to rise. It called for help.

The First Greek Bailout

Help came in the form of "emergency" grants, gifts, and loans from other EU countries in the Eurozone in 2010. Right after the first bailout, seeing how easy it was to get financial help, Greek politicians did not do what they had promised. They sold off no government assets. They reformed no labor laws. They eliminated no corruption. Years later, they are still asking for more time to "fix" their economy, and, of course, they are asking for more loans from the rest of their Eurozone partners and from the **International Monetary Fund** (of which the United States is a paying member).

Measured unemployment in Greece is about 25 percent and among youths almost 50 percent. Per-unit labor costs in Greece are higher than they are even in high-wage Germany. But many European leaders still think they can "save" Greece with more bailouts.

What we have seen in Greece are the consequences of **moral hazard.** Greek politicians know that they can always get someone else to pay for their mistakes. Hence, they are not so careful and certainly not so reform-minded as to cut government spending and thereby endanger their cushy government jobs that pay high salaries and provide expensive benefits.

Italy—A Larger Greece?

While Italy seems prosperous to many visitors, it, too, has fallen victim to the consequences of moral hazard. As just one example, for years there was a large group of Italians who could retire from government service in their early forties. Although this provision has been eliminated for new retirees, there remain half a million former government workers collecting pensions after retiring at an average age of forty-two.

Italy is also known as one of the European leaders in graft and corruption, some of which is siphoned off by different Mafia organizations. Many government-sponsored and taxpayer-funded public works projects end up unfinished, even decades later. Consider Italy's A3 highway, which was begun in the 1960s. It starts outside of Naples and goes for three hundred miles to the south. Although the A3 was officially declared to be "complete" in 2016, portions of it still resemble obstacle courses due to construction sites that linger. Some say that organized crime has been responsible for the delays. Others say that this highway represents the rotten fruits of a jobs-for-votes culture.

Italy has not asked for an EU bailout yet, but it may have by the time you read this. Mind you, Italy is not as bad off as the statistics seem to show. It has a thriving **underground economy** that may represent as much as 30 percent of GDP. What is certain is that Italian politicians know that if they do not make the reforms necessary to increase competitiveness and economic growth and to reduce wasteful government spending, other members of the Eurozone will bail them out.

SPAIN, OLÉ!

Italy's neighbor, Spain, claimed for years that it would not need a bailout. The Spanish government's borrowing costs, nonetheless, have stayed high because outside investors are worried that it will not be able to pay back its debt obligations. Although the EU had to bail out the Spanish banking system back in 2012, the Spanish government has managed to avoid defaulting on its loans—so far.

Spain talks big about "austerity." That is the word that few governments want to mention to their electorates, because austerity is supposed to mean reduced government expenditures. In Spain, heeding the wishes of the International Monetary Fund, the **European Central Bank (ECB),** and Eurozone leaders, the Spanish government declared that it would reduce many expenditures. But at the same time, it promised its citizens a 1 percent increase in pension payments per recipient in 2013. Sound familiar? It is called the don't-kick-me-out-of-office ploy that a politician can use when she or he knows that there is a bailout on the horizon. The ever-present moral hazard problem rears its ugly head again.

Spain's neighbor to the west, Portugal, may be in even worse trouble. Since joining the European Union and the Eurozone, Portuguese labor unions and government workers have succeeded in obtaining much higher salaries. The result is that Portuguese per-unit labor costs are 40 percent higher than those in Germany. Crying on the shoulders of Eurozone leaders, Portuguese politicians have shown how serious they are by not increasing government employee salaries any further. There has been little talk about reducing those bloated salaries, even though the government was happy to accept an EU bailout in late 2010. By 2016, Portuguese politicians were calling for an end to the nation's austerity measures, even though all outside observers agreed that the nation had begun to reform.

Portugal, like Spain, has seen its international borrowing costs rise because outside lenders fear that even the EU may not be able to prevent the government from defaulting on its debt.

I.O.U.s AS FAR AS THE EYE CAN SEE

Adoption of the euro meant that less-developed nations on the periphery of Europe—Greece and Portugal, just to name a few—could borrow as cheaply as core nations, such as France and Germany. Investors in the core nations poured enormous sums into the periphery, much of it spent on new houses, higher pay, pensions for more government employees, and Olympic stadiums. When recession struck in 2007, it became clear that people in Greece, Portugal, and Spain, for example, had borrowed too many euros and would have trouble paying them back.

Let's look at the results: **national debt** per person over the last twenty years skyrocketed. It increased 150 percent in Portugal and doubled in Spain, France, and Greece. The average Greek has a public debt I.O.U. of $32,000. In France that number is $35,000. Spanish citizens owe $25,000 apiece. Per capita public debt in Portugal is only $24,000, but that sum exceeds per capita income in that nation.

Calling the Money Lenders to the Rescue

Member nations in the Eurozone ceded their monetary independence to the ECB just before the Eurozone became reality. The ECB has a mission similar to that of the Federal Reserve System in the United States—to provide liquidity but never to bail out individual member states. In spite of its charter, the European Central Bank announced in the fall of 2012 that it was embarking on a plan of unlimited buying of the government debt of troubled Eurozone countries. As a consequence, the ECB effectively replaced private credit markets as a cash source for Spain and Italy, thereby lowering their borrowing costs and relieving them of the threat of **insolvency.** And this is so even though the ECB was never supposed to favor countries in crisis over countries that are not facing crises.

Moral hazard is flying around the Eurozone faster than ever. Perhaps for a while, Eurozone citizens will not understand that they are actually subsidizing the profligate ways and lack of labor market reforms in Greece, Italy, Spain, and Portugal.

The New, New Eurozone Bailout Fund

The organized bailouts started with the **Interim European Financial Stability Facility.** Then, in 2012 yet another way to provide bailouts was created. It is called the **European Stability Mechanism (ESM).** This Eurozone bailout gimmick took two years to design after leaders in the **currency union** had decided to set it up as a permanent safety net for countries in financial troubles. Its charter allows it to lend as much as €500 billion to governments that are unable to raise funds in international bond markets.

All nineteen Eurozone countries must contribute to ESM funding based on the size of their economies. Thus far, €80 billion has been contributed to the fund, which has already made loans of more than €260 billion. Indeed, the ESM now holds 50 percent of the public debt of Greece. All Eurozone countries are jointly liable for the new rescue fund. They are also jointly responsible for the ECB's liabilities. No better situation could arise for countries in trouble, such as Greece, Italy, Portugal, and Spain. These nations' governments can keep pretending to tighten their belts, keep pretending to reform their rigid labor markets, and keep pretending that they really are going to have lots of economic growth in the future. They know the truth, though, that their individual liabilities for being bailed out are going to be a small part of the joint liability of all nineteen countries.

WHY CAN'T EUROZONE COUNTRIES POLICE EACH OTHER?

Seeing the disarray in so many Eurozone countries' budgets, member-country politicians agreed in the fall of 2012 to form a so-called **fiscal pact,** which now exists as the Fiscal Stability Treaty. This Eurozone invention is supposed to involve a central entity that will oversee the budgets of each Eurozone government. Somehow, this oversight mechanism will cause less red ink to flow in each Eurozone country. The Treaty mandates that the public debts of each of its signatories will not exceed 60 percent of that nation's GDP. Almost all of the Eurozone members exceed that limit, while Italy and Portugal are currently at double the limit, with Greece leading the way at triple the limit. Fortunately, the treaty allows for transitional periods for those nations not in compliance. In practice, the treaty has so far had little visible impact on fiscal practices in the Eurozone.

BREXIT—ITS IMPACT ON THE EUROZONE

Since the EU's earliest days, it has moved toward "one Europe," a continent in which there were national borders, but in which trade, immigration, monetary and fiscal policy, perhaps even legal systems were seamless. Even though the United Kingdom (UK) was an original member of the EU, the nation has long felt itself different in important ways from the rest of Europe—culturally, legally, and economically. Eventually, the move toward complete European unification stirred serious opposition within the United Kingdom.

When British voters went to the polls in 2016 to determine whether the United Kingdom would remain within the European Union or leave it, the results stunned many throughout the world. Despite close polls leading up to the referendum, Brits who wanted to exit the EU, or "Brexit," were supposed to lose. The political analysts—and even the Irish bookies—were wrong, however. Brexit supporters won.

As a result of this surprising victory, the UK's currency, the pound sterling, immediately took a beating—dropping by more than 15 percent within short order. The pound's decline certainly made imports more expensive for British citizens, but it also made exports cheaper for those buying British cars, jet engines, and fine art. Because the UK's currency has always been the pound—even though it is a long-time member of the EU—the country was never truly part of the Eurozone. In other words, Brexit did not mean leaving the euro currency. Nonetheless, Brexit has affected the long-term viability of the euro.

For example, one Brexit financial fall-out was the EU European Council's almost immediate declaration that there would be no further attempts to construct a "United States of Europe." Simply put, there would be no true fiscal union among EU members. But such a fiscal union—with centralized spending and taxing decisions—is ultimately the key to maintaining the euro. Without fiscal union, the incentives that have thus far strained the Eurozone will ultimately end it.

By 2017, Greece and Portugal had created further woes for the Eurozone by effectively refusing to do any real fiscal housekeeping. Public expenditures in France had reached 57 percent of GDP, and its public debt was approximately 100 percent of GDP. Italy was having its own financial problems—namely, its banks had 17 percent nonperforming loans outstanding. To give you some perspective, even at the depths of the Great Recession of 2007–09 in the United States, our banks only had 5 percent nonperforming loans outstanding. By the time you read this, you may also be reading about a strong political movement in Italy to leave the Eurozone so it can repay its debts in its pre-EU currency, the lira, instead of in euros.

One thing is clear: With Brexit, British voters, knowingly or not, started the reversal of the so-called European Project of the last twenty years. We'll keep you posted as events unfold.

FOR CRITICAL ANALYSIS

1. Why would a government continue to borrow if it knew it could never pay back all of the loans, including interest?

2. Why would international bond buyers be willing to purchase government bonds from Greece, Spain, Portugal, and Italy when there appears to be some risk that those governments will not be able to pay back those loans?

3. If labor costs are extremely high in one country compared to another, what is the usual mechanism that allows the high-cost country to still be competitive in its export markets?

4. What are the benefits to the nineteen Eurozone countries of having a common currency? (*Hint:* What are the benefits of the fifty states using dollars, rather than fifty separate monies?)

5. What makes almost all government politicians everywhere in the world continue to spend more than is collected in taxes?

6. What would happen to Greece if it pulled out of the Eurozone and went back to using its former national currency, the drachma?

CHAPTER 29

The Global Power of the Big Mac

It seems obvious that the average western European or American or Canadian earns a higher income than the average resident of countries such as China and India. What is more difficult to estimate is how *much* better off the citizens are in one nation compared to another. The most obvious obstacle to creating such an estimate is the matter of national currencies. In the United States, for example, we probably want to make income comparisons in dollars. But dollars are not the national currency in Western Europe or in China or India or Japan, so we must somehow convert from one currency to another. How shall we do this?

FOREIGN EXCHANGE RATES

You know that if you take a trip to another country, you will have to pay in the currency of that country. If you go to Europe, in nineteen countries, you will buy goods with euros. If you go to India, you will pay in rupees. If you go to Russia, you will make purchases using rubles.

So, to compare the average Russian's income in rubles with the average American's income in dollars, we must convert the rubles to the equivalent amount of dollars. The data for converting are readily available on a daily basis. That is because there is a worldwide market in **foreign exchange,** or national currencies. You might find that it takes sixty rubles (or sixty rupees) to buy one dollar. So, as a first approximation, this means that to compare incomes across the world, simple arithmetic is involved. We convert, via **foreign exchange rate** tables—found on hundreds of Internet sites—other nations' average incomes in their own currencies to what they are in the U.S. currency, dollars.

For example, if the average income in France is 34,000 euros, we multiply the current euro exchange rate by that number. Suppose the exchange rate is such that one euro equals 1.10 dollars. Then average income in France is 34,000 euros times 1.1 dollars per euro, or $37,400.

When we do such calculations, we find that on an exchange-rate basis, the average American is thirty-five times richer than the average Indian, almost seven times richer than the average citizen of China, and about six times richer than the average Russian.

Problems with Using Market Exchange Rates

Foreign exchange rates are a function of world **supply and demand** (sound familiar?). But demand and supply of currencies is ultimately derived from (or determined by) the demand and supply of, among other things, **traded goods.** Traded goods (and services) are those that, as the name suggests, are traded across national borders. Some examples of traded goods are wines, automobiles, wheat, and shoes. If all goods were traded and if that trade occurred with no distortions, then exchange rates would permit us to perfectly compare incomes around the world.

But there is a complication: Not all goods and services that we consume are traded goods. **Non-traded goods** include houses, haircuts, house-cleaning services, and landscaping, as well as many others. Non-traded goods and services are not involved in exchange across countries' borders.

The existence of non-traded goods implies that bias will result if we use only exchange rates to make international comparisons. This is because in poorer countries, wages are low, and so non-traded goods (made with that low-cost labor) are likely to be the cheapest. That is, in low-income nations we expect restaurant meals, beauty salon services, and house cleaning to be much less expensive than those same items in high-income nations. Hence, if we use current exchange rates—based on traded goods—to convert incomes to a common currency, differences in average incomes between low-wage nations and high-wage nations are going to be exaggerated.

Often, you will read newspaper stories about a developing country in which the average income is, say, $1,000 a year. That number is typically derived from current foreign exchange rates. It does not take account of how cheaply residents in that country can buy basic foods and services that are not traded in international markets.

PURCHASING POWER PARITY—A SOLUTION?

Somehow we have to adjust current exchange rates to account for differences in the true cost of living across countries. To do so, we may use a concept known as **purchasing power parity,** which creates a type of adjusted foreign exchange rate.[1] The details of how the World Bank and other organizations calculate various purchasing power parity measures for two hundred countries are not important here. Suffice it to say that, in doing so, attempts are made to correct market foreign exchange rates for the relative cost of living in each country. So, on a purchasing power parity basis—taking into account the lower cost of living in India, China, and Russia—average income in the United States is only nine times higher than in India, three times higher than in China, and about 2.5 times as high as in Russia.

A major problem remains, nonetheless. Purchasing power adjustments are difficult to calculate in each country. The residents of each nation buy different combinations of goods and services or, in the alternative, they buy similar goods and services but with subtle variations in quality. Not only are the calculations difficult but also there are disputes over the best way to do them for each country, leading to doubts about whether the measures *really* account for differences in the cost of living.

It is here that a humble sandwich enters our story.

BIG MAC TO THE RESCUE

Since 1967, a monster burger called the Big Mac has been a featured item on the menu of McDonald's restaurants. A typical Big Mac is created using virtually identical ingredients around the world (although substitution occurs where religious or cultural norms rule out beef). Big Macs are produced according to a uniform process detailed in the McDonald's six hundred-page manual. As well as being a "standard product," local prices of Big Macs are not distorted by international transportation and distribution costs.

In light of these facts, since 1986, the magazine *The Economist* has developed a Big Mac Index. By using one good only—a Big Mac—*The Economist* has thereby created a means of comparing the cost of living around the world and also a means of determining how much exchange rates fail to account for non-traded goods.

---

1 Obviously, there is no market for anything measured in units of purchasing power parity.

Keeping in mind that the methods of production and the ingredients are the same in Big Macs everywhere, if we convert international Big Mac prices using exchange rates, we "should" get exactly the same price everywhere. But if, using exchange rates, we calculate that a Big Mac costs $6.60 in Switzerland, but only $5.00 in the United States, this says that a dollar does not go very far in Switzerland. That is, the cost of living in Switzerland is relatively high, most likely because non-traded goods (such as housing) are quite expensive there. Similarly, if we also find that, at current exchange rates, a Big Mac costs the equivalent of $2.80 in China, we have found that the dollar goes a long way there: The cost of living is low in China compared to that in the United States. Again, this is most likely because non-traded goods made with low-wage labor are quite cheap in China.

The upshot is that if we adjust incomes using the Big Mac index to correct for differences in the cost of living, we can get a much better idea of relative real incomes. In one recent year, for example, using exchange rates, income in Switzerland was about $80,000, compared to about $56,000 in the United States. After correcting with the aid of the Big Mac, however, we find that real income in Switzerland is only about $60,000—still higher than that in the United States, but not by much.

McWages, Real Wages, and Well-Being

Now consider creating a McWage. Given that the talent necessary to make a Big Mac is about the same everywhere, we can collect information on the wages of Big Mac preparers throughout the world. This will provide us with a comparison of the cost of hiring that uniform quality of labor across countries. If we then take McWages and divide them by the local price of a Big Mac, we can discern how many Big Mac equivalents each worker is paid per hour. This is a simple, albeit one-good specific, measure of the **real wage** for low-skill workers, that is, the wage rate for such workers adjusted for the cost of living in each nation. And this measure— "Big Macs per hour"—can be constructed without worrying about biases in exchange rates or complicated purchasing power parity calculations.

That is exactly what economists Orley Ashenfelter and Stepan Jurajda have done. They have found that low-skill workers in the United States earned about 2.5 Big Macs per hour (or BMPH), compared to the 3.1 BMPH earned in Japan. In Canada and Western Europe, workers were paid a bit under 2.2 BMPH. Using the same calculations, the authors found that workers in Russia earned about 1.2 BMPH, while Eastern European workers collected about 0.8. Workers in China earned about 0.6 BMPH, while those in India earned only about 0.4. The bottom line is that using the BMPH index, we see that standards of living among workers vary greatly around the world, but not nearly to the extent that is suggested by exchange rates.

TRENDS IN PRODUCTIVITY

A basic tenet of economics is that in competitive labor markets (and that is certainly where McDonald's gets its workers) people are paid based on what they produce. Thus, using the data mentioned above, we can infer that workers in the United States are only about 15 percent more productive than those in Canada or Western Europe, but they are about four times as productive as those in China.

We can also look at the patterns of change in the BMPH index over time to give us an idea of how **productivity** is evolving around the world. As one example, between 2000 and 2007, McWages in the United States rose by 13 percent while the price of a Big Mac jumped by 21 percent. That means that real wages for low-skill workers *fell* in the United States by about 8 percent over this period. By the same calculation for the same period, productivity and thus real wages rose 60 percent in China and by over 50 percent in India. Clearly, average productivity was rising sharply in these two countries.

Between 2007 and 2016, real wages continued to fall (but more slowly) in developed nations such as the United States, Canada, and Western Europe. In most developing nations, real wages have been rising, although much more slowly than before. The good news of this story is that developing nations are generally closing the standard of living gap. The bad news is that the world's financial crisis and its aftermath have diminished opportunities around the world for low-skill workers, a development that is surely worth monitoring in the future.

FOR CRITICAL ANALYSIS

1. Assume you are going to take a trip to Paris. You buy euros at your local bank or at the airport. Then you start spending them once you are in Paris. Every time you buy something there, you explicitly or implicitly translate the euro price into dollars. Often, you might say to yourself, "How do Parisians afford such high prices?" What is wrong with this line of reasoning? (*Hint:* In what currency do Parisians earn their income?)

2. Why don't the local prices of restaurant meals, haircuts, and gardening services affect a country's exchange rate?

3. If the same amount of materials and the same methods are used to produce Big Macs in over one hundred twenty countries, why are the prices of Big Macs not all the same, expressed in dollars?

4. Is there anything that a Big Mac preparer in a developing country can do to earn a higher real wage rate?

5. Why does McDonald's provide a six hundred-page manual to the company's franchises in every country? (*Hint:* What are the ways that any franchisor can monitor the quality of its franchisees?)

6. In a wealthy country, wages are high not only in the traded goods and services sector but also in the non-traded goods and services sector. Why? (*Hint:* Are there two separate labor markets or just one?)

CHAPTER 30

The Opposition to Globalization

The last twenty-five years has been a time of great change on the international trade front. The North American Free Trade Agreement (NAFTA), for example, substantially reduced **trade barriers** among citizens of Canada, the United States, and Mexico. On a global scale, the Uruguay Round of the General Agreement on Tariffs and Trade (GATT) was ratified by 117 nations, including the United States. Under the terms of this agreement, the **World Trade Organization (WTO),** whose membership now numbers more than 150, replaced GATT, and **tariffs** were cut worldwide. Agricultural **subsidies** were also reduced, and patent protections were extended. The WTO has also established arbitration boards to settle international disputes over trade issues.

The Gains from Trade

Many economists believe that both NAFTA and the agreements reached during the Uruguay Round were victories not only for free trade and **globalization** (the integration of national economies into an international economy) but also for the citizens of the participating nations. Nevertheless, many noneconomists, particularly politicians, have opposed these agreements. Indeed, a centerpiece of President Trump's 2016 campaign was a promise to dismantle NAFTA and start a trade war with China. In light of the chasm between economic evidence and political rhetoric, it is important to understand what is beneficial about NAFTA, the Uruguay Round, the WTO, and free trade and globalization.

Voluntary trade creates new **wealth.** In voluntary trade, both parties in an exchange gain. They give up something of lesser value to them in return for something of greater value to them. In this sense, exchanges are always unequal. But it is this unequal nature of exchange that is the source of the increased **productivity** and higher wealth that occur whenever trade takes place. When we engage in exchange, what we give up is worth less than what we get—for if this were not true, we would not have traded. What is true for us is also true for our trading partner, meaning that the partner is better off, too. (Of course, sometimes after an exchange, you may believe that you were mistaken about the value of what you just received—this is called *buyer's remorse*, but it does not affect our discussion.)

Free trade encourages individuals to employ their abilities in the most productive manner possible and to exchange the fruits of their efforts. The **gains from trade** arise from one of the fundamental ideas in economics: A nation gains from doing what it can do best *relative to other nations*, that is, by specializing in those endeavors in which it has a **comparative advantage.** Trade encourages individuals and nations to discover ways to specialize so that they can become more productive and enjoy higher incomes. Increased productivity and the subsequent increase in the rate of **economic growth** are exactly what the signatories of the Uruguay Round and NAFTA sought—and are obtaining—by reducing trade barriers and thus increasing globalization.

Keeping the Competition Out

Despite the enormous gains from exchange, some people (sometimes a great many of them) routinely oppose free trade, particularly in the case of international trade. This opposition comes in many guises, but they all basically come down to one: When our borders are open to trade with other nations, this exposes some individuals and businesses in our nation to more **competition.** Most firms and workers hate competition, and who can blame them? After all, if a firm can keep competitors out, its **profits** are sure to stay the same or even rise. Also, if workers can prevent competition from other sources, they may enjoy higher wages and perhaps a larger selection of jobs. So the real source of most opposition to globalization is that the opponents of trade dislike the competition that comes with it. This position is not immoral or unethical, but it is not altruistic or noble, either. It is based on self-interest, pure and simple.

Opposition to globalization is nothing new, by the way. In the twentieth century, it culminated most famously in the Smoot–Hawley Tariff Act of 1930. This federal statute was a classic example of **protectionism**—an effort to protect a subset of U.S. producers at the expense of consumers and other producers. It included tariff schedules for over twenty thousand products, raising taxes on affected imports by an average of 52 percent.

The Smoot–Hawley Tariff Act encouraged so-called *beggar-thy-neighbor* policies by the rest of the world. Such policies are an attempt to improve (a portion of) one's domestic economy at the expense of foreign countries' economies. In this case, tariffs were imposed to discourage imports in the hope that domestic import-competing industries would benefit. France, the Netherlands, Switzerland, and the United Kingdom soon adopted beggar-thy-neighbor policies to counter the American ones. The result was a massive reduction in international trade. According to many economists, this caused a worldwide worsening of the Great Depression.

Opponents of globalization sometimes claim that beggar-thy-neighbor policies really do benefit the United States by protecting import-competing industries. In general, this claim is not correct. It is true that *some* Americans benefit from such policies, but two large groups of Americans lose. First, the purchasers of imports and import-competing goods suffer from the higher prices and reduced selection of goods and suppliers caused by tariffs and import **quotas.** Second, the decline in imports caused by protectionism also causes a decline in *exports*, thereby harming firms and workers in these industries.

This result follows directly from one of the fundamental propositions in international trade: *In the long run, imports are paid for by exports.* This proposition simply states that when one country buys goods and services from the rest of the world (imports), the rest of the world eventually wants goods from that country (exports) in exchange. Given this fundamental proposition, a corollary becomes obvious: *Any restriction on imports leads to a reduction in exports.* Thus, any extra business for import-competing industries gained as a result of tariffs or quotas means at least as much business *lost* for exporting industries.

THE ARGUMENTS AGAINST GLOBALIZATION

Opponents of globalization often raise a variety of objections in their efforts to reduce it. For example, it is sometimes claimed that foreign companies engage in **dumping,** which is selling their goods in the United States "below cost." The first question to ask when such charges are made is: Below *whose* cost? Clearly, if the foreign firm is selling in the United States, it must be offering the good for sale at a price that is at or below the costs of U.S. firms. Otherwise it could not induce Americans to buy it. But the ability of individuals or firms to obtain goods at lower cost is one of the *benefits* of free trade, not one of its harmful aspects.

What about claims that import sales are taking place at prices below the foreign company's costs? This amounts to arguing that the owners of the foreign company are voluntarily giving some of their wealth to us, namely, the difference between their costs and the (lower) price they charge us. It is possible, though unlikely, that they might wish to do this, perhaps because this could be the cheapest way of getting us to try a product that we would not otherwise purchase. But even supposing it is true, why would we want to refuse this gift? As a nation, we are richer if we accept it. Moreover, it is a gift that will be offered for only a short time. There is no point in selling at prices below cost unless the seller hopes to soon raise the price profitably above cost!

Another argument sometimes raised against globalization is that the goods are produced abroad using "unfair" labor practices (such as the use of child labor) or production processes that do not meet U.S. environmental standards. Such charges are sometimes true. But we must remember two things here. First, although we may find the use of child labor (or perhaps sixty-hour workweeks with no overtime pay) objectionable, such practices were at one time commonplace in the United States. They were observed here for the same reason they are currently observed abroad. The people involved were (or are) too poor to do otherwise. Some families in developing nations cannot survive unless all family members contribute. As unfortunate as this situation is, if we insist on imposing our values and attitudes—shaped in part by our great wealth—on people whose wealth is far less than ours, we run the risk of making them worse off even as we think we are helping them.

Similar considerations apply to environmental standards.[1] Individuals' and nations' willingness to pay for environmental quality is very much shaped by their wealth. Environmental quality is a **normal good.** This means that people who are rich (such as Americans) want to consume more of it per capita than people who are poor. Insisting that other nations meet environmental standards that we find acceptable is much like insisting that they wear the clothes we wear, use the modes of transportation we prefer, and consume the foods we like. The few people who can afford it will indeed be living in the style to which we are accustomed, but most people in developing countries will not be able to afford anything like that style.

---

1 There is one important exception to this statement. When foreign air or water pollution is generated near enough to our borders (e.g., in Mexico or Canada) to cause harm to Americans, good public policy presumably dictates that we seek to treat that pollution as though it were being generated inside our borders.

Our point is not that foreign labor or environmental standards are, or should be, irrelevant to Americans. Instead, our point is that achieving high standards of either is costly, and trade restrictions are unlikely to be the most efficient or effective way to achieve them. Just as important, labor standards and environmental standards are all too often raised as smokescreens to hide the real motive: keeping the competition out.

THE REAL PROMISE OF PROTECTIONISM

Proponents of protectionism often claim that when international trade is reduced, trade *within* the United States expands by an even greater amount. But it doesn't, because the reduction in trade with the rest of the world reduces our overall wealth and thereby contributes to a reduction in domestic consumption, and thus production. To see why this is true, consider what would happen if we restricted or eliminated *interstate* trade within America. (After all, those autoworkers in Detroit are taking jobs away from people in Miami, Chicago, and Dallas who might otherwise be making cars.) Indeed, let's also eliminate trade between people in different *counties*. Or, perhaps we should carry the argument to its logical ending, by eliminating all trade between people, so that each of us can be fully employed producing whatever it is we might hope to consume in such a world.

The promise of protectionism is a promise of impoverishment—and it is one that will hurt the disadvantaged the most. A study of forty countries found that the richest citizens would lose 28 percent of their wealth if international trade were halted. But the poorest 10 percent of the populations would lose 68 percent of their meager incomes without international trade. It is difficult to see how a policy that harms people at every point in the income distribution will improve our well-being.

WHY ARE ANTITRADE MEASURES PASSED?

If globalization is beneficial and restrictions on trade are generally harmful, how does legislation such as the Smoot–Hawley Tariff Act and other restrictions on international trade ever get passed? The explanation is that because foreign competition often affects a narrow and specific import-competing industry, such as textiles, shoes, or automobiles, trade restrictions are crafted to benefit a narrow, well-defined group of economic agents. For example, limits on imports of Japanese automobiles in the 1980s chiefly benefited workers and owners of the Big Three automakers in this country: General Motors, Ford, and Chrysler. Similarly, long-standing quotas that limit imports of sugar benefit the owners of a handful of large U.S. sugar producers. Because of the concentrated benefits that accrue when Congress votes in favor of trade restrictions, sufficient funds can be raised in those industries to aggressively lobby members of Congress to impose those restrictions.

The eventual reduction in exports that must follow is normally spread throughout all export industries. Consequently, no specific group of workers, managers, or shareholders in export industries will be motivated to contribute funds to lobby Congress to reduce international trade restrictions. Further, although consumers of imports and import-competing goods lose due to trade restrictions, they, too, are typically a diffuse group of individuals, none of whom will be greatly affected individually by any particular import restriction. The simultaneous existence of concentrated benefits and diffuse costs led Mark Twain to observe long ago that the free traders win the arguments but the **protectionists** win the votes.

Of course, the protectionists don't win *all* the votes—after all, about one-seventh of the U.S. economy is based on international trade. Despite the opposition to free trade that comes from many quarters, its benefits to the economy as a whole are so great that it is unthinkable that we might do away with international trade altogether. Both economic theory and empirical evidence clearly indicate that, on balance, Americans are better off with freer trade achieved through such developments as NAFTA and the WTO.

For Critical Analysis

1. For a number of years, Japanese automakers voluntarily limited the number of cars they exported to the United States. What effect do you think this had on Japanese imports of U.S. cars and U.S. exports of goods and services *other than* automobiles?

2. Until a few years ago, U.S. cars exported to Japan had the driver controls on the left side (as in the United States). The Japanese (like the British), however, drive on the left side of the road, so Japanese cars sold in Japan have the driver controls on the right side. Suppose the Japanese tried to sell their cars in the United States with the driver controls on the right side. What impact would this likely have on their sales in this country? Do you think the unwillingness of U.S. carmakers to put the driver controls on the "correct" side for exports to Japan had any effect on their sales of cars in that country?

3. Keeping in mind the key propositions of globalization outlined in this chapter, what is the likely impact of international trade restrictions

on the following variables in the United States: employment, the unemployment rate, real GDP, and the price level? Explain your responses.

4. During the late 1980s and early 1990s, American automobile manufacturers greatly increased the quality of the cars they produced relative to the quality of the cars produced in other nations. What effect do you think this had on American imports of Japanese cars, Japanese imports of American cars, and American exports of goods and services other than automobiles?

5. The U.S. government subsidizes the export of U.S.-manufactured commercial aircraft. What effect do you think this policy has on American imports of foreign goods and American exports of products other than commercial aircraft? Explain.

6. Who bears the costs and enjoys the benefits of the subsidies mentioned in the previous question?

CHAPTER 31

The $750,000 Job

In even-numbered years, particularly years evenly divisible by four, politicians of all persuasions are apt to give long-winded speeches about the need to protect U.S. jobs from the evils of **globalization.** To accomplish this goal, we are encouraged to "buy American." If further encouragement is needed, we are told that if we do not voluntarily reduce the amount of imported goods we purchase, the government will impose (or make more onerous) **tariffs** (taxes) on imported goods or **quotas** (quantity restrictions) that physically limit imports. The objective of this exercise is to "save U.S. jobs."

Unlike black rhinos or blue whales, U.S. jobs are in no danger of becoming extinct. There are virtually an unlimited number of potential jobs in the U.S. economy, and there always will be. Some of these jobs are not very pleasant, and many others do not pay very well, but there will always be employment of some sort as long as there is **scarcity.** Thus, when steelworkers making $72,000 per year say that imports of foreign steel should be reduced to save their jobs, what they really mean is this: They want to be protected from **competition** so that they can continue their present employment at the same or a higher salary rather than move to different jobs that have less desirable working conditions or lower salaries. There is nothing wrong with the steelworkers' goal (better working conditions and higher pay), but it has nothing to do with "saving jobs."

THE GAINS FROM GLOBALIZATION

In any discussion of the consequences of international trade restrictions, it is essential to remember two facts. First, *we pay for imports with exports.* It is true that in the short run, we can sell off **assets** or borrow from abroad if we happen to import more goods and services than we export. But we have only a finite amount of assets to sell, and foreigners will not wait forever for us to pay our bills. Ultimately, our accounts can be settled only if we provide (export) goods and services to the trading partners from whom we purchase (import) goods and services. Trade, after all, involves a *quid pro quo* (literally, "something for something").

The second point to remember is that *voluntary trade is mutually beneficial to the trading partners.* If we restrict international trade, we reduce those benefits, both for our trading partners and for ourselves. One way these reduced benefits are manifested is in the form of curtailed employment opportunities for workers. The reasoning is simple. Other countries will buy our goods only if they can market theirs because they, too, must export goods to pay for their imports. Thus, any U.S. restrictions on imports to this country—via tariffs, quotas, or other means— ultimately cause a reduction in our exports because other countries will be unable to pay for our goods. This implies that import restrictions must inevitably decrease the size of our export sector. Thus, imposing trade restrictions to save jobs in import-competing industries has the effect of costing jobs in export industries. Most studies have shown that the net effect seems to be reduced employment overall.

The Adverse Effects of Trade Restrictions

Import restrictions also impose costs on U.S. consumers as a whole. By reducing competition from abroad, quotas, tariffs, and other trade restraints push up the prices of foreign goods and enable U.S. producers to hike their own prices. Perhaps the best-documented example of this effect is found in the automobile industry, where "voluntary" restrictions on Japanese imports were in place for more than a decade.

Due in part to the enhanced quality of imported cars, sales of domestically produced automobiles fell from nine million units in 1978 to an average of six million units per year between 1980 and 1982. Profits of U.S. automakers plummeted as well, and some incurred substantial losses. The automobile manufacturers' and autoworkers' unions demanded protection from import competition. Politicians from automobile-producing states rallied to their cause. The result was a "voluntary" agreement by Japanese car companies (the most important competitors of U.S. firms) to restrict their U.S. sales to 1.68 million units per year. This agreement—which amounted to a quota, even though it never officially bore that name—began in April 1981 and continued well into the 1990s in various forms.

Robert W. Crandall, an economist with the Brookings Institution, estimated how much this voluntary trade restriction cost U.S. consumers in higher car prices. According to his research, the reduced supply of Japanese cars pushed their prices up by $5,200 per car, measured in 2017 dollars. The higher prices of Japanese imports in turn enabled domestic producers to hike their prices an average of up to $2,100 per car. The total tab in the first full year of the program was about $11 billion. Crandall also estimated that about 26,000 jobs in automobile-related industries were protected by the voluntary import restrictions. Dividing $11 billion by 26,000 jobs yields a cost to consumers of about $420,000 *per year* for every job preserved in the automobile industry. U.S. consumers could have saved over $8 billion on their car purchases each year if instead of implicitly agreeing to import restrictions they had simply given $100,000 in cash each year to every autoworker whose job was protected by the voluntary import restraints.

The same types of calculations have been made for other industries. Tariffs in the apparel industry were increased between 1977 and 1981, preserving the jobs of about 116,000 U.S. apparel workers at a cost of $45,000 per job each year. The cost of **protectionism** has been even higher in other industries. Jobs preserved in the glassware industry due to trade restrictions cost $200,000 apiece each year. In the maritime industry, the yearly cost of trade restrictions is $290,000 per job. In the steel industry, the cost of protecting a job has been estimated at an astounding $750,000 per year. If free trade were permitted, each steelworker losing a job could be given a cash payment of half that amount each year, and consumers would still save a lot of **wealth.**

The current record holder for squandering resources to cater to a handful of workers, however, goes to Barack Obama. In 2009, in response to claims of **dumping** (see Chapter 30) by Chinese tire makers, he imposed a special tariff on tire imports from China. The cost to Americans of this policy was $1.1 billion per year. This amounts to $900,000 per year for each of the 1,200 jobs that were "saved." Of course, President Trump campaigned on the promise of even more protectionism, so perhaps by the time you read this, we'll have a new record holder.

The Real Impact on Jobs

The adverse impact of international trade restrictions is even worse than portrayed thus far. This is because none of the typical cost studies, such as those summarized above, account for the impact of import restrictions on the flow of exports, the number of workers who lose their jobs in the export sector, and thus total employment in the economy.

Remember that imports pay for exports and that our imports are the exports of our trading partners. So when imports to the United States are restricted, our trading partners will necessarily buy less of what *we* produce. The resulting decline in export sales means less employment in exporting industries. And the total reduction in trade leads to less employment for workers such as stevedores (who load and unload ships) and truck drivers (who carry goods to and from ports). On both counts—the overall cut in trade and the accompanying fall in exports—protectionism leads to employment declines that might not be obvious immediately.

Some years ago, Congress tried to pass a "domestic-content" bill for automobiles. The legislation would have required that cars sold in the United States have a minimum percentage of their components manufactured and assembled in this country. Proponents of the legislation argued that it would have protected 300,000 jobs in the U.S. automobile manufacturing and auto parts supply industries. Yet the legislation's supporters failed to recognize the negative impact of the bill on trade in general and its ultimate impact on U.S. export industries. A U.S. Department of Labor study did recognize these impacts, estimating that the domestic-content legislation would have cost more jobs in trade-related and export industries than it protected in import-competing businesses. Congress ultimately decided not to impose a domestic-content requirement for cars sold in the United States.

THE LONG-RUN FAILURE OF IMPORT CONTROLS

In principle, trade restrictions are imposed to provide economic help to specific industries and to increase employment in those industries. Ironically, in the long-term, restrictions may be totally ineffective in protecting employment in an industry. Researchers at the **World Trade Organization (WTO)** examined employment in three industries that have been heavily protected throughout the world: textiles, clothing, and iron and steel. Despite stringent **protectionist** measures, employment in these industries actually declined during the period of protection, sometimes dramatically. In textiles, employment fell 22 percent in the United States and 46 percent in the European Common Market (the predecessor of the **European Union**). Employment losses in the clothing industry ranged from 18 percent in the United States to 56 percent in Sweden. Losses in the iron and steel industry ranged from 10 percent in Canada to 54 percent in the United States. In short, the WTO researchers found that restrictions on free trade were no guarantee against employment losses, even in the industries supposedly being protected.

The evidence seems clear: The cost of protecting jobs in the short run is enormous and in the long run it appears that jobs cannot be protected, especially if one considers all aspects of protectionism. Free trade is a tough platform on which to run for office, but it is likely to be the one that will yield the most general benefits if implemented. Of course, this does not mean that politicians will embrace it. So we end up "saving jobs" at an annual cost of $750,000 each.

For Critical Analysis

1. If it would be cheaper to give each steelworker $375,000 per year in cash than impose restrictions on steel imports, why do we have the import restrictions rather than the cash payments?

2. Most U.S. imports and exports travel through our seaports at some point. How do you predict that members of Congress from coastal states would vote on proposals to restrict international trade? What other information would you want to know when making such a prediction?

3. Who gains and who loses from import restrictions? In answering, you should consider both consumers and producers in both the country that imposes the restrictions and in the other countries affected by them. Also, be sure to take into account the effects of import restrictions on *export* industries.

4. When you go shopping for a new computer, is your real objective to "import" a computer into your apartment, or is it to "export" cash from your wallet? What does this tell you about the true object of international trade—is it imports or exports?

5. Some U.S. policy is designed to subsidize exports and thus increase employment in export industries. What effect does such policy have on our imports of foreign goods and thus on employment in industries that compete with imports?

6. What motivates politicians to impose trade restrictions?

GLOSSARY

abject poverty: surviving on the equivalent of $1.90 or less of income per person per day

adverse selection: a process in which "undesirable" (high-cost or high-risk) participants tend to dominate one side of a market, causing adverse effects for the other side; often results from asymmetric information

after-tax income: income after taxes are deducted

aggregate demand: the total value of all planned spending on goods and services by all economic entities in the economy

asset: any valuable good capable of yielding a flow of income or services over time

asymmetric information: a circumstance in which participants on one side of a market have more information than those on the other side of the market; often results in adverse selection

average tax rate: total taxes divided by income

balance sheet: a written record of assets and liabilities

bank run: an attempt by many of a bank's depositors to convert checkable and savings deposits into currency because of a perceived fear for the bank's solvency

bankruptcy: a state of being legally declared unable to pay one's debts so that some or all of the indebtedness is legally wiped out by the courts

blockchain: a public ledger of all transactions that have ever been executed

bond: a debt conferring the right to receive a specific series of money payments in the future

bondholders: the owners of government or corporate bonds

book value: asset valuations that are based on the original purchase price of the asset rather than a current market value

budget constraint: all of the possible combinations of goods that can be purchased at given prices and given income

budget deficit: the excess of government spending over government revenues during a given time period

business cycles: the ups and downs in overall business activity, evidenced by changes in GDP, employment, and the price level

capital: productive assets, such as factories, equipment, and knowledge stemming from research and development

capital gains: appreciation in the value of an asset; when these are realized in the sale of an asset, they are typically subject to taxation

capital stock: the collection of productive assets that can be combined with other inputs, such as labor, to produce goods and services

capitalism: an economic and political system in which resources are chiefly owned and controlled by individuals, rather than by the government

capitalist system: see *capitalism*

cash and noncash transfers: payments and services provided by the government to individuals deemed worthy of their receipt

cash flow: cash receipts minus cash payments

cash-constrained: circumstances in which an individual cannot borrow against future income, so that the person's spending is limited to cash on hand

central bank: a banker's bank, usually a government institution that also serves as the bank for the country's treasury; central banks normally regulate commercial banks

checkable deposits: accounts at depository institutions that are payable on demand, either by means of a check or by direct withdrawal, as through an automated teller machine (ATM)

civil law system: a legal system in which statutes passed by legislatures and executive decrees, rather than judicial decisions based on precedent, form the basis for most legal rules

collateral: assets that are forfeited in the event of default on an obligation

commercial bank: a financial institution that accepts demand deposits, makes loans, and provides other financial services to the public

common law system: a legal system in which judicial decisions based on precedent, rather than executive decrees or statutes passed by legislatures, form the basis for most legal rules

comparative advantage: the ability to produce a good or service at a lower opportunity cost compared to other producers

competition: rivalrous behavior

constant-quality price: price adjusted for any change in the quality of the good or service; *see also* **quality-adjusted price**

consumer price index (CPI): a measure of the dollar cost of purchasing a bundle of goods and services assumed to be representative of the consumption pattern of a typical consumer; one measure of the price level

consumption: spending by consumers on new goods and services

core inflation: a measure of the overall rate of change in prices of goods, excluding energy and food

cost of living: the dollar cost (relative to a base year) of achieving a given level of satisfaction

creative destruction: the ultimate outcome of a competitive process in which innovation continually creates new products and firms and replaces existing firms and products

creditor: an institution or individual that is owed money by another institution or individual

cryptocurrencies: decentralized *digital currencies* that use encryption techniques for security

currency: paper money and coins issued by the government to serve as a medium of exchange

currency union: an agreement among independent governments to use a common medium of exchange

debt crisis: circumstances in which an entity that owes money is unable to repay it

default: failure to meet obligations, for example, the failure to make debt payments

default risk: an estimation combining the probability that a contract will not be adhered to and the magnitude of the loss that will occur if it is not

deficit: excess of government spending over tax receipts during a given fiscal year

deflation: a decline in the average level of the prices of goods and services

deindustrialization: a process of social and economic change caused by the removal or reduction of industrial capacity or activity in a country or region

demand: the willingness and ability to purchase goods

demand deposits: see *checkable deposits*

depository institutions: financial institutions that accept deposits from savers and lend those deposits out to borrowers

depression: a severe recession

digital currencies: any form of money that is stored digitally

digital wallet: a combination of hardware and software that can be used to make electronic commerce transactions securely and quickly

direct foreign investment: resources provided to individuals and firms in a nation by individuals or firms located in other countries

disability payments: cash payments made to persons whose physical or mental disabilities prevent them from working

discouraged workers: persons who have dropped out of the labor force because they are unable to find suitable work

discretionary spending: government spending that is decided on anew each year, rather than being determined by a formula or set of rules

disposable income: income remaining after all taxes, retirement contributions, and the like are deducted

dividends: payments made by a corporation to owners of shares of its stock, generally based on the corporation's profits

dumping: the sale of goods in a foreign country at a price below the market price charged for the same goods in the domestic market or at a price below the cost of production

dynamic economic analysis: a mode of analysis that recognizes that people respond to changes in incentives and that takes these responses into account when evaluating the effects of policies

earned income tax credit: a federal tax program that permits negative taxes, that is, provides for payments to people (instead of collecting taxes from them) if their incomes go below a predetermined level

economic growth: sustained increases in real per capita income

economic safety net: the set of government programs (such as unemployment insurance and food stamps) that people can call upon when their incomes are low

economies of scale: reductions in average costs achieved by expanding the scale of operations

elasticity: a measure of the responsiveness of one variable to a change in another variable

entitlement programs: government programs for which spending is determined chiefly by formulas or rules that specify who is eligible for funds and how much they may receive

equity: assets minus liabilities; net asset value

European Central Bank (ECB): the central bank for the group of nations that uses the euro as their monetary unit

European Stability Mechanism: a 2012 agreement among users of the euro that provides for international guarantees and transfers, for the purpose of preventing default among nations using the euro

European Union (EU): a supranational entity resulting from an agreement among European nations to closely integrate the economic, political, and legal systems of the twenty-eight individual member nations

excess reserves: funds kept on hand by commercial banks to meet the transaction demands of customers and to serve as precautionary sources of funds in the event of a bank run; may be held as vault cash or as deposits at the Fed

excess supply: an excess of the quantity supplied of a good over the quantity demanded, evaluated at a given relative price for the good

exchange rate: the price of a currency expressed in terms of another currency

expansion: a period in which economic activity, measured by industrial production, employment, real income, and wholesale and retail sales, is growing on a sustained basis

expansionary monetary policy: actions that tend to increase the level or rate of growth of the money supply

expected rate of inflation: the rate at which the average level of prices of goods and services is expected to rise

Eurozone: the group of European nations that have agreed to use the euro as their common monetary unit

face value: the denomination in terms of a unit of account expressed on a coin or unit of currency

Fannie Mae: U.S. government-sponsored enterprise established in 1938 to facilitate the market in home mortgages

federal budget deficit: the excess of the national government's spending over its receipts

federal funds rate: the nominal interest rate at which banks can borrow reserves from one another

Federal Reserve System (the Fed): the central bank of the United States

fiscal pact: an agreement among independent governments to jointly monitor the spending and taxing of the nations that are part of the agreement

fiscal policy: discretionary changes in government spending or taxes that alter the overall state of the economy, including employment, investment, and output

fiscal year: the accounting year used by a government or business; for the federal government, the fiscal year runs from October 1 to September 30

flexible exchange rates: exchange rates that are free to move in response to market forces

foreclosure: the legal process by which a borrower in default under a mortgage is deprived of his or her interest in the mortgaged property

foreign currency swap: a trade that involves the exchange of principal and interest in one currency for the same in another currency

foreign exchange: national currencies

foreign exchange rate: the relative price between two national currencies

Freddie Mac: U.S. government-sponsored enterprise established in 1970 to facilitate the market in home mortgages

freelancer: a person who is self-employed and is not necessarily committed to a particular employer long-term

gains from trade: the extent to which individuals, firms, or nations benefit from engaging in voluntary exchange

gig: a single task or project for which a worker is hired—often through an online marketplace

gig economy: an economic system in which many workers find temporary employment or companies contract with independent contractors for short-term engagements

globalization: the integration of national economies into an international economy

government-sponsored enterprise (GSE): a federally chartered corporation that is privately owned, designed to provide a source of credit nationwide, and limited to servicing one economic sector

gross domestic product (GDP): the dollar value of all new, domestically produced final goods and services in an economy

gross public debt: all public debt, including that owned by agencies of the government issuing it

hedge funds: investment companies that require large initial deposits by investors and pursue high-risk investments in the hope of achieving high returns

human capital: the productive capacity of human beings

illiquid: when used in reference to a company or person—having insufficient cash on hand to meet current liabilities; when used in reference to an asset—that which cannot be easily and cheaply converted into cash

in-kind transfer: the provision of goods and services rather than cash, as in the case of Medicare, Medicaid, or subsidized housing

incentives: positive or negative consequences of actions

income inequality: a circumstance in which the incomes of different individuals are not all identical

income mobility: the tendency of people to move around in the income distribution over time

independent contractor: a person who performs specific tasks in return for payments that are tied to the successful completion of the tasks

individual mandate: the requirement under the Affordable Care Act of 2010 that individuals purchase health care insurance or face an income-related fine; many people refusing insurance under the Act have been granted exemptions from the mandate

industrial policy: a set of government actions that attempt to influence which firms succeed and which fail

Industrial Revolution: the widespread radical socioeconomic changes that took place in England and many other nations, beginning in the late eighteenth century, brought about when extensive mechanization of production systems resulted in a shift from home-based hand manufacturing to large-scale factory production

inefficient: an outcome that fails to maximize the value of a resource

inflation: a rise in the average level of the prices of goods and services

inflation tax: the decline in the real value or purchasing power of money or government bonds due to inflation

inflationary premium: the additional premium, in percent per year, that people are willing to pay to have dollars sooner rather than later, simply because inflation is expected in the future

innovation: the transformation of something new, such as an invention, into something that creates economic benefits

inside information: valuable information about future economic performance that is not generally available to the public

insolvent: describing a financial condition in which the value of one's assets is less than that of one's liabilities

insourcing: the use of domestic workers to perform a service traditionally done by foreign workers

institutions: the basic rules, customs, and practices of society

interagency borrowings: loans from one part of the federal government to another

interest group: a collection of individuals with common aims

Interim European Financial Stability Facility: a temporary agreement among users of the euro that provided international guarantees and transfers, for the purpose of preventing default among nations using the euro; succeeded in 2012 by the European Stability Mechanism

intermediate goods: goods that contribute to present or future consumer welfare but are not direct sources of the utility themselves; typically, they are used up in the production of final goods and services

International Monetary Fund: an international association of nations created in 1945 to promote international trade and stability of exchange rates

invention: a novel product, process, or application that is clearly distinguishable from existing products, processes, or applications

investment: the creation of new machines, factories, and other assets that enable the production of more goods and services in the future

investment bank: a financial institution that helps companies or municipalities obtain financing by selling stocks or bonds on their behalf

labor force: individuals aged sixteen and over who either have jobs or are looking and are available for work

labor force participation rate: the sum of all people who are working or are available for and looking for work, divided by the population; both numerator and denominator are generally restricted to persons aged sixteen and above

labor productivity: output produced per unit of labor input

labor supply curve: a schedule showing the quantity of labor supplied at each wage rate

law of demand: the observation that there is an inverse, or negative, relation between the price of any good and the quantity of it demanded, holding other factors constant

legal tender: coins or paper money that must be accepted if offered in payment

liabilities: amounts owed; the legal claims against an individual or against an institution by those who are not owners of that institution

loophole: a provision of the tax code that enables a narrow group of beneficiaries to achieve a lower effective tax rate

lump sum tax rebates: fixed cash payments made by a government to taxpayers that are independent of taxpayer income

mandates: in the context of governments, regulations or laws that require other governments, private individuals, or firms to spend money to achieve goals specified by the government

marginal tax rate: the percentage of the last dollar earned that is paid in taxes

market valuation: the price an asset (or firm) would fetch if offered for sale

median age: the age that separates the older half of the population from the younger half

median income: the income that separates the higher-income half of the population from the lower-income half

Medicaid: joint federal-state health insurance program for low-income individuals

Medicare: federal health insurance program for individuals aged sixty-five and above

medium of exchange: any asset that sellers will generally accept as payment

mercantilists: believers in the doctrine of mercantilism, which asserted (among other things) that exports were the principal objective of international trade because they permitted the accumulation of gold

microeconomics: the study of decision making by consumers and by firms and of the market equilibria that result

minimum wage: the lowest hourly wage that firms may legally pay their workers

monetary policy: the use of changes in the amount of money in circulation to affect interest rates, credit markets, inflation (or deflation), and unemployment

money supply: the sum of checkable deposits and currency in the hands of the public

moral hazard: the tendency of an entity insulated from risk to behave differently than it would behave if it were fully exposed to the risk

mortgage-backed security (MBS): a debt obligation that pledges home mortgages as collateral

mortgages: debts that are incurred to buy a house, stipulating that if the debt is not paid, the house may be sold by the creditor and the proceeds used to pay that debt

mutual funds: pools of money that are invested in assets, often shares of stock in corporations

national debt: cumulative excess of federal spending over federal tax collections over time; total explicit indebtedness of the federal government

natural-resource endowments: the collection of naturally occurring minerals (such as oil and iron ore) and living things (such as forests and fish stocks) that can be used to produce goods and services

near-field communication (NFC): the technology that enables radio communication between smartphones and other devices that are close by, without actually touching the device

negative tax: a payment from the government to an individual that is based on that individual's income

net assets: assets minus debt

net public debt: the portion of the public debt that is owned outside of the government issuing it

net tax: taxes paid minus income transfers received

net worth: the excess of assets over liabilities

nominal: an amount expressed in terms of a nation's unit of account

nominal income: income expressed in terms of a monetary unit, such as the dollar

nominal interest rate: the premium, in percent per year, that people are willing to pay to have dollars sooner rather than later

nominal prices: the exchange value of goods, expressed in terms of a unit of account, such as the dollar or the euro

non-employer firms: self-employed individuals operating unincorporated businesses with no paid employees

non-traded goods: goods and services not exchanged across international borders

normal good: a good for which the demand increases as people's income or wealth grows

on-demand services: valuable activities that are provided specifically at the request of the person benefitting from them

open market: the market for U.S. Treasury securities

opportunity cost: the highest-valued, next-best alternative that must be sacrificed to obtain something

outsourcing: the use of labor in another country to perform service work traditionally done by domestic workers

patent: legal protection for an invention that prevents others from imitating the invention without compensating the inventor

pay-as-you-go system: a scheme in which current cash outflows are funded (paid for) with current cash inflows

payments system: the institutional infrastructure that enables payments for goods and services to be made

payroll taxes: taxes that are levied on income specifically generated by workforce participation and that are generally earmarked for spending on specific programs, such as Social Security

per capita income: GDP divided by population

per capita real net public debt: net public debt, deflated by the price level and divided by the population

perfectly inelastic: having an elasticity (or responsiveness) of zero

permanent income: the sustained or average level of income that one expects will be observed over a long period of time

personal consumption expenditures index (PCE): a measure of the dollar cost of purchasing a bundle of goods and services assumed to be representative of the consumption pattern of a typical consumer; one measure of the price level

physical capital: the productive capacity of physical assets, such as buildings

platform firm: a company whose business is operation of a an Internet-based virtual marketplace that facilitates of exchanges of goods and services by others

poverty line: an arbitrary division between income levels, used to designate individuals who have incomes below the line as living in poverty; the line varies over time, across nations, and across family sizes (with the line being higher for larger families)

price controls: government rules that limit the prices firms may charge for the goods or services they sell

price level: the average current-year cost, measured relative to the average base-year cost, of a typical basket of goods and services

productivity: output per unit of input

profits: the difference between revenue and cost

progressive tax: a tax that increases as a percentage of income as the income of the person or company being taxed increases

progressive tax system: a set of rules that result in tax collections that are a larger share of income as income rises

property and contract rights: legal rules governing the use and exchange of property and the enforceable agreements between people or businesses

proportional tax system: a set of rules that result in tax collections that are an unchanging share of income as income changes

protectionism: economic policy of promoting favored domestic industries through the use of high tariffs and quotas and other trade restrictions to reduce imports

protectionist: any attitude or policy that seeks to prevent foreigners from competing with domestic firms or individuals

public debt: the amount of money owed by a government to its creditors

purchasing power: a measure of the amount of goods and services that can be purchased with a given amount of money

purchasing power parity (PPP): the principle that the relative values of different currencies must reflect their purchasing power in their home countries

quantitative easing (QE): Federal Reserve policy that entails the purchase of various financial assets, conducted in an effort to increase aggregate demand

quota: a limit on the amount of a good that may be imported; generally used to reduce imports so as to protect the economic interests of domestic industries that compete with the imports

real gross domestic product (real GDP): the inflation-adjusted level of new, domestically produced final goods and services

real income: income adjusted for inflation; equivalently, income expressed in terms of goods and services

real interest rate: the premium, in percent per year, that people are willing to pay to have goods sooner rather than later

real per capita GDP: Gross Domestic Product per person, adjusted for inflation

real per capita income (real GDP per capita): GDP corrected for inflation and divided by the population—a measure of the amount of new domestic production of final goods and services per person

real price: price of a good or service adjusted for inflation; equivalently, the price of a good or service expressed in terms of other goods and services

real purchasing power: the amount of goods and services that can be acquired with an asset whose value is expressed in terms of the monetary unit of account (such as the dollar)

real tax rate: share of GDP controlled by the government

real value: value adjusted for inflation or, equivalently, expressed in terms of other goods and services

real wages: wages adjusted for changes in the price level

recession: a decline in the level of overall business activity

regressive tax system: a set of rules that result in tax collections that are a smaller share of income as income rises

relative prices: prices of goods and services compared to the prices of other goods and services; costs of goods and services measured in terms of other commodities

reparations: payments, in cash or in kind, that must be made from the citizens of one nation to another, often observed as part of the terms of surrender ending a war

required reserves: funds that a commercial bank must lawfully maintain; they may be held in the form of vault cash or deposits at the Fed

reserves: assets held by depository institutions, typically in the form of currency held at the institution or as non-interest-bearing deposits held at the central bank, to meet customers' transaction needs and the legal requirements of the Fed

resource allocation: the set of uses to which resources, or assets, are put

resources: any items capable of satisfying individuals' desires or preferences or suitable for transformation into such goods

revealed preferences: consumers' tastes as demonstrated by the choices they make

rule of law: the principle that relations between individuals, businesses, and the government are governed by explicit rules that apply to everyone in society

saving: an addition to wealth, conventionally measured as disposable personal income minus consumption

savings: one's stock of wealth at a given moment in time

scarcity: a state of the world in which there are limited resources but unlimited demands, implying that we must make choices among alternatives

share of stock: claim to a specified portion of future net cash flows (or profits) of a corporation

shareholders: owners of shares of stock in a corporation

Social Security: the federal system that transfers income from current workers to current retirees

solvent: describing a financial condition in which the value of one's assets is greater than that of one's liabilities

stagflation: a period of macroeconomic stagnation, combined with inflation

standard of living: a summary measure of the level of per capita material welfare, often measured by per capita real GDP

start-up capital: initial funds raised to create and begin operations of a new firm

static economic analysis: a mode of analysis that assumes for simplicity that people do not change their behavior when incentives change

stock: as applied to measurement, an amount measured at a particular moment in time; as applied to a financial instrument, the right to share in future cash flows of a corporation

stockbroker: a middleman who sells shares of stock to individuals

subprime mortgages: mortgages that entail a higher risk of loss for the lender

subsidies: government payments for the production of specific goods, generally intended to raise the profits of the firms producing those goods

supply: the willingness and ability to sell goods

supply and demand: the interaction between willingness and ability to sell, and willingness and ability to buy

systemic risk: hazard that is felt or experienced throughout an entire economy

tariff: a tax levied only on imports; generally used to reduce imports so as to protect the economic interests of domestic industries that compete with the imports

tax bracket: a range of income over which a specific marginal tax rate applies

tax credit: a direct reduction in tax liability, occasioned by a specific set of circumstances and not dependent on the taxpayer's tax bracket

tax evasion: the deliberate failure to pay taxes, usually by making a false report

tax liability: total tax obligation owed by a firm or individual

tax rate: the percentage of a dollar of income that must be paid in taxes

tax rebate: a return of some previously paid taxes

trade barrier: a legal rule imposed by a nation that raises the costs of foreign firms seeking to sell goods in that nation; they include tariffs and quotas

trade deficit: an excess of the value of imports of goods and services over the value of the exports of goods and services

trade surplus: an excess of the value of exports of goods and services over the value of the imports of goods and services

traded goods: goods and services that are exchanged across international borders

Treasury bills: short-term notes of indebtedness of the U.S. government

two-sided market: economic institutions (often Internet-based) having two distinct user groups that provide each other with benefits when they interact through the market

underground economy: commercial transactions on which taxes and regulations are being avoided

unemployment benefits: regular cash payments made to individuals, contingent on their status as being unemployed

unemployment rate: the number of persons looking and available for work, divided by the labor force

unit of account: the unit in which prices are expressed

untraded goods: goods and services that are not exchanged across international borders

voucher: a written authorization, exchangeable for cash or services

wealth: the present value of all current and future income

wealth tax: a tax based on a person's net worth

World Trade Organization (WTO): an association of more than 150 nations that helps reduce trade barriers among its members and handles international trade disputes among them

Selected References and Web Links

Chapter 1   Rich Nation, Poor Nation

Easterly, William. *The Tyranny of Experts: Economists, Dictators, and the Forgotten Rights of the Poor*. New York: Basic Books, 2014.

Easterly, William, and Ross Levine. "Tropics, Germs, and Crops: How Endowments Influence Economic Development." *Journal of Monetary Economics* 50, no. 1 (2003): 3–39.

Mahoney, Paul G. "The Common Law and Economic Growth: Hayek Might Be Right." *Journal of Legal Studies* 30, no. 2 (2001): 503–525.

Rosenberg, Nathan, and L. E. Birdzell, Jr. *How the West Grew Rich*. New York: Basic Books, 1987.

www.worldbank.org. Official Web site of the World Bank.

Chapter 2   Innovation and Growth

Aeppel, Timothy. "Economists Debate: Has All the Important Stuff Already Been Invented?" *Wall Street Journal*, June 15, 2014.

Ip, Greg. "When Tech Bites Back: Innovation's Dark Side." *The Wall Street Journal*, October 19, 2016.

Ridley, Matt. *The Evolution of Everything: How New Ideas Emerge*. New York: HarperCollins, 2015.

Van Dyke, Raymond. "Caveat Emptor: The New Patent Paradigm." *E-Commerce Times*, March 15, 2014.

Chapter 3   Outsourcing and Economic Growth

Chu, Kathy. "China Manufacturers Survive by Moving to Asian Neighbors." *Wall Street Journal*, May 1, 2013.

Council of Economic Advisers. *Economic Report of the President*. Washington, DC: Government Printing Office, 2017.

Gnuschke, John E., Jeff Wallace, Dennis R. Wilson, and Stephen C. Smith. "Outsourcing Production and Jobs: Costs and Benefits." *Business Perspectives* 16, no. 2 (2004): 12–18.

Reinsdorf, Martin, and Matthew J. Slaughter (eds.). *International Trade in Services and Intangibles in the Era of Globalization*. National Bureau of Economic Research Studies in Income and Wealth, v. 69. Chicago: University of Chicago Press, 2009.

Chapter 4   Poverty, Capitalism, and Growth

Deaton, Angus. *The Great Escape: Health, Wealth, and the Origins of Inequality*. Princeton, NJ: Princeton University Press, 2013.

Foundation for Teaching Economics. "Is Capitalism Good for the Poor?" Retrieved from www.fte.org/capitalism/index.php

Gwartney, James, Joshua Hall, and Robert Lawson. *Economic Freedom of the World: 2016 Annual Report.* Vancouver, Canada: Fraser Institute, 2016. www.freetheworld.com. Fraser Institute site on economic freedom around the world.

Ortiz-Ospina, Esteban and Max Roser. "World Poverty." November 12, 2016. Retrieved from https://ourworldindata.org/world-poverty

Chapter 5   The Threat to Growth

Council of Economic Advisers. *Economic Report of the President.* Washington, DC: Government Printing Office, 2017.

Goolsbee, Austan. "The Impact of the Corporate Income Tax: Evidence from State Organizational Form Data." *Journal of Public Economics* 88, no. 11 (2004): 2283–2299.

Harberger, Arnold C. "Three Basic Postulates for Applied Welfare Economics: An Interpretive Essay." *Journal of Economic Literature* 9, no. 3 (1971): 785–797.

Miron, Jeffrey. *U.S. Fiscal Imbalance Over Time.* Cato Institute, Washington, DC: 2016.

Norton, Rob. "Corporate Taxation." *The Concise Encyclopedia of Economics.* Retrieved from www.econlib.org/library/Enc/CorporateTaxation.html

Chapter 6   Hello Boomers, Goodbye Prosperity

Ip, Greg. "For Economy, Aging Population Poses a Double Whammy." *The Wall Street Journal*, August 3, 2016.

Maestas, Nicole, Kathleen J. Mullen, and David Powell. "The Effect of Population Aging on Economic Growth, the Labor Force and Productivity." NBER Working Paper 22452, July 2016.

National Research Council, *Aging and the Macroeconomy: Implications of an Older Population.* National Academies Press, Washington DC: 2012.

Chapter 7   What Should GDP Include?

"How to Measure Prosperity." *The Economist*, April 30, 2016.

"Sex, Drugs, and GDP." *The Economist*, May 31, 2014.

Stevenson, Betsey, and Justin Wolfers. "Economic Growth and Subjective Well-Being: Reassessing the Easterlin Paradox." *Brookings Papers on Economic Activity*, Spring 2008, pp. 1–87.

Stevenson, Betsey, and Justin Wolfers. "Subjective Well-Being and Income: Is There Any Evidence of Satiation?" *American Economic Review* 103, no. 3 (2013): 598–604.

"The Trouble with GDP." *The Economist*, April 30, 2016.

www.bea.gov/national/index.htm#gdp. GDP data from U.S. Department of Commerce, Bureau of Economic Analysis.

CHAPTER 8   What's in a Word? Plenty, When It's the "R" Word

Business Cycle Dating Committee. "The NBER's Recession Dating Procedure." National Bureau of Economic Research, 2003. Retrieved from nber.org/cycles/recessions.html

Layton, Allan P., and Anirvan Banerji. "What Is a Recession? A Reprise." *Applied Economics* 35, no. 16 (2003): 1789–1797.

www.bea.doc.gov. Web site of the U.S. Department of Commerce's Bureau of Economic Analysis.

CHAPTER 9   The Disappearing Middle Class

Pew Research Center. *The Middle Class Is Losing Ground*. Washington, DC: 2015.

Rose, Stephen J. *The Growing Size and Incomes of the Upper Middle Class*. The Urban Institute. Washington, DC: 2016.

Shah, Neil. "Wealth Gap between America's Rich and Middle Class Families Widest on Record." *The Wall Street Journal*, December 17, 2014.

Zumbrun, Josh. "Not Just the 1%: The Upper Middle Class is Larger and Richer Than Ever.'" *The Wall Street Journal*, June 21, 2016.

CHAPTER 10   Capital, Wealth, and Inequality

Armour, Philip, Richard V. Burkhauser, and Jeff Larrimore. "Levels and Trends in United States Income and Its Distribution: A Crosswalk from Market Income Towards a Comprehensive Haig-Simons Income Approach." NBER Working Paper 19110, June 2013.

Burkhauser, Richard V., et al. "A 'Second Opinion' on the Economic Health of the American Middle Class." *National Tax Journal* 65, no. 1 (2012): 7–32.

Chetty, Raj, et al. "Where Is the Land of Opportunity? The Geography of Intergenerational Mobility in the United States." National Bureau of Economic Research Working Paper No. 19843, 2014.

Congressional Budget Office. *The Distribution of Household Income and Federal Taxes, 2010*. Washington, DC: December 2013.

Marx, Karl. *Capital: A Critique of Political Economy*. London: Penguin Classics, 2004 (translation of the original from 1867).

Pew Charitable Trusts, Economic Mobility Project. "Women's Work: The Economic Mobility of Women Across a Generation." 2014. Retrieved from www.pewtrusts.org/en/research-and-analysis/reports/2014/04/01/womens-work-the-economic-mobility-of-women-across-a-generation

Proctor, Bernadette D., Jessica L. Semega, and Melissa A. Kollar. "Income and Poverty in the United States: 2015." Report Number P60-256, United States Census Bureau, September 13, 2016.

CHAPTER 11   The Great Stagnation

Barro, Robert J. "Why This Slow Recovery Is Like No Recovery." *Wall Street Journal*, June 4, 2012.

Kravis, Marie-Josee. "What's Killing Jobs and Stalling the Economy," *The Wall Street Journal*, June 3, 2016.

Morath, Eric. "Seven Years Later, Recovery Remains the Weakest of the Post-World War II Era." *The Wall Street Journal*, July 29, 2016.

Mulligan, Casey B. "The Safety Net, Work Incentives, and the Economy since 2007." Testimony for the Committee on the Budget, U.S. House of Representatives Hearing on "Strengthening the Safety Net," April 17, 2012.

"Welfare Reform as We Knew It." *Wall Street Journal*, September 19, 2012.

CHAPTER 12   The Case of the Missing Workers

Autor, David H., and Mark G. Duggan. "The Growth in the Social Security Disability Rolls: A Fiscal Crisis Unfolding." *Journal of Economic Perspectives* 20, no. 3 (2006): 71–96.

Congressional Budget Office. *Social Security Disability Insurance: Participation and Spending*, Congress of the United States, Washington, DC: 2016.

Darby, Michael R. "Three-and-a-Half Million U.S. Employees Have Been Mislaid: Or, an Explanation of Unemployment, 1934–1941." *Journal of Political Economy* 84, no. 1 (1976): 1–16.

Eberstadt, Nicholas. "The Idle Army: America's Unworking Men," *The Wall Street Journal*, September 1, 2016.

Maestas, Nicole, Kathleen J. Mullen, and Alexander Strand. "Does Disability Insurance Receipt Discourage Work? Using Examiner Assignment to Estimate Causal Effects of SSDI Receipt." *American Economic Review* 103, no. 5 (2013): 1797–1829.

Sparshott, Jeffrey. "As Low-Skilled Jobs Disappear, Men Drop Out of the Workforce," *The Wall Street Journal*, June 20, 2016.

Wallis, John Joseph, and Daniel K. Benjamin. "Public Relief and Unemployment in the Great Depression." *Journal of Economic History* 41, no. 1 (1981): 97–102.

CHAPTER 13   The Gig Economy

Aloni, Erez. "Pluralizing the Sharing Economy." *Washington Law Review*. Vol. 91, March 31, 2016.

Burtch, Gordon, et al. "Can You Gig It? An Empirical Examination of the Gig-Economy and Entrepreneurial Activity." Ross School of Business, Paper No. 1308. March 7, 2016.

Calin, Gabriel, et al. "Comparative Analysis of the Online Recruiting Platforms Using Utility-Related Factors." *Informatica Economica*, 20, no. 2 (2016): 15.

D'Cruz, Premilla, and Ernesto Noronha. "Positives Outweighing Negatives: The Experiences of Indian Crowd-Source Workers." *Work Organization Labour & Globalization*, 10, no. 1 (Spring 2016): 44–63.

DeGeorge, Gail. "Numbers Don't Measure the 'Gig Economy'." *Sage Business Researcher*, November 15, 2016.

Eichhorst, Werner, et al. "How Big Is the Gig? Assessing the Preliminary Evidence on the Affects of Digitalization of the Labor Market," No. 17, Institute for the Study of Labor (IZA), 2016.

Torpey, Elka, and Andrew Hogan. "Working in a Gig Economy," U.S. Bureau of Labor Statistics, May, 2016.

CHAPTER 14   Mobility in America

Becker, Gary S., and Richard A. Posner. "How to Make the Poor Poorer." *Wall Street Journal*, January 26, 2007, p. A11.

Chetty, Raj, Nathaniel Hendren, Patrick Kline, and Emmanuel Saez. "Where is the Land of Opportunity? The Geography of Intergenerational Mobility in the United States." *The Quarterly Journal of Economics*, 129, no. 4 (December 2014): 1553–1623.

Chetty, Raj, Nathaniel Hendren, Patrick Kline, Emmanuel Saez, and Nick Turner. "Is the United States Still a Land of Opportunity? Recent Trends in Intergenerational Mobility." *American Economic Review* 104, no. 5 (2014): 141–147.

Jacoby, Tamar. "This Way Up: Mobility in America." *Wall Street Journal*, July 18, 2014.

U.S. Department of the Treasury. *Income Mobility in the U.S. from 1996 to 2005*. Washington, DC: Government Printing Office, 2007.

CHAPTER 15   Inflation and the Debt Bomb

Alchian, Armen A., and Reuben Kessel. "The Effects of Inflation." *Journal of Political Economy* 70, no. 6 (1962): 521–537.

Keynes, John Maynard. *The Economic Consequences of the Peace*. New York: Harcourt, Brace & Company, 1920.

Rattner, Steven. "The Dangerous Notion That Debt Doesn't Matter." *New York Times*, January 20, 2012.

Spiers, Elizabeth. "The World's Worst Inflation." *Fortune*, August 18, 2008, p. 36.

Timiraos, Nick. "Debate Over U.S Debt Changes Tone." *The Wall Street Journal*," July 24, 2016.

CHAPTER 16   Is It Real, or Is It Nominal?

Bresnahan, Timothy F., and Robert J. Gordon (eds.). *The Economics of New Goods*. NBER Studies in Income and Wealth no. 58. Chicago: University of Chicago Press, 1997.

Goklany, Indur M., and Jerry Taylor. "A Big Surprise on Gas." *Los Angeles Times*, August 11, 2008.

www.bls.gov. Web site of the Bureau of Labor Statistics, U.S. Department of Labor.

www.eia.doe.gov. Web site of the Energy Information Administration, U.S. Department of Energy.

CHAPTER 17   Can We Afford the Affordable Care Act?

Cox, Cynthia, Michelle Long, Ashley Semanskee, Rabah Kamal, Gary Claxton, and Larry Levitt. "2017 Changes in Insurer Participation in the Affordable Care Act's Health Insurance Marketplaces." The Henry J. Kaiser Foundation,

November 1, 2016. Retrieved from http://kff.org/health-reform/issue-brief/2017-premium-changes-and-insurer-participation-in-the-affordable-care-acts-health-insurance-marketplaces/

Goodnough, Abby. "Many See I.R.S. Penalties as More Affordable Than Insurance." *The New York Times*, November 7, 2016.

Ip, Greg. "The Unstable Economics in Obama's Health Care Law." *The Wall Street Journal*, August 19, 2016.

Radnofsky, Louise. "Number of Uninsured in U.S. Dropped Below 10% for First Time in 2015." *The Wall Street Journal*, May 17, 2016.

Somashekhar, Sandhya, and Ariana Eunjung Cha. "Insurers Restricting Choice of Doctors and Hospitals to Keep Costs Down." *Washington Post*, November 20, 2013.

CHAPTER 18   Who *Really* Pays Taxes?

Congressional Budget Office. "The Distribution of Household Income and Federal Taxes, 2013." Congress of the United States: Washington, DC: June, 2016.

Hollenbeck, Scott, and Maureen Keenan Kahr. "Ninety Years of Individual Income and Tax Statistics, 1916–2005." *Statistics of Income Bulletin*, Winter 2008. Retrieved from www.irs.gov/uac/IRS-Issues-Winter-2008-Statistics-of-Income-Bulletin

http://federalbudgetinpictures.com/. An array of spending, tax, and deficit facts, Prepared by the Heritage Foundation and conveniently displayed in pictures.

www.taxpolicycenter.org. Research on taxes, conducted and published by the Urban Institute and the Brookings Institution.

CHAPTER 19   Are You Stimulated Yet?

Cogan, John F., and John B. Taylor. "The Obama Stimulus Impact? Zero." *Wall Street Journal*, December 9, 2010.

Friedman, Milton, and David Meiselman. "The Relative Stability of Monetary Velocity and the Investment Multiplier in the United States, 1897–1958." In *Commission on Money and Credit: Stabilization Policies*. Englewood Cliffs, NJ: Prentice-Hall, 1963, pp. 165–268.

Merrick, Amy. "Rejecting Stimulus, States Forgo Rail Funds." *Wall Street Journal*, December 10, 2010, p. A6.

Peltzman, Sam. "The Effect of Government Subsidies-In-Kind on Private Expenditures: The Case of Higher Education." *Journal of Political Economy* 81, no. 1 (1973): 1–27.

Saving, Jason. "Can the Nation Stimulate Its Way to Prosperity?" *Economic Letters: Insights from the Federal Reserve Bank of Dallas* 6, no. 8 (2010): 1–3.

CHAPTER 20   Higher Taxes Are in Your Future

Council of Economic Advisers. *Economic Report of the President*. Washington, DC: Government Printing Office, 2017.

Lazear, Edward P. "America's Coming Tax Increase." *The Wall Street Journal*, April 27, 2016.

The 2016 Annual Report of the Board of Trustees of the Federal Old-Age and Survivors Insurance and Federal Disability Insurance Trust Funds. Washington, DC: Government Printing Office, 2016.

"The State Taxathon," *The Wall Street Journal*, October 26, 2016.

http://www.usdebtclock.org/#. One of many private Web sites that track the U.S. national debt.

http://www.treasurydirect.gov/NP/debt/current. U.S. Treasury Web site, giving you the current status of the national debt and enabling you to find that status on any working day for the past 20 years.

CHAPTER 21   The Myths of Social Security

Congressional Budget Office. "Social Security: A Primer." September 2001. Retrieved from www.cbo.gov/showdoc.cfm?index=3213&sequence=0

Engelhardt, Gary V., and Jonathan Gruber. *Social Security and the Evolution of Elderly Poverty.* NBER Working Paper No. 10466. Boston: National Bureau of Economic Research, 2004.

Oshio, Takashi. *Social Security and Trust Fund Management.* NBER Working Paper No. 10444. Boston: National Bureau of Economic Research, 2004.

The 2016 Annual Report of the Board of Trustees of the Federal Old-Age and Survivors Insurance and Federal Disability Insurance Trust Funds. Washington, DC: Government Printing Office, 2016.

https://www.ssa.gov/history/briefhistory3.html. A history of the background and development of Social Security, written by the Social Security Administration.

CHAPTER 22   The Fed and Financial Panics

Friedman, Milton, and Anna J. Schwartz. *A Monetary History of the United States, 1867–1960.* Princeton, NJ: Princeton University Press, 1963.

Goodman, Peter. "Taking a Hard New Look at a Greenspan Legacy." *New York Times*, October 9, 2008.

Lowenstein, Roger. *America's Bank: The Epic Struggle to Create the Federal Reserve.* New York: Penguin, 2015.

Norris, Floyd. "Plan B: Flood Banks with Cash." *New York Times*, October 10, 2008.

CHAPTER 23   The Fed Feeding Frenzy

Hilsenrath, Jon. "After Crisis, U.S. Is Set to Rethink Fed's Role." *Wall Street Journal*, May 18, 2009, p. A12.

Hilsenrath, Jon, and Pedro Nicolai Da Costa, "Fed Sets October End for Bond Buying." *Wall Street Journal*, July 9, 2014.

Lang, Jia Lynn, Neil Irwin, and David S. Hizenrath. "Fed Aid in Financial Crisis Went Beyond U.S. Banks to Industry, Foreign Firms." *Washington Post*, December 2, 2010.

www.federalreserve.gov/monetarypolicy/mpr_default.htm. Every six months the Federal Reserve System is required to submit a report to Congress on its current monetary policy. You can find the latest version at this address.

CHAPTER 24   Deposit Insurance and Financial Markets

Allen, Franklin, and Douglas Gale. "Competition and Financial Stability." *Journal of Money, Credit and Banking* 36, no. 3 (2004): S453–S480.

Bordo, M., H. Rockoff, and A. Redish. "The U.S. Banking System from a Northern Exposure: Stability versus Efficiency." *Journal of Economic History* 54, no. 2 (1994): 325–341.

Diamond, D., and P. Dybvig. "Bank Runs, Deposit Insurance, and Liquidity." *Journal of Political Economy* 91, no. 3 (1983): 401–419.

Friedman, Milton, and Anna J. Schwartz. *A Monetary History of the United States, 1867–1960.* Princeton, NJ: Princeton University Press, 1963.

CHAPTER 25   Revolutionizing the Way We Pay

Castronova, Edward, and Joshua A. T. Fairfield. "The Digital Wallet Revolution," *International New York Times*, September 12, 2014.

Cunningham, Ellen. "Digital Wallets: Intro to Apple Pay, Android Pay, Chase Pay, and More," August 29, 2016. Retrieved from www.cardfellow.com/digital-wallets-apple-pay-samsung-pay-paypal/

Eavis, Peter. "Digital Currencies Have Yet to Prove Themselves." *International New York Times*, April 2, 2014, p. 16.

Helft, Miguel. "The Death of Cash," *Fortune*, July 23, 2012, p. 118ff.

"Less Coin to Purloin." *The Economist*, April 5, 2014, p. 66.

Mansfield, Heather. "Mobile for Good: How Mobile Wallets Will Transform Fundraising." NonProfit Technology Network, April 16, 2014.

Sidel, Robin. "Card Issuers Jump Onto Apple Pay Bandwagon." *Wall Street Journal*, September 12, 2014.

CHAPTER 26   Cryptocurrencies

Ciaian, Pavel, et al. "The Economics of Bitcoin Price Formation." *Applied Economics* 48, no. 16 (2015): 1799–1815.

Dibrova, Alina, "Virtual Currency: New Step in Monetary Development." *Proceedings, Social and Behavioral Sciences* 229 (2016): 42–49.

Elendner, Herrmann, et al. "The Cross-Section of Crypto-Currencies as Financial Assets: An Overview." *SFB 649 Discussion Paper 2016-038*, October 3, 2016.

Mushkin, Martin, et al. "Virtual Currency Is Here to Stay: Legal Aspects of the Bitcoin Evolution," April 2, 2014. Retrieved from http://www.mushkinlaw.com/virtual-currency-is-here-to-stay1/

"Shedding Light on the Dark Web." *The Economist*, July 16, 2016. Retrieved from http://www.economist.com/news/international/21702176-drug-trade-moving-street-online-cryptomarkets-forced-compete

CHAPTER 27   The Value of the Dollar

Clark, Peter, et al. *Exchange Rates and Economic Fundamentals.* IMF Occasional Paper no. 115. Washington, DC: International Monetary Fund, 1994.

Eichengreen, Barry. *Exorbitant Privilege: The Rise and Fall of the Dollar and the Future of the International Monetary System.* New York,: Oxford University Press, 2012.

Grant, James. "Is the Medicine Worse than the Illness?" *Wall Street Journal*, December 20, 2008.

www.exchange-rates.org. One of many private currency converters available online.

Chapter 28   The Eurozone after Brexit

Charlemagne, "SimEurope: Some Fantasies for the Future of Europe May Cause More Problems than They Resolve." *The Economist*, September 22, 2012, p. 64.

Fidler, Stephen. "Spanish Bailout Is No Fix for Italy's Woes." *Wall Street Journal Europe*, October 5–7, 2012, p. 4.

Gianviti, Francois, et al. "A European Mechanism for Sovereign Debt Crisis Resolution: A Proposal." *Bruegel Blueprint Series*, vol. X, 2010.

"The Emperor Creates No Jobs." *Wall Street Journal*, May 28, 2013.

www.esm.europa.eu Website of the European Stability Mechanism

Chapter 29   The Global Power of the Big Mac

Ashenfelter, Orley, and Stepan Jurajda, "Comparing Real Wages." NBER Working Paper No. 18006, 2012. Retrieved from www.nber.org/papers/w18006

Ashenfelter, Orley, and Stepan Jurajda, "Cross-Country Comparisons of Wage Rates: The McWage Index." Princeton, NJ: Industrial Relations Section, August 2009.

Clementi, Fabio, et al. "A Big Mac Test of Price Dynamics and Dispersion of Across Euro Area,." *Economic Bulletin* 30, no. 3, August (2010): 2037–2053.

www.economist.com/content/big-mac-index Website for the Big Mac index

https://www.statista.com/statistics/275235/big-mac-worldwide-cities-working-time/ Recent data on the number of minutes of work required to pay for a Big Mac

Chapter 30   The Opposition to Globalization

Althaus, Dudley, and Christina Rogers. "Donald Trump's Nafta Plan Would Confront Globalized Auto Industry." *The Wall Street Journal*, November 10, 2016.

Frankel, J. A., and D. Romer. "Does Trade Cause Growth?" *American Economic Review* 89, no. 3 (1999): 379–399.

Makki, Shiva S., and Agapi Somwaru. "Impact of Foreign Direct Investment and Trade on Economic Growth: Evidence from Developing Countries." *American Journal of Agricultural Economics* 86, no. 3 (2004): 795–801.

"Pirates v Economists." *The Economist*, July 12, 2014, p. 42.

Reynolds, Alan. "What the China Trade Warriors Get Wrong." *The Wall Street Journal*, October 26, 2016.

Trivedi, Anjani. "In Trump's China, Industrial Subsidies Loom Large." *The Wall Street Journal*, November 16, 2016.

CHAPTER 31   The $750,000 Job

Congressional Budget Office. "The Pros and Cons of Pursuing Free-Trade Agreements." July 2003. Retrieved from www.cbo.gov/showdoc.cfm?index=4458&sequence=0

Crandall, Robert W. "The Effects of U.S. Trade Protection for Autos and Steel." *Brookings Papers on Economic Activity* 1987, no. 2 (1987): 271–288.

Eberstadt, Nicholas. "The Idle Army: America's Unworking Men." *The Wall Street Journal*, September 1, 2016.

Jordan, Miriam and Santiago Perez. "Small Businesses Lament There Are Too Few Mexicans in U.S., Not Too Many." *The Wall Street Journal*, November 24, 2016.

"Stolen Jobs? Offshoring." *The Economist*, December 13, 2003, p. 15.

Turner, Taos, and Paul Kiernan. "How Latin America Pays the Price for Protectionism." *The Wall Street Journal*, November 25, 2016.

INDEX

A

AARA (American Recovery and Reinvestment Act of 2009), 128, 130–131
Abject poverty, 23–24
ACA (Affordable Care Act), 113–119
Acemoglu, Daron, 6
Adverse selection, 114–115, 159–160
Affordability index, 107–108
Affordable Care Act (ACA), 113–119
Afghanistan War, 30, 129
Africa
    institutions in, 6, 7
    per capita income in, 26
    poverty in, 24
    standard of living in, 24
African Americans, income mobility of, 94–95
After-tax income, 33–34
Aggregate demand, 76
    deposit insurance and, 158
    Federal Reserve and, 151, 152–154
Agricultural subsidies, 198
AIG (American International Group), 149, 151, 153
Airbnb, 88–89
Air pollution, 201
American Dream, 86
American International Group (AIG), 149, 151, 153
American Recovery and Reinvestment Act of 2009 (AARA), 128, 130–131
Antipoverty programs, 91–92
Apparel industry, 207
Apple, 32
Apple Pay, 166
Argentina, 24, 25, 136–137
Arts, GDP and, 48
Ashenfelter, Orley, 195
Assets, 4
    in Argentina, 137
    of banks, 148, 158
    of elderly, 140
    Federal Reserve and, 153
    globalization and, 205–206
    net, 66
    rate of return on, 64
Asymmetric information, 159
Auerbach, Alan, 67
Austerity, 187, 189

Australia, 4, 5–6, 24
Automatic teller machines (ATMs), 168
Automobiles
    government bailouts for, 134
    innovations in, 14
    insourcing for, 20
    protectionism for, 202
    quality improvements to, 108
    trade barriers for, 206–207
Average income, 25–26, 66, 96, 193, 194
Average per capita income, 25
Average tax rate, 121–124

B

Baby boomers, 37–41
    retirement of, 83
    Social Security and, 141, 142
Bailouts. See Government bailouts
Balance sheets, 149, 153
Bank panics, 148
    Panic of 1907, 147
    Panic of 2008, 76–77, 149, 152, 157, 159
Bank runs, 147
    deposit insurance and, 157–159
    in Great Depression, 139, 148, 158, 159
Bankruptcy
    bitcoin exchanges, 171–172
    from debt crisis, 184
    risk and, 180
Banks. See also Central banks
    assets of, 148, 158
    commercial banks, 148, 149–151
    deposit insurance at, 157–162
    in EU, 187, 188, 189
    Federal Reserve and, 147–151
    fractional reserve banking system, 168
    government regulation of, 189
    risk categories for, 162
Barrett, Craig, 18
Barro, Robert, 131
Bear Stearns, 153
The Beatles, 181–182
Beggar-thy-neighbor, 200
Behavior, taxes and, 34
Bernanke, Ben, 148, 149
Big Mac Index, globalization and, 192–196
Bitcoin miners, 170–172

Bitcoins (BTC), 169, 170–172
    exchanges, 171–172
    as investments, 173
Blockchains, 170–171, 172
Bloomingdale's, 166
BLS (Bureau of Labor Statistics), 79, 87
BMW, 20
Boeing Corporation, 181–182
Bondholders, 180
Bonds. See also Treasury bonds
    currencies for, 180
    of elderly, 140
    inflation and, 100, 102
    Panic of 2008 and, 149
    rate of return for, 180
Brazil, 4
Brexit, 189–190
Budget constraint, 30, 98, 133
Budget deficit, 30, 185
    economic stimulus packages and, 126, 134
    interest rates and, 129
    tax cuts and, 127
Burden, of taxes, 120–121
Bureau of Labor Statistics (BLS), 79, 87
Bush, George W.
    economic stimulus packages of, 126, 134, 135
    government regulation and, 76
    government spending and, 30, 35, 76
    national debt and, 98, 100
    tax cuts of, 127
Business cycle
    GDP and, 45–49
    Great Stagnation and, 71–77
    income mobility and, 91–96
    national debt and, 98–103
    nominal prices and, 105–109
    real prices and, 105–109
    recessions and, 51–54
    unemployment rate and, 79–84
Buyer's remorse, 199

C

Cambodia, 19
Canada, 4, 24, 180
    Big Mac Index, 195
    globalization and, 198, 201
Capital, 64
    human, 3
    physical, 3
    social, 94

Capital in the Twenty-First Century (Piketty), 64
Capitalism
  in China, 28
  economic growth and, 23–28
  income and, 23–28
  income inequality in, 64–69
  institutions and, 24
  per capita income and, 26
  in South Korea, 27
  wealth and, 64–69
  in West Germany, 27–28
Capital stock, 3
Cash-constrained, 131
Cash transfers, 74
CBO (Congressional Budget Office), 65, 134
CCC (Civilian Conservation Corps), 80
Central banks, 184. *See also* Federal Reserve System
  ECB, 187, 188
Checks, 164
Chetty, Raj, 94, 96
Child labor, 201
Chile, 25
China
  Big Mac Index in, 195
  capitalism in, 28
  Communism in, 28
  economic growth in, 6
  national debt and, 99, 100
  outsourcing to, 18
  productivity in, 196
  real wages in, 195
  standard of living in, 24
  trade and, 19
Chrysler, 134, 202
Civilian Conservation Corps (CCC), 80
Civil law system, 4–5, 6
Clinton, Bill, 75
Coca-Cola, 12
Coins, 164–167
Coldplay, 182
College Recruiter, 88
Colonial growth, 5–6
Commercial banks, 148, 149–151
Common law system, 4, 5
Communism, 26, 27–28
Comparative advantage, 199
Competition
  for employment, 205
  globalization and, 199–200
  income inequality and, 68
  profits and, 199
  protectionism and, 203
Computers. *See also* Internet and Internet commerce
  cryptocurrencies, 168–173
  hacking, bitcoins and, 173
  for payments systems, 164–167

Congress
  domestic-content bill in, 208
  economic stimulus packages of, 126, 130
  inflation tax and, 99
  national debt and, 98, 101
  outsourcing and, 16
  protectionism by, 203
  Social Security and, 140, 141, 142, 143
  taxes during Great Recession, 76
  unemployment benefits and, 74–75
Congressional Budget Office (CBO), 65, 134
Constant-quality price, 108
Construction industry, 47, 72, 73–74, 186
Consumer price index (CPI), 141, 155
Consumers
  currencies and, 178–179
  revealed preferences of, 105
  tax cuts and, 127–128
Consumption
  economic stimulus packages and, 134
  in GDP, 48
  government spending and, 129
  PCE, 154–155
  PPP and, 25
  taxes and, 76
Contract employment, 85–89
Contract rights, 4–5
Corporate taxes, 31
Corruption, 185, 186
Costa Rica, 25
Cost of living
  CPI and, 141
  foreign exchange rates and, 194–195
  poverty line and, 92
Counterfeiting, of cryptocurrencies, 171
CPI (Consumer price index), 141, 155
Crandall, Robert W., 207
Credit card companies, Apple Pay and, 166
Creditors, 158
Credit risks, profits from, 160–161
Cryptocurrencies, 168–173
  adverse aspects of, 172–173
  value, 169–170, 171–172
Cryptography, 169
Currency
  bank runs and, 157
  cryptocurrencies, 168–173
  demand for, 181
  foreign exchange rates for, 177–182

  interest rates and, 180
  payments systems and, 164–167
  PPP of, 179
  price level for, 179
  purchasing power of, 179, 181
  supply of, 181
  trade of, 177
Currency union, 188

D

Darby, Michael, 80
Darkcoin, 169
Davy, Humphrey, 9, 32
Debt, national. *See* National debt
Debt crisis, 184
Decision-making process, gig economy and, 89
Default
  on national debt, 102
  risk, 180
Defense Department (United States), 16
Deficit, government. *See* Budget deficit
Deflation, 154
Demand. *See also* Aggregate demand; Supply; Supply and demand
  aggregate, 76, 152, 153, 154, 158
  for currencies, 177–182
  law of, 90, 110
Demand deposits, 102
Department of Defense (United States), 16
Department of Labor (United States), 208
Department of State (United States), 16
Deposit insurance
  adverse selection with, 159–160
  bank runs and, 157–159
  at banks, 157–162
  fees for, 161–162
  moral hazards with, 160–161
Depository institutions, 102, 157, 168
Depth, of recessions, 53
Developing countries
  employment in, 201
  hard currency in, 181
  moral hazards with, 160
  standard of living in, 196
Digital chips, payment cards with, 166
Digital currencies, 168–173
Digital wallets, 165–167
Disability payments, 47, 83
Discouraged workers, 80–82
Diseases, in colonies, 6
Dispersion, of recessions, 53

Disposable income, 107–108, 127
Dodd-Frank Act, 150
Dollars, 177–182
Domestically produced goods and services, 46
Domestic-content bill, 208
Dumping, 200–201
Duration, of recessions, 53

E
Earned income tax credit, 92
Easterly, William, 5–6
East Germany, 27–28
ECB (European Central Bank), 187, 188
Economic growth
　baby boomers and, 38
　capitalism and, 23–28
　contract rights and, 4–5
　failure of, 6
　from globalization, 199
　government spending and, 30–35
　innovation and, 9–14, 32
　institutions for, 3, 5–6
　investment and, 64
　in Italy, 187
　outsourcing and, 16–21
　population growth and, 54
　poverty and, 23–28
　property rights and, 3–7
　threat to, 30–35
　trade barriers and, 17–18
Economic safety net, 74–75
Economic Stimulus Act of 2008, 127, 128
Economic stimulus packages, 126–132, 134
Economies of scale, 165
The Economist, 194
Edison, Thomas, 9, 32
Education
　for economic growth, 27
　government regulation of, 76
　government spending on, 128–129
　income mobility and, 94
　SSI and, 82
Egypt, 4
Elderly persons. See also Pensions; Retirement; Social Security
　baby boomers, 37–41
　poverty and, 139–140
Elections, 120, 124
Embedded chips, payment cards with, 166
Employment. See also Productivity; Retirement; Unemployment rate
　ACA and, 118
　aging workforce, 37
　benefits, 86, 89

competition for, 205
in developing countries, 201
disability payments and, 82–83
in Europe, 21
free trade and, 207–209
globalization and, 205–209
in Great Recession, 71
labor force participation rate, 37–38
labor productivity, 37–38
licensing for, 47
mentorship and workplace experience, 39–40
outsourcing and, 16–21
protectionism and, 207–209
in recessions, 21, 52
scarcity and, 205
in United States, 21
Employment benefits, 86, 89
Entertainment industry, GDP and, 48
Entitlement programs, 30
Environment, globalization and, 201
EU. See European Union
Europe
　aging workforce in, 40
　employment in, 21
　innovation in, 12–13
　taxes in, 31
European Central Bank (ECB), 187, 188
European Common Market, 208
European Stability Mechanism (ESM), 188–189
European Union (EU)
　banks in, 187, 188, 189
　capitalism in, 25
　euros in, 177–182, 184–190
　fiscal pact in, 189
　GDP in, 46
　globalization and, 184–190
　Great Recession and, 189
　national debt in, 188
　R&D in, 32
　recessions in, 188
　taxes in, 31
　textile industry in, 208
Euros, 177–182, 184–190
Eurozone, globalization and, 184–190
Excess reserves, 149–150, 152
Excess supply, of housing, 74
Exchange rates, flexible, 177
Expansion, of economy, 54
Exports, 19, 178–179, 200, 203
Extractive institutions, 6, 7

F
Facebook, 32–33
Failure of nations' economic growth, 6
Fair share, of taxes, 120–121

Family
　in developing countries, 201
　income mobility and, 94
Fannie Mae, 149, 153
The Fed. See Federal Reserve System
Federal Deposit Insurance Corporation (FDIC), 158–159
Federal Reserve System, 147–151
　assets and, 153
　CPI and, 155
　Great Recession and, 72
　inflation and, 102–103, 153–155
　interest rates and, 155
　QE and, 152–155
Federal Savings and Loan Insurance Corporation (FSLIC), 158
Final goods and services, 45, 46, 133
Finland, 25
Fiscal pact, 189
Fiscal policy
　ACA and, 113–119
　economic stimulus packages and, 126–132
　Social Security and, 139–143
　taxes and, 120–124, 133–137
Fiscal Stability Treaty, 189
Fitzgerald, F. Scott, 95
Fixed income, Social Security as, 140–141
Flexible exchange rates, 177
Food, stocks of, 7
Food stamps, 75
Ford Motor Company, 134, 202
Foreign currency swaps, 153
Foreign exchange rates, 192–196
　cost of living and, 194–195
　for currencies, 177–182
　PPP and, 194
　productivity and, 196
　real wages and, 195–196
　supply and demand with, 193
Fractional reserve banking system, 168
France, 4, 187–190
Fraser Institute, 24
Freddie Mac, 149, 153
Freelancers, 85–89
Freelancers Union, 87
Freelancer (website), 88
Free trade
　competition and, 199
　employment and, 207–208
　globalization and, 198–199
　opposition to, 203, 207–208
Friedman, Milton, 148
FSLIC (Federal Savings and Loan Insurance Corporation), 158
Fuller, Ida Mae, 142

G

Gains from trade, 199
Garten, Jeffrey E., 18
Gasoline, price of, 105–108
Gates, Bill, 13, 32
GATT. *See* General Agreement on Tariffs and Trade
GDP. *See* Gross domestic product
General Agreement on Tariffs and Trade (GATT), 198
General Motors (GM), 134, 202
Genetically modified organisms (GMOs), 12
Germany, 27–28, 47, 101
Gig economy, 85–89
Glassware industry, 207
Globalization
  assets and, 205–206
  Big Mac Index and, 192–196
  competition and, 199–200
  dollars and, 177–182
  employment and, 205–209
  environment and, 201
  EU and, 184–190
  free trade and, 198–199
  gains from, 205–206
  opposition to, 198–203
  productivity and, 40
  protectionism and, 199–200, 205–209
  trade and, 198–199
GM (General Motors), 134, 202
Goklany, Indur, 107–108
Gold, as currency, 169–170
Goods and services
  final, 45, 46, 133
  in GDP, 45–46
  illegal, 46–48
  intermediate, 48
  non-traded, 193
  normal, 201
  traded, 193
Google Wallet, 166
Government bailouts, 30, 134
  of Greece, 186
  of Ireland, 32
  of Italy, 186–187
  of Spain, 187
Government regulation, 25
  of banks, 147–151, 189
  economic growth and, 38
  of education, 76
  Great Recession and, 76–77
Government spending
  in Argentina, 136–137
  consumption and, 129
  economic growth and, 30–35
  in economic stimulus packages, 129
  in EU, 185, 186, 187
  in Great Recession, 76
  incentives and, 30–32
  interest rates and, 129

in Italy, 187
taxes and, 30–31, 35, 134–135
Great Britain. *See* United Kingdom
Great Depression
  bank runs in, 139, 148, 158, 159
  economic stimulus packages in, 131
  Federal Reserve in, 148
  Great Recession and, 72
  tariffs and, 200
  unemployment rate in, 79–80
Great Gatsby curve, 95
Great Recession
  comparison to Eurozone situation, 189
  economic safety net in, 74–75
  government regulation and, 76–77
  government spending in, 76
  Great Stagnation after, 71–77
  housing in, 73–74
Great Stagnation, 71–77
Greece, 4, 185–190
Greenspan, Alan, 148–149
Gross domestic product (GDP), 45–49. *See also* Real gross domestic product
  AARA and, 131
  baby boomers and real per capita GDP, 38
  budget deficit and, 185
  economic stimulus packages and, 126
  in Eurozone, 185, 187, 190
  government spending and, 30, 135
  happiness and, 48–49
  of Italy, 187
  measurement of, 45–49
  R&D and, 48
  underground economy and, 46–48
Growth, economic, 3–4
Guru (website), 88

H

Hacking, bitcoins and, 173
Happiness, income and, 48–49
Hard currency, 181
Health insurance, ACA and, 113–119
Heinze, Otto, 147
Hewlett, Bill, 33
High-income people
  luck of, 66–67, 93
  taxes of, 35, 120–124
Homemakers, 46, 47
Honda, 20
Hong Kong, 3, 24
Hoover, Herbert, 148
Hospitals, ACA and, 116

Housing, in Great Recession, 73–74
Human capital, 3
Hyperinflation, 101

I

Illegal goods and services, 46–48
Illegal transactions, cryptocurrencies and, 172–173
Illiquidity, 158
Imports. *See also* Trade barriers
  beggar-thy-neighbor policies, 200
  of Japanese automobiles, 202, 206–207
  quotas on, 200, 205
  trade restrictions and, 203
Incentives
  for future investments, 6
  government spending and, 30–32
  innovation and, 11
  for property rights, 6, 7
  with TANF, 75
  taxes and, 30–32, 34
  in Zimbabwe, 7
Inclusive institutions, 6
Income. *See also* High-income people; Per capita income; Real per capita income; Wages
  after-tax, 33–34
  average, 25–26, 66, 96, 192
  average per capita, 25
  capitalism and, 23–28
  disposable, 107–108, 127
  of elderly, 140
  fixed, Social Security as, 140–141
  happiness and, 48–49
  inequality, 64–69
  marginal tax rates on, 65
  mobility, 66–67, 91–96
  nominal, 107
  PPP and, 25, 179, 194
  real, 52, 66, 107
  taxes and, 120–124
Income inequality, 64–69, 94, 96
Income mobility, 66–67, 91–96
Income taxes
  credits, 136
  cuts, and economic stimulus packages, 127–128
  cuts in, 135
  earned income tax credit, 92
  economic stimulus packages and, 127–128
  liability, 127
  lump sum tax rebates, 127
  real tax rate, 135
Independent contractors, 85–89
India, 4, 16, 18–19, 20
Individual mandate, with ACA, 114

Indonesia, 19
Industrial production, in recessions, 52
Industrial Revolution, 11, 23–24
Infant mortality, 26–27
Inflation
  CPI and, 141
  Federal Reserve and, 101, 102–103, 153–155
  GDP and, 52
  gold and, 170
  hyperinflation, 101
  interest rates and, 180
  national debt and, 98–103
  nominal prices and, 106–107, 109
  PPP and, 179
  prices and, 106–107, 109
  Social Security and, 140
  stagnation and, 73
  tax, 99–103
In-kind transfers, 92
  food stamps, 75
  Medicaid, 113, 114, 117, 118, 119
  Medicare, 65, 119
Innovation, 9–14
  in automobiles, 14
  economic growth and, 9–14, 32
  future of, 13–14
  incentives and, 11
  in Industrial Revolution, 23
  invention and, 9–10, 13–14
  markets for, 12–13
  patents and, 12
  productivity and, 33
  profit from, 13
  property rights to, 14
  R&D and, 10–11
  real per capita income and, 23
  standard of living and, 10–11
  taxes and, 13, 33–34
  wealth and, 32–33
Insolvency, 158. See also Bankruptcy
  in Eurozone, 188
Insourcing, 20
Institutions
  capitalism and, 24
  depository, 102, 157
  economic growth and, 3, 5–6
  extractive, 6, 7
  inclusive, 6
  in Industrial Revolution, 24
  wealth and, 6, 7
  in Zimbabwe, 7
Intellectual property, 48
Interest on reserves, banks paying, 150–151
Interest rates, 150
  currencies and, 180
  default risk and, 180
  Federal Reserve and, 155

government spending and, 129
  inflation and, 180
  real interest rates, 180
  in recession, 73
  risk and, 160
Interim European Financial Stability Facility, 188
Intermediate goods, 48
Internal Revenue Service (IRS), 87, 100, 123, 135, 136
International Monetary Fund, 186
Internet and Internet commerce
  gig economy and, 85–89
  innovation, 9, 12
  outsourcing and, 16–17
  ride-sharing, 12, 172
Invention, 9–10
  innovation and, 9–10, 13–14
  patents for, 12
Investment
  bitcoins as, 173
  in capital, 64
  currencies for, 180
  for economic growth, 3, 64
  in human capital, 3
  in physical capital, 3
  rate of return on, 64, 159
  in R&D, 48
Iraq War, 30
Ireland, 31, 32
IRS (Internal Revenue Service), 87, 100, 123, 135, 136
Israel, 4
Italy, 4
  Eurozone and, 186–187, 189
  GDP, 46

J
Japan, 21, 25
  aging workforce in, 40
  automobiles from, 202, 206–207
  deflation in, 154
Jobs. See Employment
Jobs, Steve, 32
Jurajda, Stepan, 195

K
Das Kapital (Marx), 64
Kennedy, John F., 35, 127, 128
Kirchner, Cristina, 136
Kotlikoff, Lawrence, 67

L
Labor Department (United States), 208
Labor force, 79. See also Employment
  participation rate, 37–38, 83–84
  unemployment, 79–84
Labor productivity, 37–38. See also Productivity

Labor supply curve, 81
Lady Gaga, 48
Lasers, 10
Laws of supply and demand, 110
  gold and, 169–170
La'zooz, 172
Legal systems, 3–7
  for economic growth, 3, 4–5
  patents in, 12
  rule of law and, 3, 7
Legal tender, 164
Lender of last resort, 148, 149
Levine, Ross, 5–6
Liabilities, 158
  bank deposits, 168
Licensing, occupational, 47
Life cycle pattern of earnings, 66–67, 93
Life expectancy, 26–27
Light bulb, invention of, 9, 10, 13, 32
Litecoin, 169
Loyalty points, with digital wallets, 166–167
Luck, 66–67, 93, 95
Lump sum tax rebates, 127
Luxembourg, 3
Lyft, 12, 88

M
Macy's, 166
Mafia, 186
Mahoney, Paul, 4, 5
Marginal cost, gold mining, 170
Marginal tax rates, 35, 123–124
  on income, 65
  reduction of, 135
  tax cuts and, 127
  underground economy and, 48
Markets
  for innovation, 12–13
  for scarce resources, 24
Market valuation, 88
Market value, 45
Marx, Karl, 64
McDonald's restaurants, 166
  Big Mac Index, globalization and, 192–196
McKinsey Global Institute, 87
McWages, 195–196
Median age, 93
Medicaid, 113, 114, 117, 118, 119
Medicare, 65, 119
Mentorship, and workplace experience, 39–40
Mercedes-Benz, 20
Mexico, 4, 5, 20, 198, 201
Microsoft Corporation, 13, 32
Midwest states, 94
Minimum wage, 97
Mobility, income, 91–96
Monero, 169

A Monetary History of the United States (Friedman and Schwartz), 148
Monetary policy
    deposit insurance and, 157–162
    Federal Reserve and, 147–155
    payments systems and, 164–167
Money supply, 103, 152, 158
Moral hazards, 115, 186
    with deposit insurance, 160–161
    in Eurozone, 188
Morgan, J. P., 147
Mortgage-backed securities (MBS), 153, 157
Mortgages, 86, 149
Mt. Go, 171
Mugabe, Robert, 7

N
NAFTA (North American Free Trade Agreement), 198, 199, 203
Nakamoto, Satoshi, 169
National Bureau of Economic Research (NBER), 51–54
National Credit Union Share Insurance Fund (NCUSIF), 158
National debt
    AARA and, 130–131
    economic stimulus packages and, 126, 130–131
    in EU, 188
    euro, effect of, 188
    inflation and, 98–103
Natural-resource endowments, 3
NBER (National Bureau of Economic Research), 51–54
NCUSIF (National Credit Union Share Insurance Fund), 158
Near-field communication (NFC), 166
Neither employed nor in education or training (NEET), 82
Net assets, 66
Netherlands, 46
Net tax, 67
Net worth, 35
New goods and services, 45–46
New York Times, 10
New Zealand, 4, 5–6, 24
NFC (Near-field communication), 166
Nominal income, 107
Nominal prices, 105–109
    declining, 109
Noncash transfers, 74
Non-employer firms, 87
Non-traded goods and services, 193
Normal goods, 201
North America, colonies in, 5–6

North American Free Trade Agreement (NAFTA), 198, 199, 203
North Korea, 27

O
Obama, Barack, 75. *See also* American Recovery and Reinvestment Act of 2009
    economic stimulus and, 126, 129–130, 134
    food stamps and, 75
    government regulation and, 76–77
    government spending and, 30, 35, 76
    national debt and, 98, 100
Obamacare (ACA), 113–119
On-demand services, 87
Open market, 152
Opportunity cost, 83
Outsourcing
    economic growth and, 16–21
    prices and, 19–20

P
Packard, David, 33
Panic of 1907, 147
Panic of 2008, 76–77, 149, 152, 157, 159
Patents and patent law, 32
    innovation and, 12
Pay-as-you-go system, 142
Payments systems, 164–167
Payroll taxes, 141, 143
PCE (personal consumption expenditures) price index, 154–155
Peercoin, 169
Pensions. *See also* Social Security
    in Argentina, 136–137
    as assets, 140
    in EU, 184, 186, 188
    government spending on, 30
Per capita growth, reductions in, 39
Per capita income, 26. *See also* Real per capita income
    average, 25
    average annual growth, 17–18
Personal consumption expenditures (PCE) price index, 154–155
Physical capital, 3
Platform firms, 87–88
Political stability, 3, 5
Political systems, 3, 5
Pollution, 201
Population growth, 54
Portugal, 187–190
Poverty
    in Africa, 24
    average income and, 25–26
    economic growth and, 23–28

of elderly, 139–140
    Industrial Revolution and, 23–24
    in Russia, 3
    Social Security and, 65
    in United States, 91–92
Poverty line, 92
PPP (Purchasing power parity), 25, 179, 194
Pre-existing conditions, ACA and, 115–116
Price levels, 140
    for currencies, 179
    GDP and, 45
Prices, 105–109. *See also* Price levels
    Big Mac Index and, 194–195
    CPI, 155
    declining nominal prices, 109
    for gasoline, 105–108
    inflation and, 106–107, 109
    law of demand and, 90, 110
    nominal prices, 105–109
    outsourcing and, 19–20
    PCE, 154–155
    product quality and, 108
    unit of account for, 99
Productivity, 37–38
    adverse effects on, 38–39
    Big Mac Index and, 196
    disposable income and, 107–108
    experience and, 39
    foreign exchange rates and, 196
    income inequality and, 68
    innovation and, 33
    from voluntary trade, 198
Product quality, prices and, 108
Profits
    competition and, 199
    from credit risks, 160
    of hospitals, 116
    for innovations, 13
    Panic of 1907 and, 147
Progressive tax policies, 67
Property rights, 3–7
    bank deposits, 168
    incentives for, 6, 7
    to innovation, 14
    in Zimbabwe, 7
Prostitution, 46, 47
Protectionism
    competition and, 203
    cost of, 207
    employment and, 207–209
    globalization and, 199–200, 205–209
    in Japan, 21
Protection of persons and property, 5
Purchasing power, 141, 179, 181
Purchasing power parity (PPP), 25, 179, 194

Q
Quality, of products, 108
Quantitative easing (QE), 152–155
Quid pro quo (something for something), 206
Quotas, on imports, 200, 205

R
Radio frequency identification (RFID), 166
Rate of return
on bonds, 180
on investments, 64, 159
on Social Security, 142
R&D (research and development), 10–11, 32, 48
Reagan, Ronald, 127, 128
Real gross domestic product (real GDP), 45, 46, 71
in recessions, 51–52, 72–73
Real income, 52, 66, 107
Real interest rates, 180
Real per capita GDP, baby boomers and, 38
Real per capita income, 5, 23, 28, 49
in recessions, 54
in Zimbabwe, 7
Real price, 107
Real purchasing power, 140
Real tax rate, 135
Real value, 103
Real wages, 81–82, 195–196
Recessions, 51–54. *See also* Great Recession
bank runs in, 157–158
business cycle and, 51–54
discouraged workers in, 81
economic stimulus packages in, 126–132
employment in, 21
in EU, 188
Federal Reserve for, 147, 148, 149, 151
interest rates in, 73
productivity and, 40
unemployment rate in, 80, 81
Recovery, economic, 40
Relative prices, 105–109
Reparations, 101
Required reserves, 149–150, 152
Research and development (R&D), 10–11, 32, 48
Reserves, banks, 149–150, 152
Resource allocation, digital wallets and, 167
Retail sales, in recessions, 52
Retirement, 83, 136, 139–140. *See also* Pensions; Social Security
Revealed preferences, of consumers, 106

Revolutionary War, 101–102
RFID (radio frequency identification), 166
Ride-sharing, 12, 172
Risk
categories of, for banks, 162
credit, 160–161
default, 180
Robinson, James, 6
Rocky Mountain states, 94
Rowling, J. K., 48
Rule of law, economic growth and, 3, 7
Russia, 3, 18
Rust Belt states, 94

S
SAIF (Savings Association Insurance Fund), 158
Satisfaction, GDP and, 49
Savings, 159
bank runs and, 139
for retirement, 136
Savings Association Insurance Fund (SAIF), 158
Scarce resources, 24
Scarcity, 205
Schools and schooling. *See* Education
Schwartz, Anna, 148
Segregation, 94–95
Semiconductors, 33
Senior citizens. *See* Elderly persons
September 11, 2001, 149
Services. *See* Goods and services
Shares of stock, 3, 147, 157
of elderly, 140
SimplyHired, 88
Singapore, 24
Single-parent households, 94
Smartphones, 9
economies of scale with, 165
payments systems and, 164–167
Smoot-Hawley Tariff Act of 1930, 199–200, 202
Social capital, 94
Social Security, 139–143
CPI and, 141
income inequality and, 65
rate of return on, 142
Social Security Administration (SSA), 83
Social Security Disability Insurance (SSDI), 83
Social Security Trust Fund, 141–142
Software development, outsourcing and, 16, 17
Solvency, 158
Something for something (*quid pro quo*), 206

South America, 6
Southern states, 94
South Korea, 27
Spain, 187–190
SSA (Social Security Administration), 83
SSDI (Social Security Disability Insurance), 83
SSI (Supplemental Security Income), 83
Stagnation, 73
Standard of living, 24
in developing countries, 196
from economic growth, 3
R&D and, 10–11
rise of, 64, 68
wealth and, 33
Start-up capital, 88
State Department (United States), 16
Stevenson, Betsey, 48–49
Stimulus packages, economic, 126–132, 134
Stocks and stockholders. *See* Shares of stock
Stocks of food, in Zimbabwe, 7
Subsidies, 30
for agriculture, 198
Sugar, 202–203
Supplemental Security Income (SSI), 83
Supply. *See also* Supply and demand
of currencies, 177
excess, 74
labor supply curve, 81
money, 103, 152, 158
Supply and demand
with foreign exchange rates, 193
gold and, 169–170
Sweden, 4
Switzerland, 3, 24, 179, 195

T
Tablet devices, 165
TANF (Temporary Assistance to Needy Families), 75
Tariffs
for employment, 205
in Smoot-Hawley Tariff Act of 1930, 200
WTO and, 198
Tax credits, 31, 136
Tax cuts, 127–128, 135
Taxes. *See also* Income taxes; Tariffs; Tax rates
after-tax income, 33–34
behavior and, 34
consumption and, 76
corporate, 31
credits, 31, 136
cryptocurrencies and, 173

Taxes (*continued*)
cuts, 127–128, 135
earned income tax credit, 92
in EU, 190
in Europe, 31
evasion, 31
government spending and, 30–31, 35, 134–135
during Great Depression, 76, 80
of high-income people, 35, 120–124
incentives and, 30–32, 34
incidence, 120
income and, 120–124
income inequality and, 67
increases in, 133–137
inflation, 98–103
innovation and, 13, 33–34
liability, 127
net tax, 67
payroll, 141, 143
progressive tax policies, 67
R&D and, 32
rebates, 92
Tax evasion, 31
Taxicab companies, 88–89
Tax incidence, 120
Tax liability, 127
Tax rates, 67. *See also* Marginal tax rates
average tax rate, 121–124
real tax rate, 135
Tax rebates, 92
Taylor, Jerry, 107–108
Taylor, John B., 128
Temporary Assistance to Needy Families (TANF), 75
Terrorism, 149
Textile industry, 208
TIPS (Treasury Inflation Protected Securities), 100
Topel, Robert, 81
Toyota, 20
Trade. *See also* Free trade; Imports; Trade barriers
China and, 19
of currency, 177
exports, 19, 178–179, 200, 203
gains from, 199
globalization and, 198–199
India and, 19
liberalization in foreign nations, 19
outsourcing and, 16–21
voluntary, 198–199, 206, 207
wealth from, 21
Trade barriers
adverse effects of, 206–207, 208–209

economic growth and, 17–18
NAFTA and, 198
outsourcing and, 17
per capita income and, 17–18
Traded goods and services, 193
Transfers, cash and noncash, 74–75
Transistors, 10
Treasury bills, 152
Treasury bonds
inflation and, 101–102
in Social Security Trust Fund, 141–142
Treasury Inflation Protected Securities (TIPS), 100
Two-sided market, 88
Two-tier health-care system, 117

U
Uber, 12, 88–89
Underground economy, 31, 46–48, 186–187
Unemployment benefits, 47, 74–75, 134, 135
Unemployment rate, 79–84
discouraged workers and, 80–82
food stamps and, 75
in Great Depression, 72, 139
in Great Recession, 71
in recessions, 81
United Copper Company, 147
United Kingdom, 4, 7, 46–47, 182, 189–190
United States
automobiles from, 206
capitalism in, 25
dollars and, 177–182
economic stimulus packages of, 126–132
employment in, 21
GDP in, 46, 47
government spending in, 30–35
income mobility in, 91–96
inflation in, 179
legal system in, 4
NAFTA and, 198, 203
national debt of, 98–103
outsourcing and, 16–21
patents in, 12
poverty in, 91–92
productivity in, 196
protectionism by, 199–200
real per capital income in, 5
real wages in, 196
textile industry in, 208
United States dollar, value of, 177–182
Unit of account, 99
Upwork, 87, 88

Uruguay Round (of GATT), 198, 199
U.S. Bureau of Labor Statistics (BLS), 87
U.S. Department of Defense, 16
U.S. Department of Labor, 208
U.S. Department of State, 16

V
Value and valuation
cryptocurrencies, 169–170, 171–172
market valuation, 88
market value, 45
real value, 103
United States dollar, value of, 177–182
Venezuela, 101
Vietnam, 19
Voluntary trade, 198–199, 206, 207
Vouchers, 75

W
Wages
minimum, 97
outsourcing and, 16–21
real, 81–82, 195–196
Walmart, 20
Water pollution, 201
Wealth
capitalism and, 64–69
of elderly, 140
income inequality and, 64–69
innovation and, 32–33
institutions and, 6
of nations, 3–7
natural-resource endowments and, 3
protectionism and, 207
standard of living and, 33
taxes and, 31
from trade, 21
from voluntary trade, 198
Wealth tax, 35
Welfare, 75
West Germany, 27–28
Wholesale sales, in recessions, 52
Winfrey, Oprah, 32
Wolfers, Judson, 48–49
Workplace experience, 39
Works Progress Administration (WPA), 80
World Trade Organization (WTO), 198, 203, 208

Z
Zcash, 169, 171, 172
Zimbabwe, 7, 25, 101
Zuckerberg, Mark, 32–33